MODULAR ORIGAMI

18 Colorful and Customizable Folded Paper Sculptures

Tung Ken Lam

Other Schiffer Books on Related Subjects
Folding Polyhedra, Alexander Heinz, ISBN 978-0-7643-6157-9
Paper Sculpture, Richard Sweeney, ISBN 978-0-7643-6214-9

© 2022 Design and layout, BlueRed Press
© 2022 Text and illustrations Tung Ken Lam
All photography by Richard James of thisisrichard.co.uk

Library of Congress Control Number: 2022940865

Produced by BlueRed Press Ltd. 2022
Designed by Insight Design
Type set in Fira Sans

ISBN: 978-0-7643-6551-5
Printed in India

Published by Schiffer Publishing, Ltd.
4880 Lower Valley Road
Atglen, PA 19310
Phone: (610) 593-1777; Fax: (610) 593-2002
Email: *Info@schifferbooks.com*
Web: *www.schifferbooks.com*

For our complete selection of fine books on this and related
subjects, please visit our website at www.schifferbooks.com.
You may also write for a free catalog.

Schiffer Publishing's titles are available at special discounts
for bulk purchases for sales promotions or premiums.
Special editions, including personalized covers, corporate
imprints, and excerpts, can be created in large quantities
for special needs. For more information, contact the publisher.

We are always looking for people to write books on new
and related subjects. If you have an idea for a book, please
contact us at *proposals@schifferbooks.com.*

Note
Italics are used to identify pieces outlined in the step-by-step exercises
later in the book—e.g., *Six Symmetrical Prisms.*
References such as (Lang 03) and (Maekawa 08) refer to specific books
as shown in "Further Reading" and the bibliography, p. 126.

CONTENTS

INTRODUCTION

Modular Origami presents eighteen modular origami projects for you to make. This technique involves folding paper into simple shapes known as modules or units. You then put these modules together—without using sticky tape or glue—to create amazing and attractive ornaments and sculptures.

The eighteen projects in this book begin at a very simple level, so that everyone can succeed straightaway. Then, you develop your skills a bit at a time, so that when you reach the last project you will be folding and assembling something really extraordinary. Every design can be customized by using different kinds of paper and combinations of colors, so that each finished ornament will be a unique and personal expression of the design. A bonus feature of some models is that they move, spin, or change shape!

Many models can be varied and extended into new works. For example, the face units of a cube can be joined into an irregular hexahedron (a six-sided triangular bipyramid), or thirty modules could be joined into a pseudo-stellated icosahedron (twenty faces). The unit can also be generalized to construct other polygons (e.g., from a square to a hexagon).

As you work through the projects, you will find that your knowledge and skills with geometry will improve. To make this clearer, see pages 6-7, which show how the regular and semiregular polyhedra are related to each other.

For ease of folding, all the models in this book use straight folds. Curling paper and curved folds are harder to achieve but can give spectacular results: see the "Further Reading" chapter for some ideas.

USEFUL TERMS

Compound origami
Origami made from folded pieces of paper that are dissimilar

Concave
A polygon is concave if some vertices point inward (are reentrant). Imagine wrapping the polygon with string and tightening it: there will be some gaps between the string and the polygon.

Convex
A polygon is convex if all the vertices point outward. Imagine wrapping the polygon with string and tightening it: the string will always touch the edges.

A polyhedron is convex if all the vertices point outward. Place a face of the polyhedron on a flat table: the table will be in full contact with that face only. This is true for every face of the polyhedron. Know that all Platonic and Archimedean Solids are convex.

Edge
The outside limit of an object. The edge defines the outline of the shape. For a polyhedron, an edge is where two faces meet.

Face
A plane (flat) surface enclosed by edges

Module
Module and unit are interchangeable terms for the same thing: a piece of paper folded into a shape that combines with others to form another shape.

Platonic Solids
The five convex regular polyhedra are known as the Platonic Solids.

The cube and octahedra are duals. The dodecahedron and icosahedron are duals. The tetrahedron is self-dual. This pattern stands out in the table as the swapping of the number of faces and vertices; the number of edges is the same for the duals.

Polygons are named using the number of edges. Some regular polygons have special names (e.g., a regular quadrilateral (4-gon) is a square).

n	Regular polygon name of n-gon
3	equilateral triangle
4	square
5	pentagon
6	hexagon
7	heptagon (or septagon)
8	octagon
9	Nonagon (or enneagon)
10	decagon
11	hendecagon (or undecagon)
12	dodecagon
13	triskaidecagon
14	tetrakaidecagon
15	pentadecagon
16	hexakaidecagon
17	heptadecagon
18	octakaidecagon
19	enneadecagon
20	icosagon

A polyhedron and its dual can form a compound (e.g., the cube and octahedron and the dodecahedron and icosahedron). The compound of two tetrahedra is the stella octangula, also known as Kepler's Star.

Polyhedron	Faces	Vertices	Edges
Regular tetrahedron	4	4	6
Regular hexahedron (cube)	6	8	12
Regular octahedron	8	6	12
Regular dodecahedron	12	20	30
Regular icosahedron	20	12	30

Archimedean Solids

The thirteen convex semiregular polyhedra are known as the Archimedean Solids. Five are truncated regular polyhedra (i.e., they can be derived from cutting off parts of the "corners" of regular polyhedra).

The other eight can be grouped into those related to the cube/octahedron and those related to the dodecahedron/icosahedron.

The polyhedron common to the compound of the cube and octahedron is the cuboctahedron. Two polyhedra are possible when a cuboctahedron is truncated along the planes of a rhombic cuboctahedron: the great and the small rhombicuboctahedron.

The polyhedron common to the compound of the dodecahedron and icosahedron is the icosidodecahedron. Two polyhedra are possible when an icosidodecahedron is truncated along the planes of a rhombic triacontahedron: the great and the small rhombicosidodecahedron.

A dual exists of each Archimedean Solid. Two notable duals are those of the cuboctahedron and the icosidodecahedron, which are the rhombic dodecahedron and the rhombic triacontahedron, respectively. Note that the dual of an Archimedean Solid is not an Archimedean Solid, unlike the duals of Platonic Solids, which are also Platonic Solids.

Polyhedron	Snub	Regular	Truncated	Great Small Rhombi-		
Tetrahedron		1	6			
Cube	17	2	7	cuboctahedron 11	12	13
Octahedron		3	8			
Dodecahedron	18	4	9	icosidodecahedron 14	15	16
Icosahedron		5	10			

Polygon

A flat shape with straight sides (see the table of polygon names on p. 5).

Polyhedron

(Plural polyhedra) A 3-D shape that has flat (planar) faces

A polyhedron is concave if some vertices point inward. Place the polyhedron on a flat table: in one or more positions there will be a hollow gap between the table and the polyhedron. The Stella Octangula is a concave polyhedron.

No:	Polyhedron	No. of Polygons with no. of edges					
		3	4	5	6	8	12
1	Regular tetrahedron	4					
6	Truncated tetrahedron		4		4		
2	Regular hexahedron (cube)		6				
7	Truncated hexahedron	8				6	
8	Cuboctahedron	8	6				
3	Regular octahedron	8					
9	Truncated octahedron		6		8		
10	Rhombicuboctahedron	8	18				
11	Rhombitruncated cuboctahedron		12		8	6	
4	Regular dodecahedron			12			
12	Truncated dodecahedron	20					10
13	Icosidodecahedron	20		12			
5	Regular icosahedron	20					
14	Truncated icosahedron			12	20		
15	Rhombicosidodecahedron	20	30	12			
16	Rhombitruncated icosidodecahedron		30		20		10
17	Snub cube	32	6				
18	Snub dodecahedron	80		12			

Some consider the Kepler-Poinsot polyhedra (not shown) to be regular polyhedra.

A regular polyhedron has identical faces and identical vertices. "Identical" can be interpreted in different ways (e.g., the polygons at every vertex arranged in the same order. One "layer" of a great rhombicuboctahedron can be rotated to create Miller's Solid, which is not usually regarded as a regular polyhedron.

Regular Polygon

A regular polygon has equal edges and equal angles.

Side

Paper has two sides.

(Mathematics) For a polygon (a 2-D object with straight edges), edge and side are equivalent. However, for a 3-D object such as a polyhedron, side is ambiguous—we use the terms "face" and "edge."

Stellate

Resembling a star

Unit

Module and unit are interchangeable terms for the same thing: see unit.

Vertex

(Plural vertices) The point where edges meet

ORIGAMI

The Japanese word for paper folding, 折紙 (*origami*), literally means fold (*oru*) paper (*kami*). In English, it is usually taken to mean "the Japanese art of folding paper," even when applied to paper folding from places other than Japan. For example, some French speakers prefer to use the French term, *pliage de papier*, instead of origami. This books uses the word "origami" for all kinds of paper folding, wherever its origin.

The roots of paper folding probably date back to the invention of paper, which is generally agreed to have been in China around 105 CE. However, other foldable materials may have been used in origami-like ways (e.g., cloth, pastry, leather, and even sheet metal). For example, there is evidence that European napkin folding may have developed independently from Asian paper folding.

Paper has been folded for practical, ceremonial, educational, and recreational purposes for a long time. Recreational and artistic origami has become particularly popular since the mid-twentieth century, when origami pioneer Akira Yoshizawa (1911–2005) succeeded in making others see origami as a valid artistic (and educational) medium. He was renowned for making lifelike animals and figures: note that this means lifelike in the sense of being alive, not necessarily a detailed and accurate replica of the subject.

Yoshizawa may have been an impetus for modern origami in the West, but curiously, the German educationist Friedrich Froebel (1782–1852) may have been the instigator for the development of Japanese origami in the preceding century. Froebel founded the kindergarten schooling system and included paper folding as an educational and artistic activity for children. Japanese kindergartens may have used Froebel's paper for folding, which led to Japanese origami paper being white on one side and printed with a color on the other side.

Although animals and birds are timeless and popular subjects, origami particularly lends itself to geometric subjects (e.g., folding a point to another point makes a straight line; folding an edge to a crease creates an angle bisector). These mathematical operations cause polygons and polyhedra to be inevitably made, even if the results are not purely geometric.

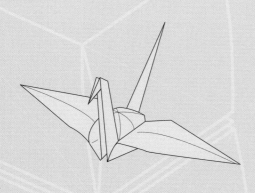
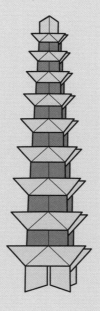
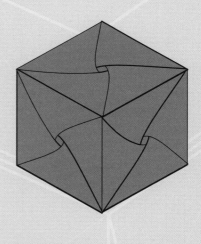

MODULAR ORIGAMI

Origami is usually thought of as being made from one sheet of paper (e.g., the traditional crane: above, left). However, using more than one sheet is not unprecedented. The roots of modular origami may lie in cut and glued models such as *tamatebako* cube (above, right) and compound origami such as the pagoda (above, center).

Modern modular origami probably began in the 1960s and 1970s as a number of folders—such as Kenneth Kawamura, Lewis Simon, and Robert Neale—created what have become classic works. In particular, in the 1980s, Tomoko Fuse triggered a wave of interest with her elegant and diverse modular origami.

TECHNIQUES OF MODULAR ORIGAMI

Most modular origami uses a system of flaps and pockets to assemble the modules without glue; namely, the flap of a module is inserted into the pocket of another module. Depending on the model, you may need to make extra folds to lock the units together: either fold the pieces together as in the Twelve-Piece Carousel or by tucking, as used in the Pentagram.

Almost all of the modular origami in this book use a single type of unit, although some need units that are mirror images. However, compound origami uses dissimilar units: Six Symmetrical Prisms is typical in using one kind of unit for the cube and another for the prisms.

Although this book shows you how to assemble specific numbers of units, you may be able to assemble a different number into other forms.

THE CASE FOR MODULAR ORIGAMI

Some folders believe that origami must be made from a single square without cutting or gluing; also, that using more than one sheet is inferior. However, relaxing these rules can really open up creative possibilities:

- More colors. A single square can have different colors on each side: the finished model can have a maximum of two colors (unless the paper is decorated or is translucent). Wanting more than two colors means using more than one sheet. However, some modular origami looks better using a restricted palette (e.g using a single color for the Starfish and a stella octangula makes the arms of the stars the same color).

- More efficient. A measure of efficiency is the ratio of the size of the finished model compared with the original sheet of paper. Another measure is how much of the original paper appears on the surface of the finished model: the less that is visible, the more that has been hidden away inside. Intriguingly, modular origami can make models that are larger than the starting sheets of paper.

- Synergy. The complexity of a model can be distributed among the units and the assembly. This can be a way of avoiding inelegant and inefficient bulky layers.

- A kind of puzzle. Most origami can be considered to be a kind of puzzle, but the assembly of units has its own particular satisfaction.

- This is a practical way to explore polyhedra and space, while at the same time learning geometry.

- A common method for making polyhedral models is to cut and glue thin card (see Wenninger 71). Modular origami can be a safe and accessible alternative: no scissors, knives, or solvents are needed. Coloring the model is achieved by folding colored paper instead of decorating the paper. Furthermore, folded models can be quicker to make and stronger than those made with cuts and glue.

- A move away from realism. Some paperfolders like to make origami that is as realistic as possible (e.g., a bird that has individual claws and feather details). Usually this requires complex folding and large sheets of special paper. However, modular origami usually favors subjects such as polyhedra and stars. Realism cannot be the focus, but other criteria might be (e.g., the elegance of the folding sequence, how the layers of paper are used and appear in the finished model, novel use of symmetry).

- Even origami creators known for complex single-sheet works, such as Robert Lang (see Lang 03) and Jun Maekawa (see Maekawa 08 and 13), have made modular works.

WHAT MAKES FOR GOOD MODULAR ORIGAMI?

This can be a matter of personal taste, but many folders would agree with at least some of these criteria:

- Respect for the paper. Do not force the paper to do things that it does not want to do (e.g., fold thirty-two layers of paper at the same time). Sometimes an idea does not work well in practice (e.g., inserting a flap that is too thick into a pocket will result in a poor join).

- Simplicity and elegance. Simple methods are preferred to complicated ones, since they are usually quicker and less error prone.

- Efficiency. The more paper that is visible in the final result, the more efficient the model. However, a smaller result may be better if the paper is distributed more evenly or if the folding sequence is better.

- Convenient starting shapes. Another aspect of efficiency is to choose starting paper that is appropriate (e.g., the geometry of a silver rectangle naturally relates to that of cubes). (Alternatively, the geometry may be embedded in a different type of rectangle, such as a square.) Squares are popular because they are the same all over the world, but oblongs are not always the same.

- Folding sequence and surprise. The folding sequence should be smooth and logical (e.g., rotating and turning the paper over should be minimized). However, unexpected moves, results, or forms are more pleasurable than tired and familiar ones. This may be why 60° geometry may be more pleasing than 22.5° geometry. Some of the best models seem to be obvious—but they may be obvious only in hindsight.

- Novelty. The element of pleasant surprise applies not only to the folding sequence but also to the overall form and the joining method. Sometimes these are obvious and can become overfamiliar. Unpromising starting points or unusual geometry can sometimes give pleasing results.

- Stable forms. Ideally the assembled form should be strong. Very strong assemblies can be thrown about without falling apart (e.g., the Skeletal Octahedron; see page 94). However, most models need more careful handling (e.g parts of *Surprise!* [page 102] can come apart if pulled too hard).

- Minimal creasing. Fold the paper only as much as needed. There are several reasons. First, why waste effort on creases that are not needed? Second, the less you handle the paper, the less the paper will be affected by dirt and oil from your hands. Also, the paper may become weaker with prolonged handling. Third, extraneous creases can spoil the finished appearance of a model and also affect its structural integrity (unless the creases are deliberate; e.g., creased pentagrams in the faces of a regular dodecahedron). A common technique is to use pinch marks instead of full creases. Another technique is to use a template (see page 23).

Getting Started

PAPER

You should be able to make all of the models in this book using commonly available paper. Ordinary 80 gsm A4, or US letter-sized photocopy paper, is readily available in a variety of colors. For squares, cut your own from oblongs. Alternatively, use square paper from memo cubes or 6 in. (15 cm) origami paper.

In general, choose papers that are strong (so will not rip easily), are not too thick (makes thick layers and causes inaccuracy), and will take and hold a crease well. This means you should normally avoid newsprint, paper-backed foil, and card stock. However, if you want to make large models, then you might need to use slightly thicker paper.

Reusing paper like junk mail and flyers is fine, especially for practice, but be careful if the paper has personal data. You can fold paper from magazines, but this can be unpleasant since the coating can rub and crack off. For fine work, choose acid-free paper that will not discolor with age.

PAPER COLOR AND PATTERNS

Commercially produced origami paper usually has a different color on each side: this can be really helpful when you follow diagrams, since the two sides are clearly differentiated. Ordinary origami paper is white on one side and printed with a color on the other side: it can enhance the appearance of some finished models (e.g., *Double Equilateral Triangle Unit*). However, it can be a disadvantage for other models (e.g., *Twelve-Piece Carousel*), unless duo paper is used, since this has different nonwhite colors on each side.

Paper that is the same color on both sides is usually easier to obtain and works better for some models—for example, it can prevent the white side of the paper showing in models such as *WXYZ*. This kind of paper is sometimes called mono paper. Another benefit is that if

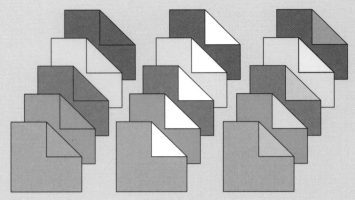

Mono Paper is the same color on both sides

Origami Paper is colored on one side and white on the other

Duo paper is colored on one side and non-white on the other.

you are folding modules where orientation is important, you can easily convert a left-handed module into a right-handed module (and vice versa) by changing mountain folds into valleys and valleys into mountains. With origami or duo paper, the colors would also change.

You can use plain paper for all of the models in this book. Patterned paper can enhance some models if you choose suitable paper, but avoid busy patterns that can be distracting and overwhelm and spoil the effect of the finished model.

Usually, you use different colors for units that are next to each other. For flat models with an even number of units using two different colors is convenient and attractive. For prime numbers such as five, you can use all-different colors. If you have an insufficient number of colors, a single color can be effective.

PAPER SIZE

Convenient paper sizes are suggested for each model so that the result fit your hands. You can usually use squares or rectangles at least 3 in. (75 mm) wide. If you want to know the size of the result for other paper sizes, use the finished model ratio given in the diagrams. This ratio is usually the longest length in the largest configuration. If the starting rectangle is not square, the shortest length is assumed to be 1.

PREPARING PAPER

Most of the models use rectangles of convenient proportions, but sometimes you will need to cut paper. The illustrations show how to fold and cut a square from an oblong. They also show how to make two kinds of rectangles that have special geometric properties: the silver (1:√2) and bronze (1:√2) rectangles. Silver rectangles are common in most of the world because paper in the ISO A series standard has sides in the ratio 1:√2. Folding a silver rectangle in half (shorter edges together) makes a rectangle that is geometrically similar to the original rectangle (having the same proportions). Two A5 sheets make an A4 sheet, two A4 make A3, etc: A0 is defined to have an area of 1 m². A bronze rectangle

can be cut into three similar rectangles. For more details, see *Star Origami* (Lam 21).

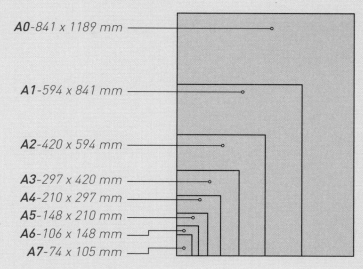

A0-841 x 1189 mm
A1-594 x 841 mm
A2-420 x 594 mm
A3-297 x 420 mm
A4-210 x 297 mm
A5-148 x 210 mm
A6-106 x 148 mm
A7-74 x 105 mm

SYMBOLS AND PROCEDURES

The diagrams in this book use symbols based on standards developed by Akira Yoshizawa, Robert Harbin, Samuel Randlett, and others. If you take some time to understand these symbols, they will soon become second nature. Not only will this save you time and make following diagrams more pleasant, you will also be able to fold from diagrams in languages that you cannot read. Additionally, you'll develop the valuable skill of folding imaginary paper in your mind.

At each step you can usually look ahead to see the result that you are aiming for. However, sometimes you will need to look carefully at the symbols. Most often you will need to distinguish valley (concave) and mountain (convex) folds: the former uses a dashed line and a plain arrowhead; the latter uses a line of dashes and dots with a hollow half arrowhead.

Even the standard symbols have some quirks. The turnover symbol might evoke turning over the model but taken literally would turn the model over again. The cut symbol uses scissors, but using a knife is usually better in practice—the scissors are a familiar design trope for cutting coupons out of magazines and such.

Since the diagrams in this book use different shading for the two sides of the paper, most diagrams omit the symbol for colored side up/down. Repeat symbols are rarely used since it's usually obvious where you need to repeat the steps—read the text for specific information about repeats. For a similar reason, the enlarged view symbol is not always used; and curiously, no standard reduced-view symbol exists.

Some common compound folds are given special names (see opposite). This book refers to only a few procedures by name: the squash fold, (inside) reverse fold, and waterbomb base. Most models use valley and mountain folds with only a few squash and reverse folds.

There is some other shorthand: a blintz fold means folding all the corners of a square to the center. A kite fold is a square with two adjacent edges folded to a diagonal: this can fly as a working kite when rigged with cord. Informally, a kite fold is the result of bisecting an acute angle of an isosceles right-angled triangle. The meeting point of the 22.5° fold and the edge is known as a kite point.

You will find two other procedures used in some models (page 18): dividing a length into equal parts and folding 60°. It is easy to divide a length into halves, quarters, and eighths, but thirds and fifths can also be made without a ruler. A good way is Shuzo Fujimoto's iterative method. Folding 60° is a special case of Abe's trisection of an acute angle.

FOLLOWING THE INSTRUCTIONS

Diagrams are like a comic strip that you follow, performing the folds in each step. Do not let the origami terminology intimidate you: you can usually tell what's required by looking ahead to the next step. Try turning the paper to make it easier to fold—the paper does not have to be in the same orientation as the diagram. For example, to make a mountain fold you might find it easier to turn the paper over, valley-fold, and then turn over again. Or a vertical valley fold is easier to make if you rotate the paper 90° so that you are folding away from your body.

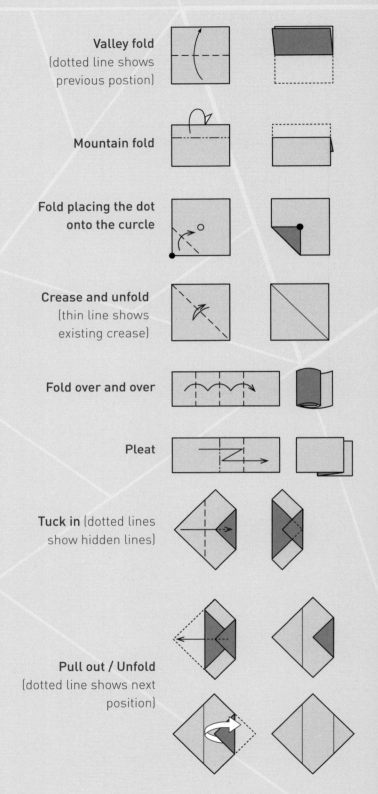

Valley fold
(dotted line shows previous postion)

Mountain fold

Fold placing the dot onto the curcle

Crease and unfold
(thin line shows existing crease)

Fold over and over

Pleat

Tuck in (dotted lines show hidden lines)

Pull out / Unfold
(dotted line shows next position)

Squash fold

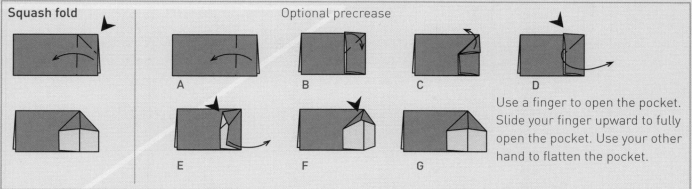

Optional precrease

Use a finger to open the pocket. Slide your finger upward to fully open the pocket. Use your other hand to flatten the pocket.

Inside reverse fold

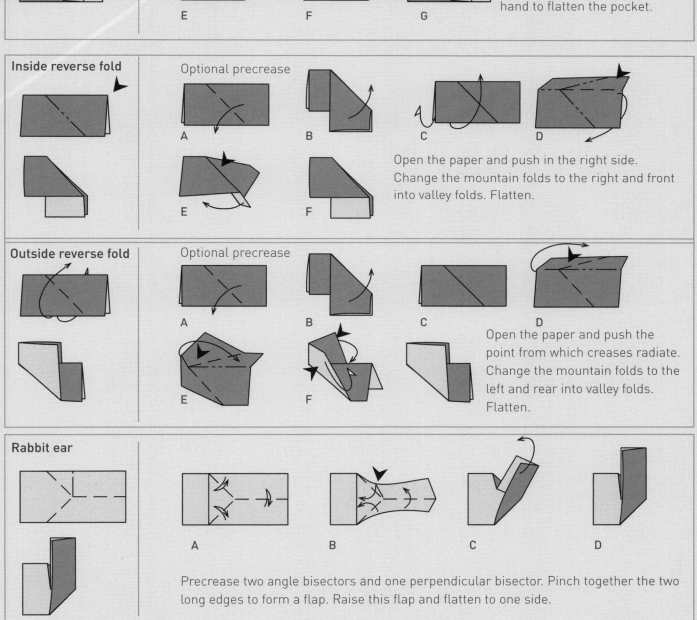

Optional precrease

Open the paper and push in the right side. Change the mountain folds to the right and front into valley folds. Flatten.

Outside reverse fold

Optional precrease

Open the paper and push the point from which creases radiate. Change the mountain folds to the left and rear into valley folds. Flatten.

Rabbit ear

Precrease two angle bisectors and one perpendicular bisector. Pinch together the two long edges to form a flap. Raise this flap and flatten to one side.

If you are a beginner, then start with the simpler models first. Early models in the book have more detailed instructions. Later models tend to be briefer, not only because it saves space, but also because as you become more experienced, you can work with larger chunks of information. In general, the simpler models are at the beginning of each group of models.

Also note that some models have different levels of difficulty for folding the modules and for assembling them.

Beginners usually appreciate the detailed text in each step, especially for assembling the modules. Many experienced folders skip the words in each step: besides fluency, one reason is that they often fold from diagrams written in languages that they cannot read, so manage without reading the words. Even so, the words can still help you by using your verbal communication channel and working memory. Sometimes the words give helpful tips that you might miss if you don't read the diagram carefully, such as "Fold only between the existing crease lines."

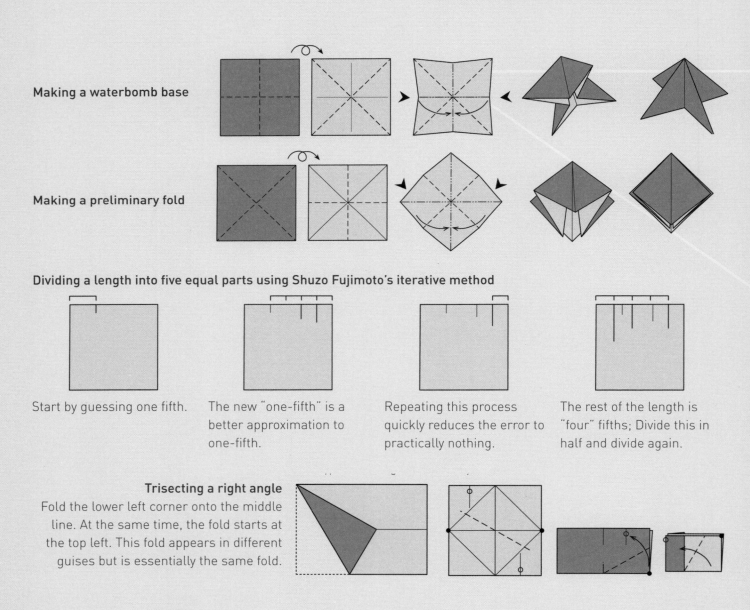

Making a waterbomb base

Making a preliminary fold

Dividing a length into five equal parts using Shuzo Fujimoto's iterative method

Start by guessing one fifth.

The new "one-fifth" is a better approximation to one-fifth.

Repeating this process quickly reduces the error to practically nothing.

The rest of the length is "four" fifths; Divide this in half and divide again.

Trisecting a right angle
Fold the lower left corner onto the middle line. At the same time, the fold starts at the top left. This fold appears in different guises but is essentially the same fold.

18

Note that diagrams are usually drawn with the layers of paper slightly spread out, even if they are meant to align exactly. This helps you understand how the layers are arranged. If you are meant to leave gaps, this will be specifically highlighted. As mentioned elsewhere, diagrams use different colors to distinguish the two sides of the paper. However, for most models you can use paper that is the same color on both sides: look at the final model to decide which kind of paper you should use.

If you are stuck, study the diagram carefully: Is there a line or arrow that you've missed? Do the flaps and layers of paper correspond to the paper in your hand? If taking a break and trying again doesn't work, ask someone else for help. It doesn't have to be an origami expert, since a fresh pair of eyes might be all that's needed. If nobody is able to help, try starting again from the beginning, carefully following every symbol and instruction. Despite the best intentions of all involved, diagrams may have mistakes, so see if you can work around the problem: Can you carry on even though you've missed out a step?

Symbols between diagrams

Turn over (dotted lines show hidden lines)

Rotate (by the angle shown)

Open up (completely unfold)

Enlarged view

Reduced view

Change of view

Other symbols

Cut

Repeat three times (or by the number of strokes)

Hold the locations indicated by the circles and perform the action described (e.g., pull the flap, reposition, and flatten)

Edge divided into equal divisions (e.g., thirds)

hidden line, previous/next position or imaginary line

paper clip

start with the colored side of the paper up/down

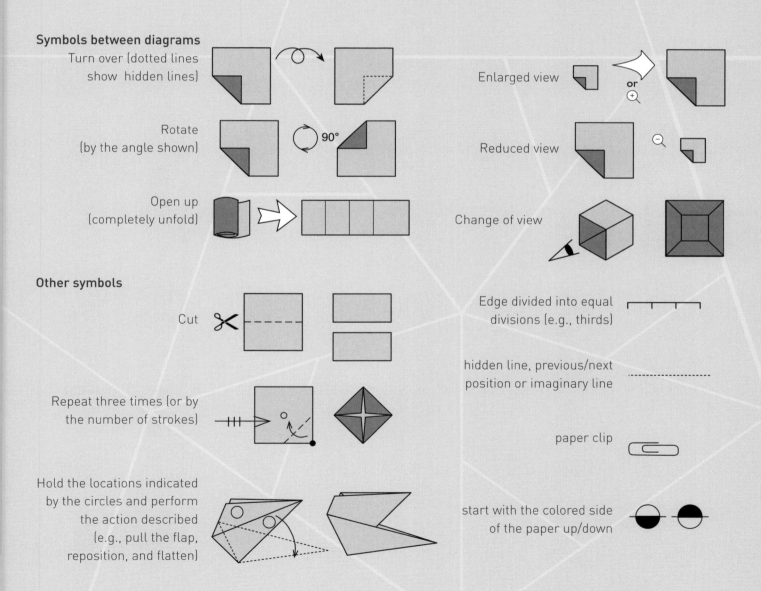

For cutting paper, certain kinds of envelope openers are convenient to use. They are small and portable, have no exposed blade, and are relatively easy to use. You fold the paper where you want to cut and then slide the envelope opener along the folded edge. However, they work best for cuts perpendicular to a raw edge and are not so good for other angles, such as 60°. Remember not to crease too hard or the blade will not catch properly. A sharp nonserrated knife will also work, but adult supervision may be needed.

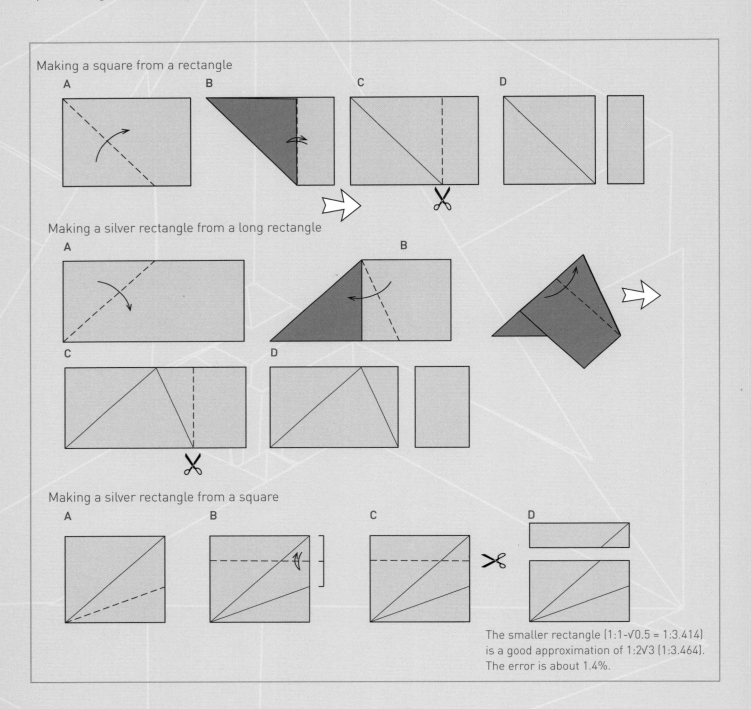

Making a square from a rectangle

A   B   C   D

Making a silver rectangle from a long rectangle

A   B

C   D

Making a silver rectangle from a square

A   B   C   D

The smaller rectangle ($1:1-\sqrt{0.5} = 1:3.414$) is a good approximation of $1:2\sqrt{3}$ ($1:3.464$). The error is about 1.4%.

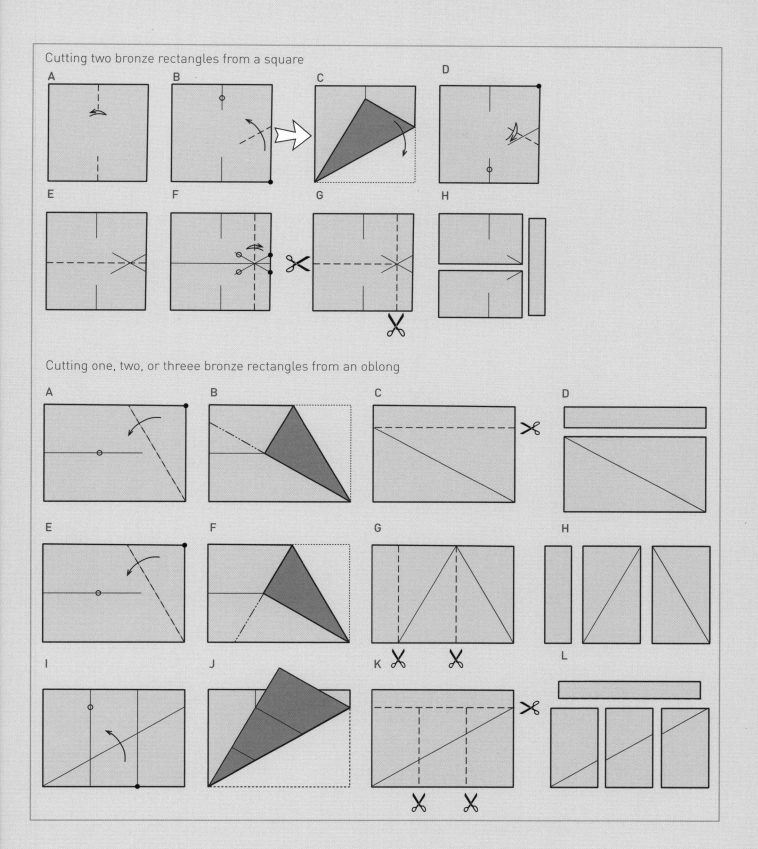

Cutting two bronze rectangles from a square

Cutting one, two, or threee bronze rectangles from an oblong

21

FOLDING

- Fold on a hard surface. To fold the diagonal of a square (see diagram 1, right): put the paper on a clean and hard surface such as a table or hardback book. Then sweep the paper, picking up the lower corner and placing it on the upper corner, sweeping downward and creasing from the center outward.

- Make firm folds. Most geometrical folds require you to make sharp creases with a finger or thumbnail.

- Fold accurately by precisely lining up edges or corners.

- To fold the diagonal of a square: instead of trying to fold through two corners, join opposite corners together and make the crease by sweeping the paper flat away from the joined corners.

- To fold a square in half with opposite edges together. Instead of trying to align the corners, join the opposite edges together and make the crease by sweeping the paper flat away from the joined edges (see diagram 2, below right).

- Manipulate the paper for convenience. Fold on a hard surface so that it supports the paper for you. Positioning the paper is important. For example, to fold a square into a 2-by-1 rectangle, it's easier to "book fold" with the "spine" closest to the body, not farthest away.

- Halving: for bisecting an angle, concentrate on lining up the edges or crease lines.

- Reverse folds. If you find these difficult, it may be caused by the original crease being too soft. Folding backward and forward will help reinforce the crease and achieve success.

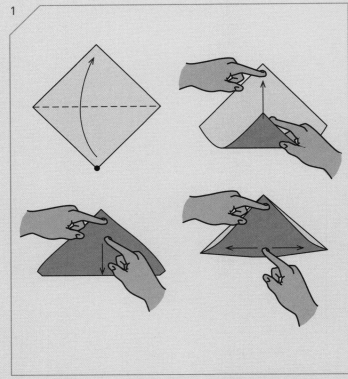

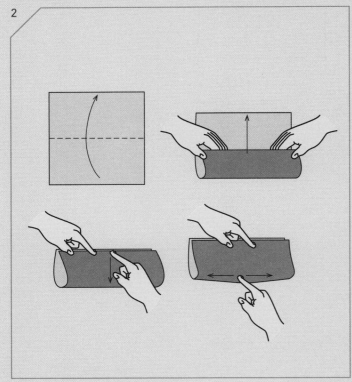

- Grain. Machine-made paper has grain: it is stronger in one direction and weaker in the perpendicular direction. You can ignore the grain most of the time. However, sometimes you may wish to orient the grain for accurate folds and for strength in the finished forms. For example, folding the thin flaps in steps 8 and 10 of the *Double Equilateral Triangle Units* is easier if the grain is vertical in step 1 (instead of horizontal).

Grain can also explain why precut square paper might not be square. Paper with grain does not expand equally in all directions when it is wetted. Different humidity levels have a similar but lesser effect, so the paper may have been square when it was cut, but not square if it is in an environment with a different humidity level.

- Sharpness of folds. Sharp folds usually make for accurate models. Sometimes, creasing sharply with your fingernails can scrape the surface of the paper, making it lose color: a softer fold using finger pressure may be better.

- Folding card. Very thin matte card usually folds well. However, some card cracks when folded, usually thicker card or card that has been coated for printing. Cracking is structurally weak and looks bad, leaving the fold looking crinkled, and any printed color is lost.

The solution is to score the card. This means making a groove in the card so that the fold is controlled—so less stress and strain is put on the card. Sometimes a single groove is not enough: two grooves with a small gap spread the stress even better.

Use a ballpoint pen that has run out of ink to score: run the pen along a ruler to make the groove. You can also use the blunt side of a knife or scissors, but remember not to cut the surface of the card.

- Coping with creep. Although origami diagrams might instruct you to fold an edge to a crease, sometimes you need to leave a small gap so that the paper is not crushed in the later steps (e.g., step 6 of *Pentagram*).

- Using a template. Reasons for using a template are to save time and minimize extraneous creases. You make one template and use it to make all the modules. For example, you could fold one unit up to a particular step and then use that to transfer a fold to a new sheet of paper.

A second type of template: for the *Pinwheel Cube*, fold a square in half (opposite edges together) and use this to fold a quarter on a new square.

A third type of template uses a pin or needle to prick through a specific point (e.g., the center of the square).

- Trade-off between accuracy and speed. Layers of paper can affect accuracy (e.g., folding a square in half and in half again can be a poor way of creasing quarters). Folding and unfolding the paper at each step is usually more accurate. However, there is a trade-off between accuracy and speed, but accuracy is usually worth the time.

If you are in a hurry, you may be able to get away with folding two sheets together and then separating them to make two units in one go. This tends to work best for simple units such as Robert Neale's *Skeletal Octahedron*, or for units that can forgive small inaccuracies.

- Mass manufacturing. Another technique for speeding up folding is to fold several units on a single sheet of paper and then cut the paper into individual modules. Instead of folding complete units, folding the main construction creases may suffice in speeding up the folding.

  For example, you may find yourself cutting A4 paper into four A6 rectangles for *Dodecahedron No. 14* (Easy Module). You might as well add the main folds before cutting (creasing the long edge of the A4 sheet into quarters and the short edge into eighths). This way the first two steps of the module are easy to make (see diagram 3, below).

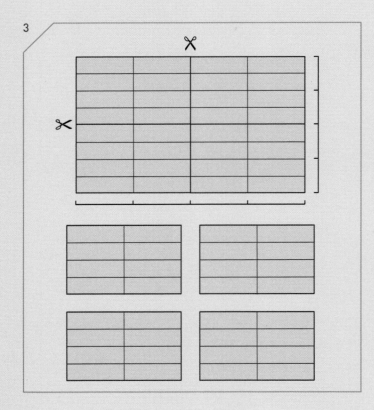

FOLDING THE MODULES

You can fold paper almost anywhere, but if you have a choice, then use a bright and comfortable place for folding. Make sure you have enough suitable paper and have clean hands before you begin. Paper absorbs moisture and oil from your fingers, so try to handle the paper as little as possible.

Sharp, accurate folding will make assembly much easier. Fold on a hard surface and be careful to keep edges or location marks lined up as you fold: don't let them slip.

As you fold more units, you should find your accuracy improves as your muscle memory learns the steps. Also, you may find better ways to make the units than the diagrams suggest. This is why you should normally avoid an assembly line method of folding, such as step 1 on each sheet of paper, then step 2 on each sheet, then step 3 on each sheet, etc. Not only is this dull and unsatisfying compared with making complete modules one at a time, you might find that you've made the same mistake on all of the modules!

ASSEMBLY

Once you have made two modules, try joining them together, since this makes folding the modules more motivating. It also lets you find out if you need to make any minor adjustments to the modules, perhaps because of the size and thickness of your paper. Usually, it is better to keep adding modules to the same model. Do not make separate subassemblies and then join them together—this can become confusing and is often inefficient.

However, for some models it is better to have all the modules ready before assembling. These are usually models that do not hold well until all the units are assembled, when they collectively get structural strength (e.g., Double Equilateral Triangle Unit models and the *Six-Part Stellated Rhombic Dodecahedron*). Otherwise, you can assemble the units as you fold them.

2-D models are mostly straightforward to assemble, but joining the last module can be hard at first. You might need to gently bend the model or flip the first modules forward to access them. This means lifting the first module and pulling it toward you; otherwise you will make a helix that could go on forever. When you pull the last module toward you, it then usually goes inside the first module. Put simply, join the first and last units in the same way that all of the other units are joined.

Sometimes, it is useful to remove the first unit and use it as a new "last" unit. You know that this last unit joins well with the "first" unit (i.e., the old second unit). This is useful where a locking fold is made during assembly (e.g., Decagon Ring).

3-D models are usually harder to assemble than 2-D models. If the last module is hard to add, loosen the other modules and try again.

For difficult and awkward assemblies, you might need some tools. The first type of tool lets you poke and tuck flaps in difficult places—cocktail sticks and nail files work well.

The second type of tool temporarily holds modules together. You can use paperclips, mini clothespins, or pressure-sensitive masking tape (depending on the model). Some models are almost impossible without paperclips (e.g., some Double Equilateral Triangle Unit models and Six Symmetrical Prisms). You might also find paperclips useful for your first attempt at assembling the Skeletal Octahedron. Paperclips can leave marks, so don't leave them in place for too long. Also, do not leave masking tape on for too long either, since it might bond with the paper and rip when removed.

LEVELS OF DIFFICULTY

Some units are easy to fold but hard to assemble (e.g., Card Cube and Six Symmetrical Prisms).

MODULE

Easy ◈ — Valley and mountain folds only, no more than about a dozen steps (e.g., Dodecagon Ring and Skeletal Octahedron).

Medium ◈◈ — Only a few compound folds such as reverse folds and squash folds (e.g., Magic Star).

Hard ◈◈◈ — Several compound folds like reverse folds and squash folds (e.g., Pinwheel Cube and WXYZ).

Difficult ◈◈◈◈ — High accuracy is essential. May have a few tricky folds (e.g., Jitterbug) or may need extensive precreasing (e.g., Six-Part Stellated Rhombic Dodecahedron by David Mitchell.

ASSEMBLY

Easy ◈ — Each unit attaches easily to the next and does not come apart easily (e.g., Decagon Ring and Starfish).

Medium ◈◈ — Each unit attaches fairly easily to the next but is only partially stable (e.g., Pinwheel Cube), or some care is needed not to make the connection neither too tight nor too loose, such as Magic Star by Robert Neale and Caterpillar.

Hard ◈◈◈ — Each unit attaches fairly easily to the next but is not particularly stable until several units are combined (e.g. Business Card Cube). Or attaching each unit is not straightforward (e.g., 12-Piece Carousel), or the last unit is difficult to attach (e.g., WXYZ). Or you need to take special care with the symmetry of the model so that adjacent units do not have the same color (e.g., Dodecahedron by Silvana Betti Mamino).

Difficult ◈◈◈◈ — Careful attention required for the order of joining or access is not always straightforward (e.g., Six Symmetrical Prisms and the Tetrahedron and Octahedron from the Windowed Icosahedron and Snub Series).

Projects

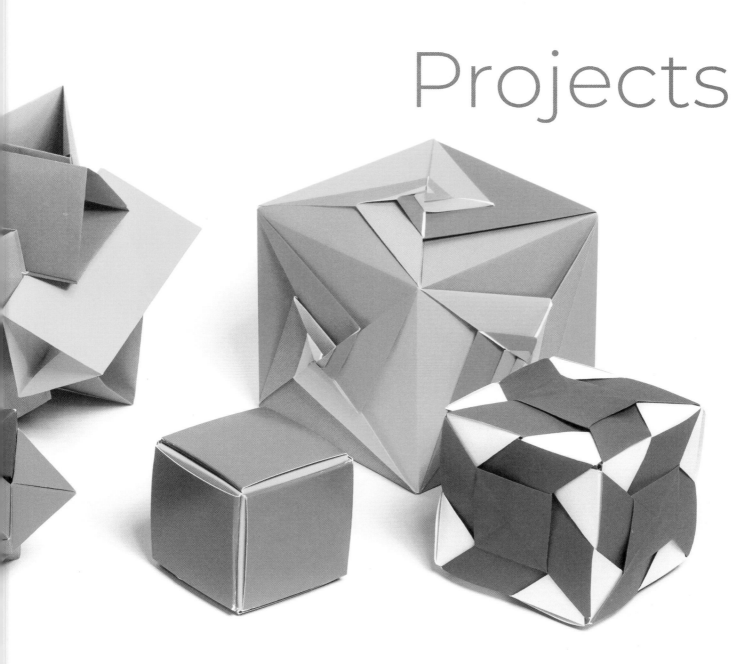

THE PROJECTS

Modular origami naturally lends itself to geometric subjects. However, flowers, animals, and other figurative subjects are possible. The models are a selection made by me and other creators. Some of the models are well known, but I am pleased to introduce some classics that may have been overlooked.

RINGS AND STARS

Rings and stars are a natural subject for modular origami: each module makes a segment or point and can be made from a different color. The geometry to make the required angles and lengths can be fascinating, and joining the units into a continuous loop can be very satisfying.

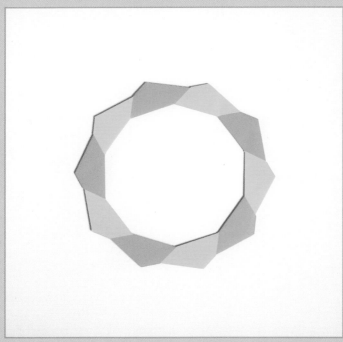

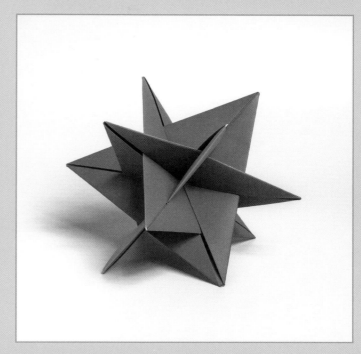

DECAGON RING ⬢

Paper requirements: ten 3 in. (75 mm) squares or larger
Finished model ratio: 2.5

This model's starting point is Nakano's *Flying Saucer 4* (Nakano 85). However, instead of using glue to join the units, a simple lock suffices. Try linking two rings or making a chain of rings.

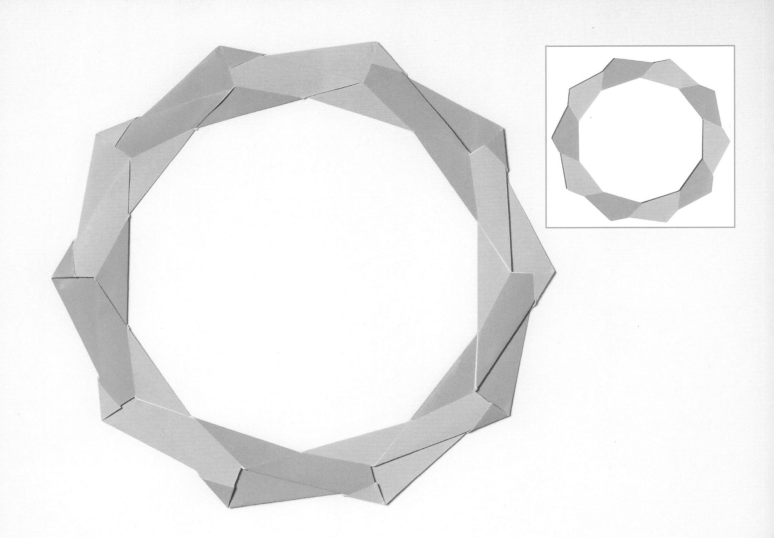

MODULE ⬡

1 Fold in half, bringing opposite edges together.

2 Fold the diagonal with both layers of paper.

3 Unit complete

ASSEMBLY ⬡

1 Insert the second unit into the pocket of the first unit.

2 Notice how the top edge of the second unit touches inside the pocket. Fold the raw edges of the second unit to lie on the diagonal of the first unit.

3 Tuck the layers of the second unit between the layers of the first unit.

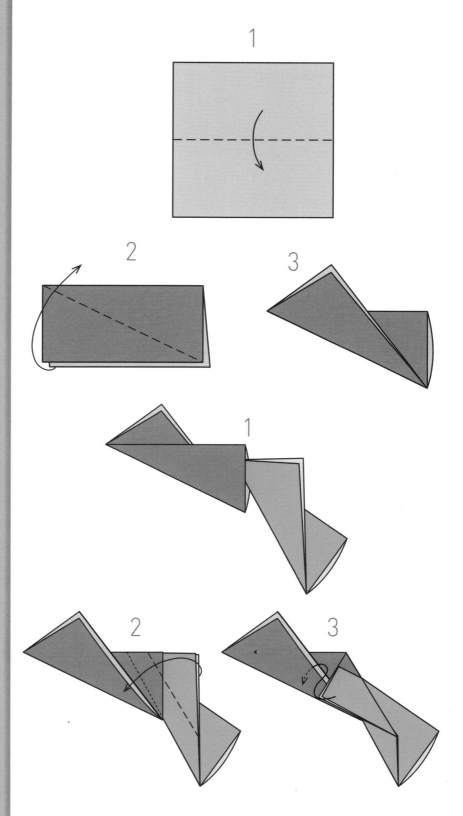

STARFISH

Paper requirements: five A8 rectangles or larger. Alternatively, use longer rectangles and a different number of units.
Finished model ratio: 1.2

This folding method generalizes to rectangles that are longer than silver rectangles. For bronze rectangles there is no excess paper to fold in steps 4 and 7, since the right angle is trisected. Longer rectangles (e.g., 2:1) have the excess paper on the lower right instead of the center in step 4.

MODULE ⬡

1 Fold the lower right corner to top left corner and unfold.

2 Fold the diagonal by folding the left end of the crease line onto the right end.

3 Fold the lower right flap to align with the raw edge behind.

4 Fold the tip of the flap down along the crease made in step 1.

5 Fold in half by mountain-folding the bottom behind.

6 The next steps are similar to steps 3 and 4. Fold the right flap over the raw edge.

7 Fold the tip of the right flap up to match the folded edge behind.

8 Open the paper and return to step 3 by undoing steps 7, 6, 5, 4, and 3.

ASSEMBLY ⬡

1 Slide the flap of the right-hand unit underneath the raw edge of the left-hand unit. Turn the paper over to repeat this on the other side.

2 Valley-fold to lock the units together. Add more units.

When adding the last unit, you may need to flatten the flaps so that you can join it to the first unit. When finished, shape the completed model so that it is symmetrical.

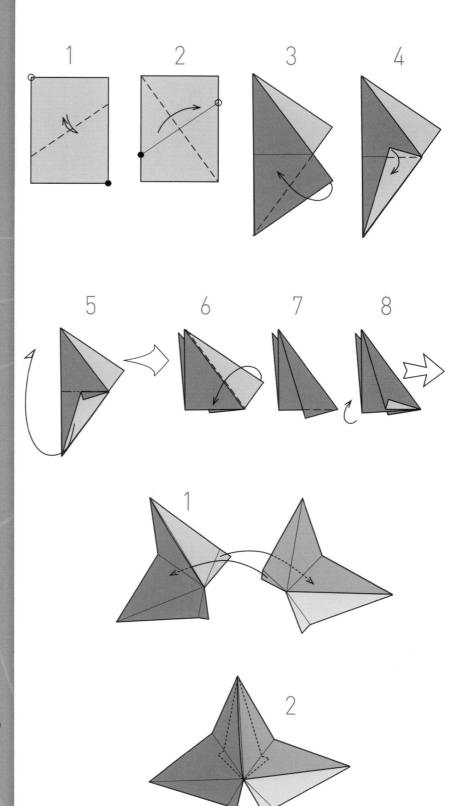

PENTAGRAM ◈

Paper requirements: five 4 in. (100 mm) squares
Finished model ratio: 1.9

An earlier version of this model used the 1:3 approximation for dividing a right angle into fifths. However, this version uses a more accurate method, which is important for the little locking flaps. For extra accuracy, with larger paper the midpoint lands just below the diagonal in step 5.

MODULE ⬡⬡

1 Diagonally fold, top left to bottom right corner.

2 Bisect the lower right 45° angle but do not fold all the way. Only on the right edge, new pinch.

3 Pinch halfway up to the pinch from step 2.

4 Pinch the midpoint of the left edge and then quarter point.

5 Crease through the top right corner and the midpoint of the two closest pinches.

6 Fold right edge up to the crease just made.

7 Fold over.

8 Fold creased edge back down onto the diagonal.

ASSEMBLY ⬡⬡⬡

1 Slide the second unit into the first.

2 Fold the small flap of the first unit over the second to lock.

3 Add more units in a clockwise direction.

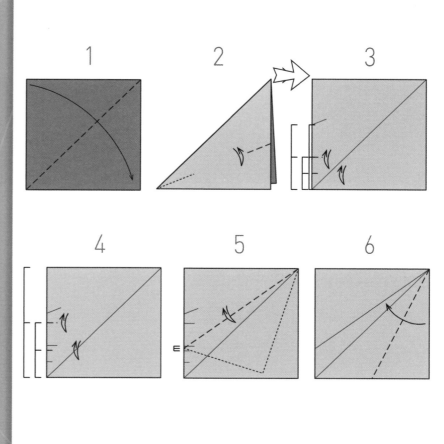

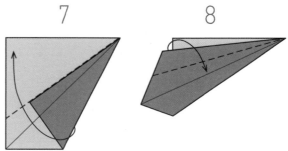

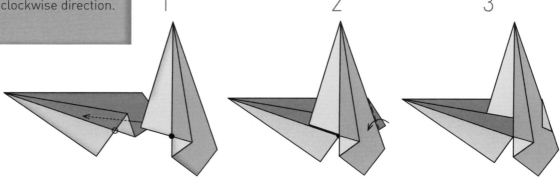

WXYZ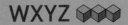

Paper requirements: twelve squares
Finished model ratio: 1.0

This was the result of experimenting with skeletal cuboctahedra, which can be seen as four intersecting regular hexagons. But what happens if the hexagons are transformed into equilateral triangles? Use four colors so that each triangle is a different color. Sizes from 3 in. (75 mm) up are effective.

MODULE ⬡⬡

1 Pinch middle and bottom.

2 Unfold so that the white side is uppermost.

3 Pinch one quarter at bottom right.

4 Valley in half upward.

5 Use the mountain at the center to help locate the fold.

6 Fold the bottom left edge to meet the edge just folded.

7 Fold the right edge just folded to meet the left edge.

8 Unfold the right flap.

9 Fold the right corner to the left corner.

10 Squash the flap to the right.

11 Mountain-fold the right flap behind.

12 Fold the left flap to the right.

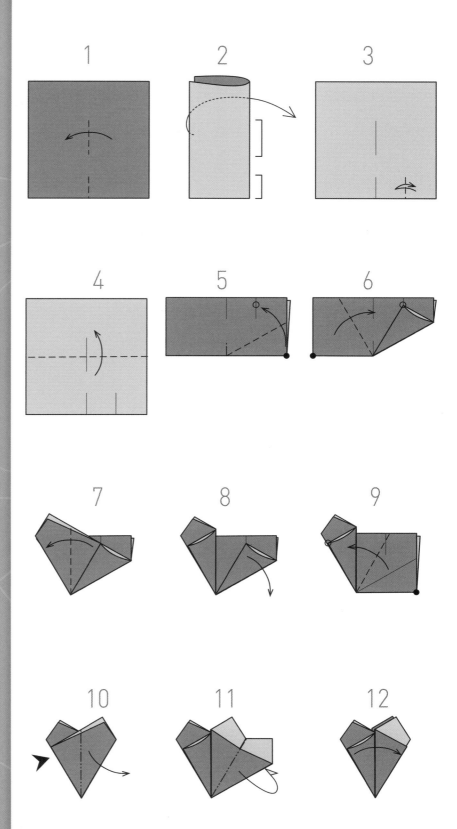

13 Squash the flap to the left.

14 Fold the left flap behind.

15 Fold down the white flaps against the colored raw edges.

16 Stand the flaps at right angles.

ASSEMBLY ●●●

1 Every unit has a pair of pockets on each side. Tuck two flaps of the second unit into one pair of pockets.

2 Two units joined. Add two more so that you have a ring of four units, each a different color. Add more units to extend each plane of color so that you have four triangles, each a different color.

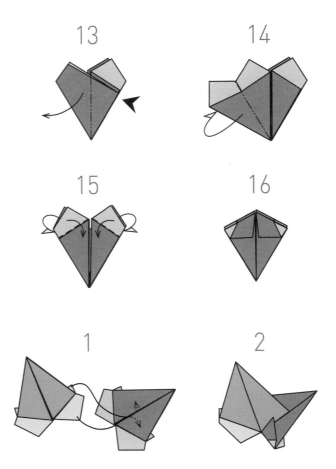

POLYHEDRA

The cube may be mundane, but modular origami can show different aspects of geometry in an appealing way (e.g., rotational or mirror symmetry). Other polyhedra can be more immediately attractive, especially if they use equilateral triangles or regular pentagons. Instructions are given for all of the convex regular polyhedra. In some cases, a single unit can make several models when different numbers of modules are used. See "Useful Terms" (pages 5–7) for details and data.

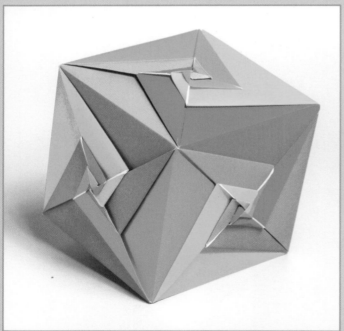

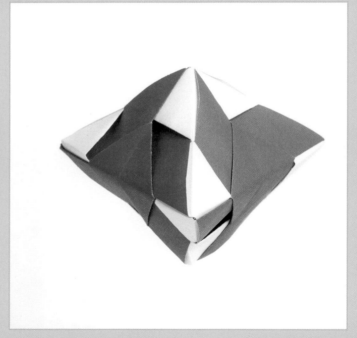

CARD CUBE 🔲

Paper requirements: twelve oblongs of thin card per cube. Use rail tickets 3.4 x 2 in. (85 x 54 mm), business cards, postcards, or other similar oblongs of thin card. You need at least six units to make the cube: for a stable cube, you need another six units to "clad" the cube.

If you are using card that cracks when folded, then you may need to score the card before folding. You can use a ballpoint pen that has run out of ink as a scoring tool. Another possible tool is the back (noncutting) edge of a knife: the aim is to press a groove into the card without cutting the surface.

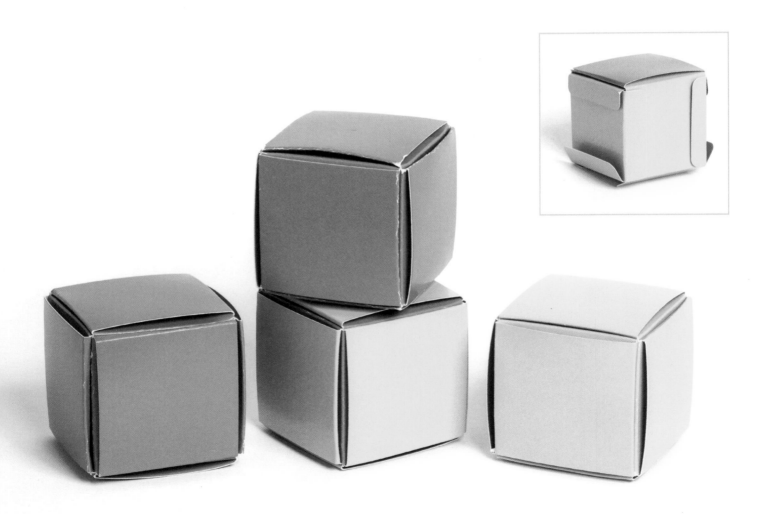

MODULE MADE BY FOLDING THIN CARD ⬡

1 Place two cards together, back to back. Fold the edges of one card around the other card to form simple tabs. The edges of the front card fold behind, and the edges of the rear card fold to the front.

2 Separate and keep the tabs at right angles.

3 Two units completed.

4 You need six for the cube and another six for the cladding (now continue to step 1 of Assembly).

MODULE MADE BY SCORING AND FOLDING THICKER CARD ⬡

1 Use one card as a template. Place the template (gray) onto the target card. Score along the top edge of the template and then move the template down slightly (about 2 mm).

2 Score along the top edge of the template.

3 Fold the top edge down.

4 Score along the bottom edge of the template.

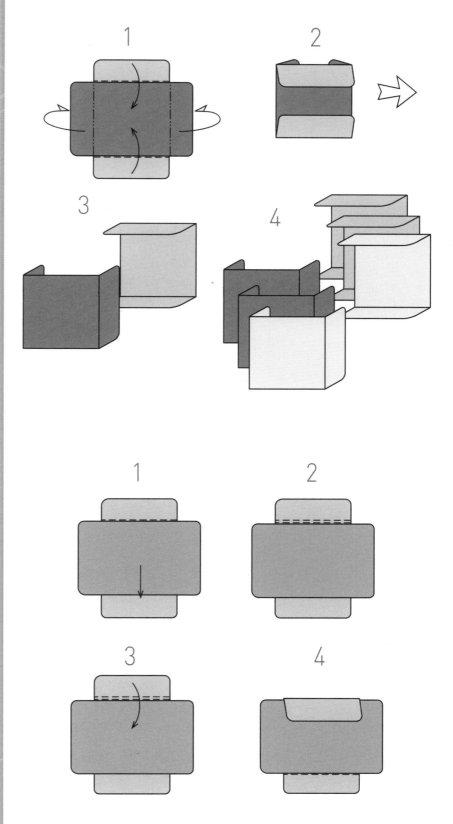

43

5 Move the template down slightly (about 2 mm).

6 Score along the bottom edge of the template. Then fold the bottom edge up.

7 Unfold the card and remove the template.

8 The ridges in the card are similar to those in some packaging such as cereal boxes.

ASSEMBLY ◆◆◆

This method of making cubes has been known since at least the nineteenth century, when they were made from playing cards.

1 Position the units so that the tabs will be on the outside of the cube. Join three around one vertex of the cube.

2 Three units positioned. Hold this in the palm of one hand or place on the surface of a table so that you have a hand free to place the other units.

3 Carefully slide the other units into place with your free hand. If the model comes apart, redo step 2. If you need to, use masking tape to temporarily hold the units in place.

4 Six units joined. The next steps are optional.

5 Secure the cube by cladding with the extra six units.

6 Here the top and bottom faces have been clad. Add more units to fully secure the cube.

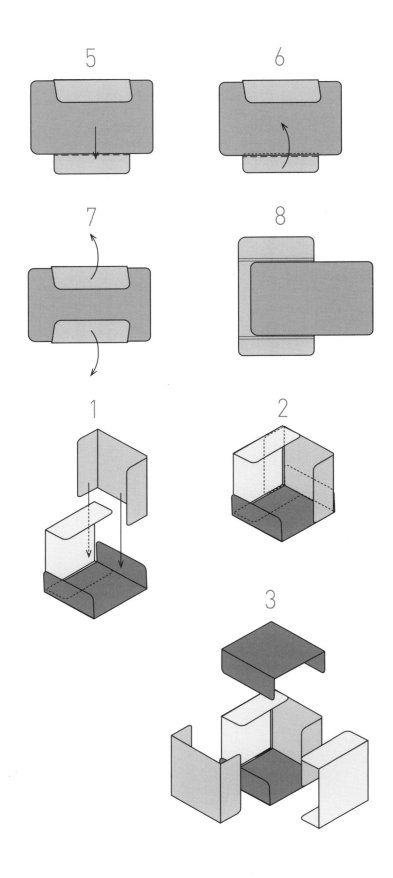

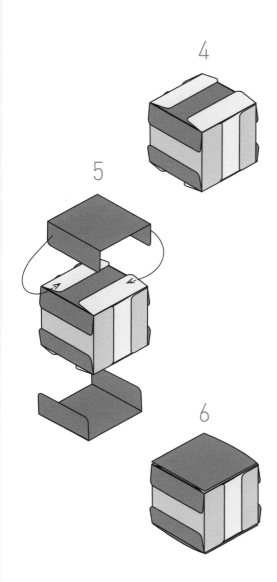

4

5

6

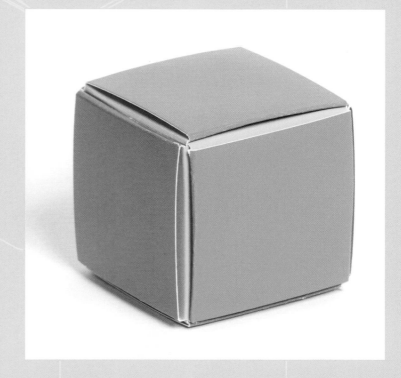

SPIRAL CUBE ◆◆◆

Paper requirements: twenty-four squares about 4 in. (10 cm) in four colors
Finished model ratio: 2.3

This cube uses a simple and efficient unit. The larger the paper, the more spiral turns you can make. You can use three or four colors. Four units (two or four colors) make a square coaster.

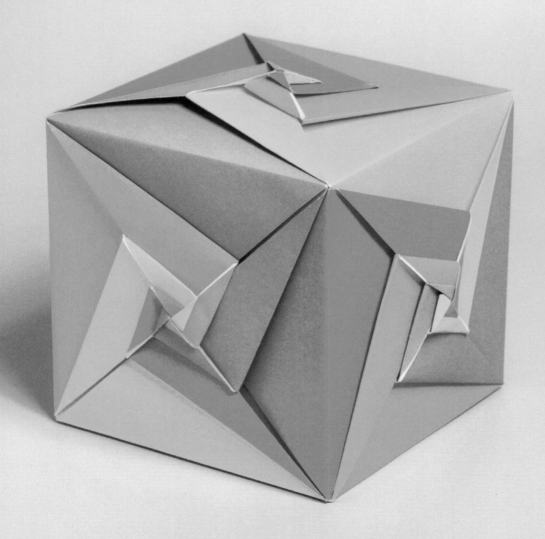

MODULE ⬡

1 Fold the bottom corner to the top corner to fold the diagonal.

2 Fold in half, joining left and right corners, and unfold.

3 Repeat steps 1 and 2 on a second square. Interleave the two units with the vertical creases as valleys.

4 Turn over top to bottom.

5 Fold the bottom left flap onto the diagonal raw edges of the top square. Rotate 180°.

6 Repeat step 5.

7 Fold the small tip onto the diagonal raw edge of the bottom square.

8 Fold the small tip onto the diagonal creased edge.

9 Rotate 180°.

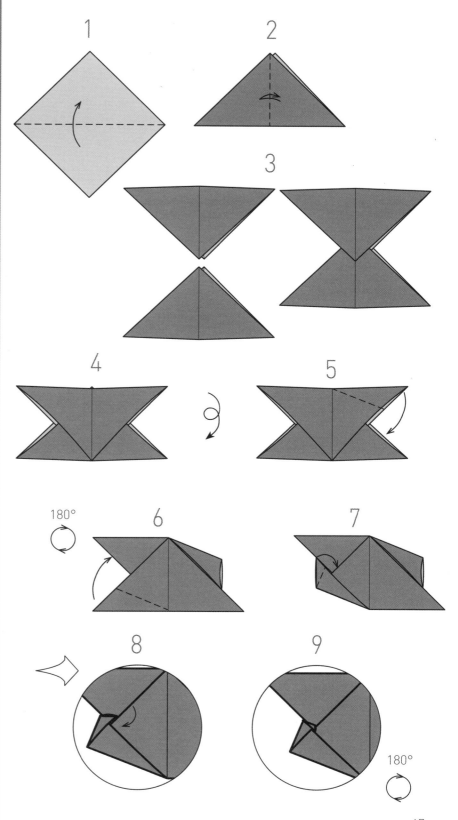

10 Separate the pieces so that you can fold to the edge of the square.

11 Repeat steps 7 and 8 and then push the two pieces back together.

12 Unfold the tips and the unit is complete.

ASSEMBLY ◆◆◆

1 Turn over four of the units and arrange them as the four corners of a square. Tuck the flap of each unit into the next unit in a clockwise direction.

2 The flaps for the spiral are on the other side.

3 Turn over.

4 The next steps magnify the center to show you how to make the spiral.

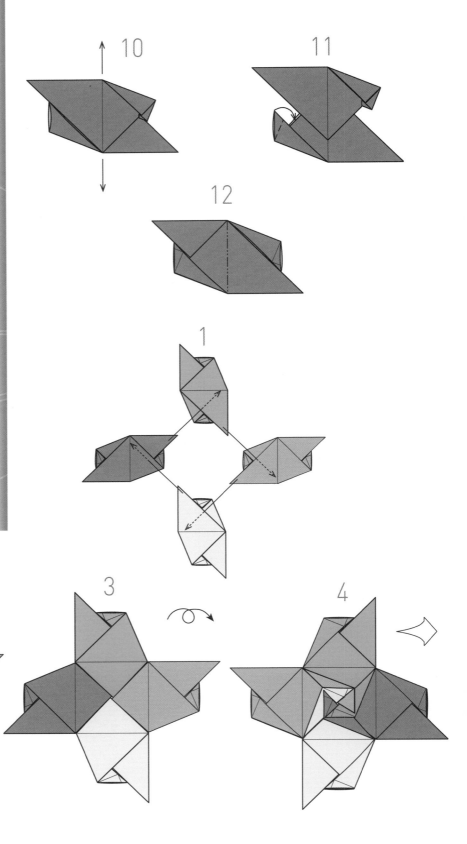

5 Fold and interleave the arms of the spiral.

6 To complete the spiral, bend the tips and position them before flattening to firm the creases.

7 The completed spiral. The next step is zoomed out to show all of the units.

8 Turn over.

9 Fold the outer halves of the units and make them stand up at right angles.

10 The remaining units do not need to be tucked in (like the first four in step 1). Put the next four units into position but do not tuck any flaps. Then add the top four units.

11 When the cube is secure, you can undo each partial spiral and make a full spiral using all of the precreases.

12 Complete

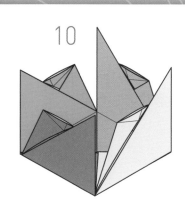

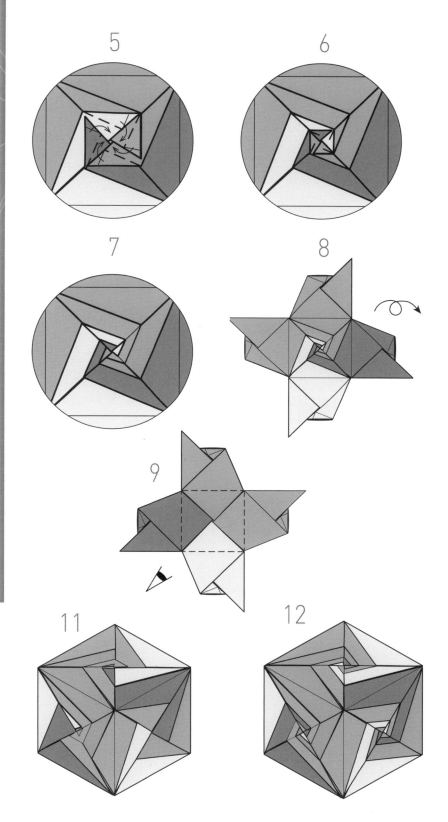

FOUR COLORS

1 Connect four units, one of each color, to form the base of the cube.

2 For the vertical edges, choose a color not already at the vertex.

3 For the top four units, the colors are the same as the base but rotated by 90°.

FOUR COLORS—TOP AND BASE THE SAME

1 The opposite edges are the same color.

2 The vertical edges are the third color.

3 The colors of the top four units are the same as the base.

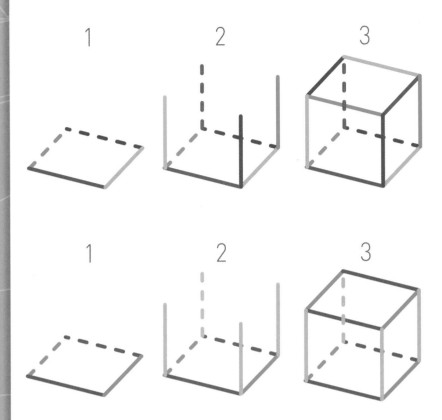

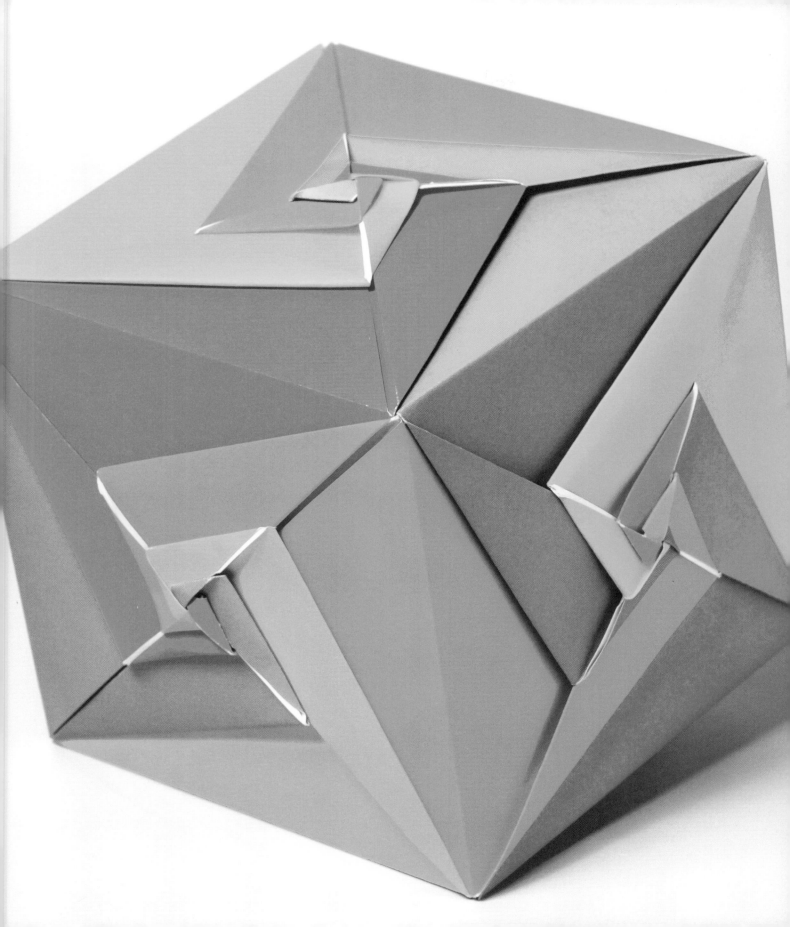

PINWHEEL CUBE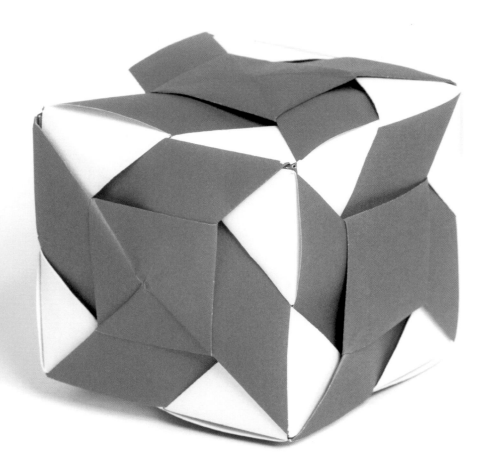

Paper requirements: six squares 3 in. (75 mm) or larger
Finished model ratio: 1.4 (square), 0.9 (cube), 0.6 (hexahedron)

As well as a cube, this unit can make other shapes. For example, two units make a flat coaster, and three units make an irregular hexahedron when a diagonal fold is added to each unit.

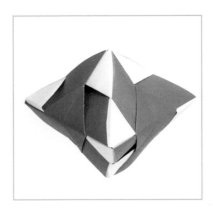

MODULE

1 Crease the diagonals, but only at the corners and the center: try to avoid creasing elsewhere.

2 Fold the edges in one quarter and unfold. Turn over.

3 Fold the bottom edge up by three-eighths to touch the horizontal crease line and unfold: crease only between the diagonals. Repeat on the other three edges to crease the inner square.

4 Squeeze the mountain folds of the diagonals and the outer square. Form a box shape.

5 Rotate the arms clockwise and flatten.

6 Valley-fold the tips along the outline of the square.

7 Unfold the tips.

8 Turn over.

9 Unit complete

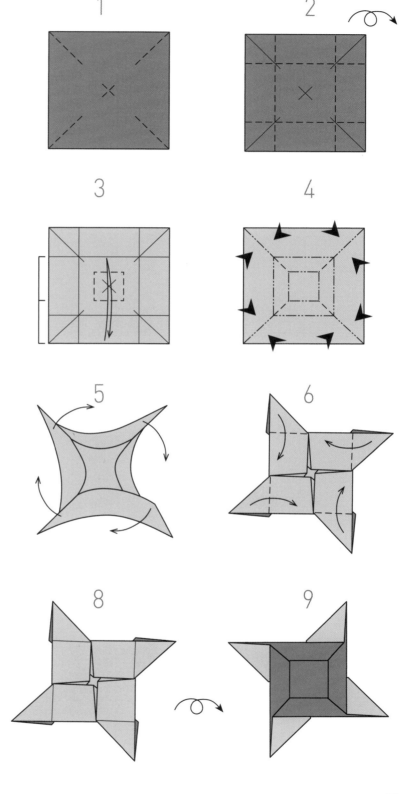

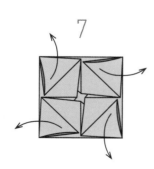

53

SQUARE ASSEMBLY 🎲

1 Take two units. Place them back to back.

2 Tuck the flaps into the pockets.

3 Complete

CUBE ASSEMBLY 🎲🎲

1 You need six units. Insert the bottom right flap of the first unit into the bottom left pocket of the second unit. At the same time, insert the top left flap of the second unit into the top right pocket of the first unit.

2 Join the third unit to the second.

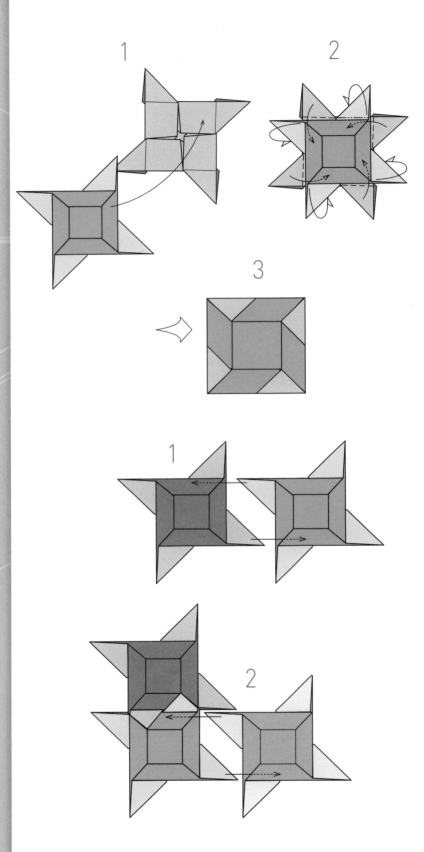

3 Form one-half of the cube by joining the first and third units. You will make mountain folds to create a 3-D shape.

4 Turn over.

5 Add more units.

6 Completed cube

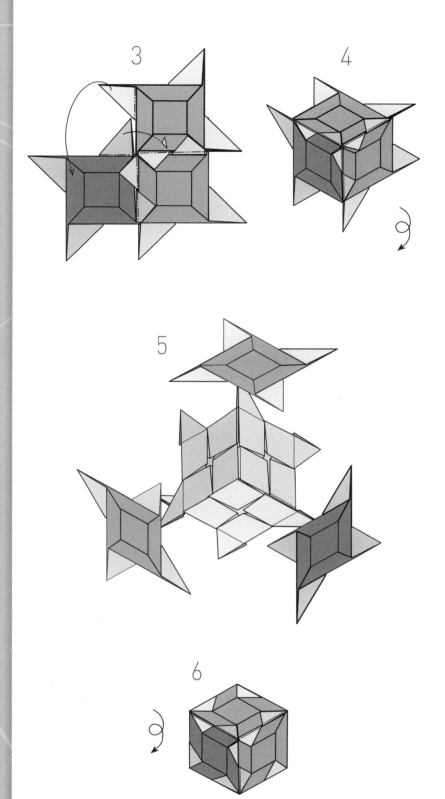

55

HEXAHEDRON ASSEMBLY ◈◈◈

1 You need three units. Make a single mountain fold on the diagonal of each unit. Then join in the same way as the cube.

2 Join the first and third units. You are making mountain folds to make a 3-D shape.

3 Mountain-fold the diagonals of each unit so that they touch each other. Turn over.

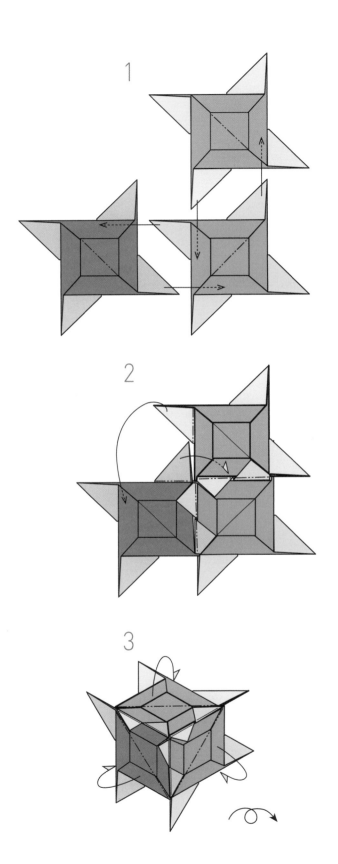

4 Tuck the three flaps into the pockets around the vertex, opposite the first vertex that you joined.

5 Bend and tuck the flaps into the pockets. You might find this easier to do when viewed from the side.

6 Completed hexahedron

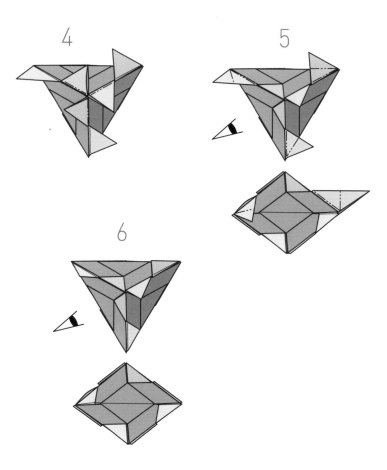

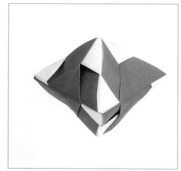

SIX SYMMETRICAL PRISMS ◇◇◇◇

Paper requirements:
Twelve squares at least 3 x 3 in. (75 x 75 mm)
Optional paperclips
Finished model ratio: 0.7

The starting folds are familiar from several traditional models such as the *sampan* boat and *masu* box (for reference, see the many online guides).The cube needs six squares: you may need to use paperclips during assembly. Use another six squares for the prism hats.

CUBE MODULE

1 Crease the diagonals. Turn over.

2 Fold the corners to the center and unfold. Turn over.

3 Crease left and right flaps 3/8. Turn over.

4 Fold the bottom corner up 1/8 and then fold on the crease made in step 2. Rotate the paper 180° and repeat.

5 Turn over.

6 Pleat.

7 Unfold the left and right corners and let it stand at 90°.

8 Unit complete. Make six in total.

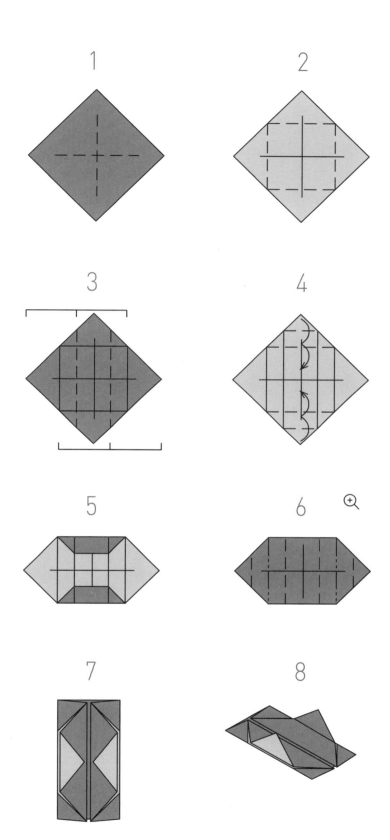

59

CUBE ASSEMBLY ⬡⬡⬡

1 Hook the small flap of the first unit into the pocket of the second unit.

2 Paper clips may help during assembly.

3 Add the third unit.

4 The assembled cube is strong. You can vary the positions of the flaps. (4a–c)

PRISM MODULE ⬡

1 Crease the diagonal and pinch the center.

2 Fold the corners to the center and unfold.

3 Fold in half and then open up.

Complete.

ASSEMBLY ⬡

1 Insert the flaps from the cube into the prism module.

2 Complete

60

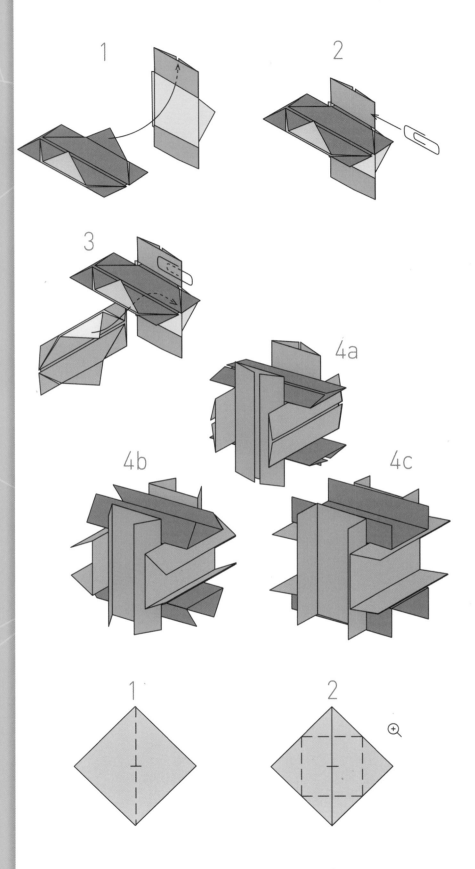

3

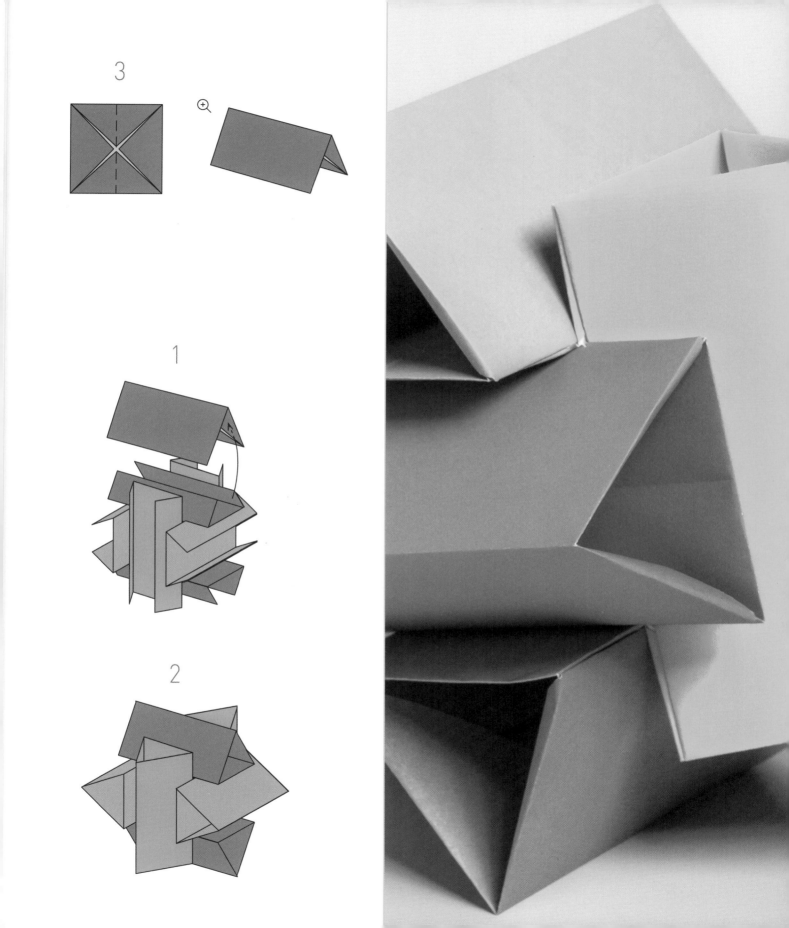

1

2

WINDOWED ICOSAHEDRON AND SNUB SERIES ◈◈◈

Paper requirements: Bronze rectangles with a short side, about 2.9 in. (7.5 cm).
Finished model ratio: 0.8 (octahedron), 0.9 (icosahedron), 1.4 (snub cube), 2.4 (snub dodecahedron)

This unit and the next one both use 60° geometry. This unit uses a rectangle that has the proportions 1:√3. You can make a pair of these bronze rectangles from a square with little waste (see page 21).

The tetrahedron uses a simplified unit from half of a bronze rectangle: this unit works for the other assemblies. The simplified unit is not as bulky as the full unit. However, assembly may be harder since the pockets are less secure. In some ways this unit is almost as versatile as the famous Sonobe unit.

MODULE ⬢

1 Bring the long edges together and crease only the central portion. Unfold. Fold the top and bottom edges to the middle.

2 Mountain-fold the left flap behind to fold in half.

3 Crease the diagonals on the upper flap. Repeat behind.

4 Unfold the rear flap.

5 Fold the flaps in a clockwise direction.

6 Reinforce the mountain folds to complete the unit.

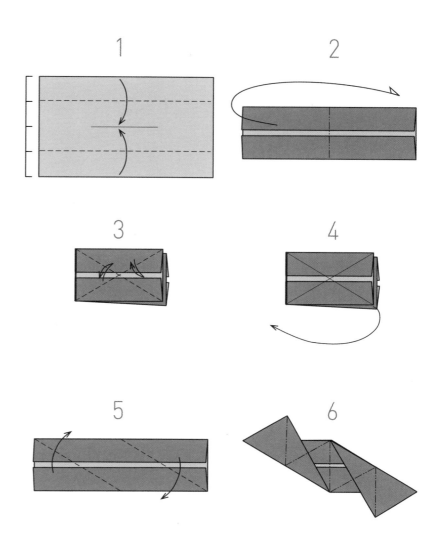

ICOSAHEDRON (SNUB TETRAHEDRON) ASSEMBLY ◆◆◆

1 You need six units. Take three units. Insert the flap of each unit into the pocket of the next to form an equilateral triangle.

2 Reinforce the mountain folds. Add the three remaining units.

3 Make a third equilateral triangle by inserting the flap into the pocket. This makes a triangular window. The flaps are on the outside of the icosahedron so the assembly will be convex.

4 A view looking down onto the triangular window. Turn over.

5 A view of the concave interior. Valley-fold the flaps and interlock. Tuck in the last set of flaps.

6 Complete. Observe the four triangular windows. The icosahedron can be thought of as a snub tetrahedron.

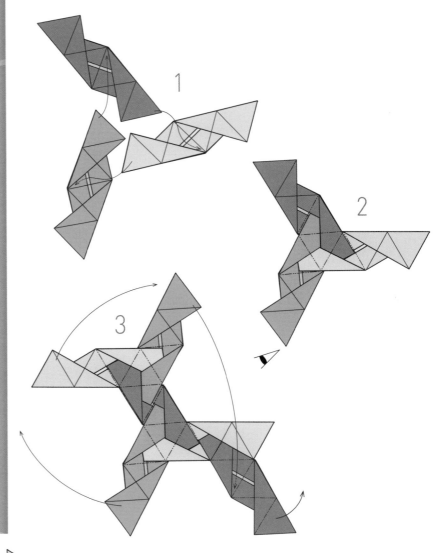

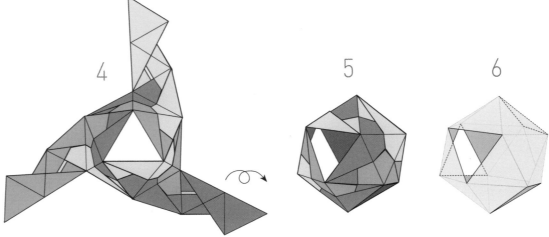

SNUB CUBE ASSEMBLY ◆◆◆

1 You need twelve units. Assemble eight units into three complete equilateral triangles and complete the fourth to make a square window.

2 The flaps are on the outside of the snub cube. Each unit corresponds to an edge of a cube. The next view is from the side looking down at the square window.

3 Add the remaining four units. These correspond to the bottom four edges of the schematic cube.

4 The completed model with a view showing the hidden faces.

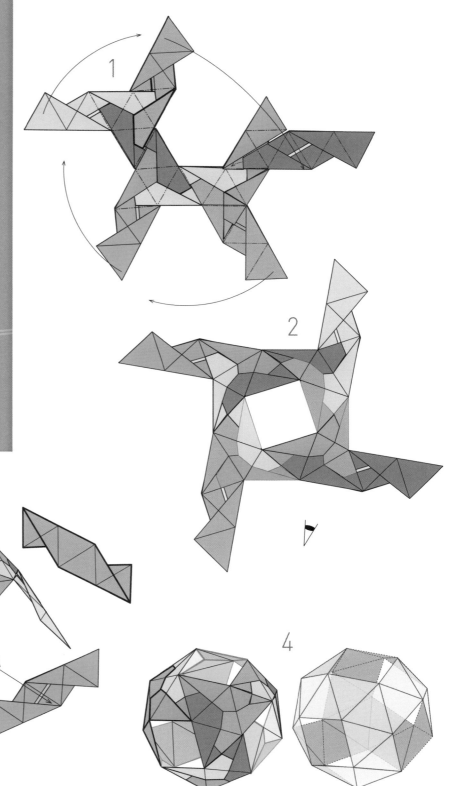

SNUB DODECAHEDRON ASSEMBLY

You need thirty units in either five or six colors (below left and right). These instructions use five colors. See *Dodecahedron No. 14 (Easy Module)* on page 80 for detailed instructions on how to arrange the colors.

You may find it helpful to make the icosahedron and snub cube before making the snub dodecahedron.

To make the snub dodecahedron, assemble the units to make one pentagonal window. Then add more units to make the "vertices" of the dodecahedron.

OCTAHEDRON ASSEMBLY

Although this octahedron uses only three units, you may find you need the experience of making the previous polyhedra in order to understand the assembly. It is harder than the others because the windows are now slits, instead of polygons.

1 Join three units to form an equilateral triangle. Then mountain-fold the flaps and form an equilateral triangle on the other side. Turn over so that you can put the flaps into position. To make this easier, you can put your finger into the slits to open them and pull the flaps into place. The slits are shown in heavy line in the schematic diagram of the octahedron. (1a–c)

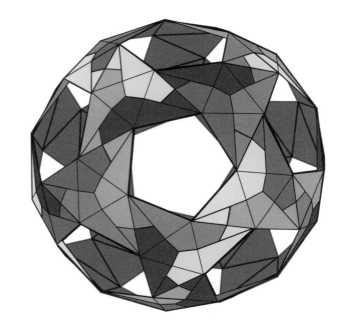

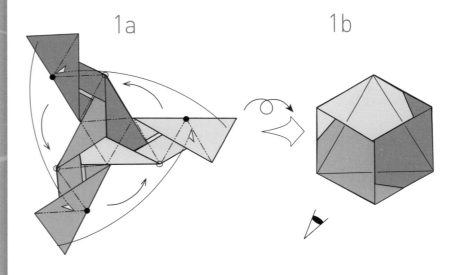

1a

1b

1c

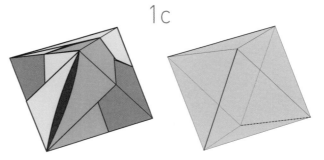

TETRAHEDRON ASSEMBLY ◇◇◇◇

This is the hardest assembly even though it uses only one unit. The reason is that the assembly is like trying to close a door from the inside.

1 Start with a 1:√3 rectangle cut in half (i.e. 1:2√3), and fold from step 2. Make valley folds in step 6.

2 Bring the ends together. Tuck the right flap under the left and slide the left flap between the layers of the right flap.

3 You may need to flatten the paper into a tube to make it easier to join the ends. A tetrahedron made from a full bronze rectangle is possible, but harder.

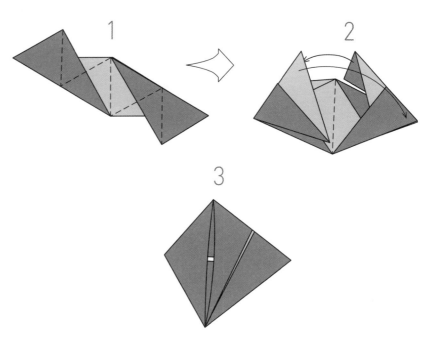

DOUBLE EQUILATERAL TRIANGLE UNIT ◆◆◆

Paper requirements: Squares about 4 in. (10 cm)
Finished model ratio: 0.5 (tetrahedron), 0.8 (octahedron),
1.0 (icosahedron), 1.2 (stella octangula).

This module can make several models, including the Platonic Solids, that are deltahedra. The tetrahedron (A), icosahedron (C), and trigonal trapezohedron (E) need equal numbers of units that are mirror images of each other. The other polyhedra need units folded in the same orientation: the octahedron (B) needs four units, and the stella octangula (D) twelve. The unit could be made from a double bronze rectangle. However, embedding it in a square makes for a convenient starting shape and also means the flaps are easier to tuck since they have a truncated tip.

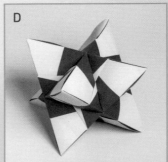
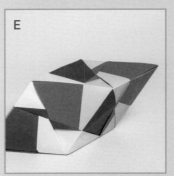

MODULE ⬢

1 Pinch midpoints of the top and bottom edges. Fold the top and bottom edges together and unfold. Turn over.

2 Pinch quarter marks on the central crease.

3 Fold the bottom left corner onto the right-hand quarter mark; at the same time, pivot the fold through the bottom midpoint.

4 Unfold the flap.

5 Rotate 180°.

6 Repeat step 3.

7 Refold the right flap.

8 Fold the top layer along a line through the two points.

9 Pull out the hidden flap.

10 Fold the flap to match.

11 Mountain-fold in half and unfold.

12 Mountain-fold the top left flap and unfold. Repeat with the lower right flap.

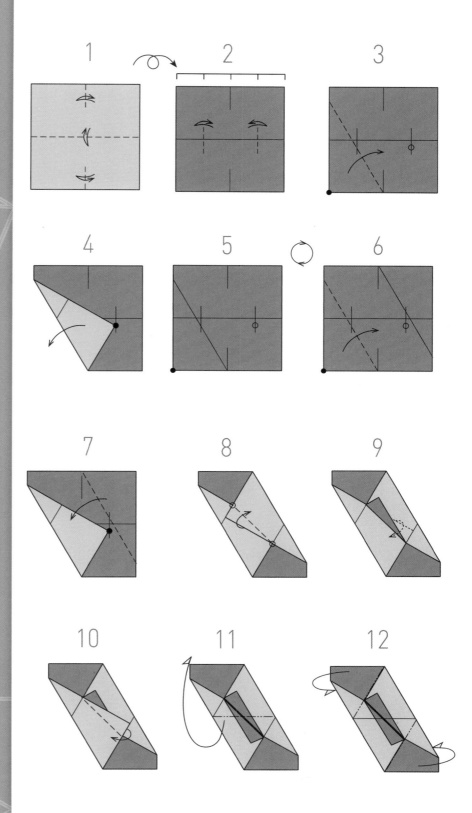

TETRAHEDRON ASSEMBLY 🔷

1 Make a second unit that is a mirror image of the first (i.e., in step 3, fold the bottom right corner onto the left-hand quarter mark).

2 Tuck the top right flap of the second unit into the pocket of the first unit.

3 Tuck the top left flap of the first unit into the pocket of the first unit. You will need to use three existing mountain folds. The result is 3-D.

4 Mountain-fold flap of the second unit around and to the rear.

5 Mountain-fold the flap of the first unit to lie on the tetrahedron. Rotate the tetrahedron so that you can see the loose flaps.

6 Completed tetrahedron

OCTAHEDRON ASSEMBLY 🔷🔷🔷

1 Tuck the tips of the first and second units into the pockets behind them to secure the regular tetrahedron.

2 Take four units. Insert the flap of the second unit into the pocket of the first unit.

3 Add the third and then the fourth unit.

4 Insert the flap of the first unit into the pocket of the fourth unit. You will make a 3-D shape that is half of the octahedron.

5 Look inside the half octahedron.

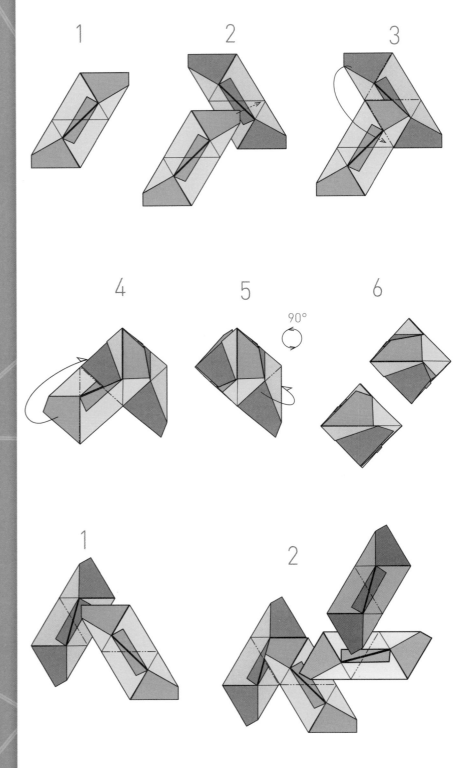

6 Interlock the flaps so that the flap of each unit is on top of the next unit (in a clockwise direction).

7 Tuck the flap of each unit into the pocket of the unit below.

8 Completed octahedron

TETRAHEDRA AND OCTAHEDRA

An octahedron can be surrounded by four tetrahedra to form a larger tetrahedron (A and B, below right). Another way of looking at this is that one small red tetrahedron has had the lengths of its edges doubled to make the larger tetrahedron. This is analogous to taking a cube and doubling the lengths to make a cube that has eight times the volume of the smaller cube. Therefore, the larger tetrahedron has a volume that is eight times that of the smaller tetrahedron. Also, the central octahedron is half of the volume of the larger tetrahedron. Why?

Doubling the length makes the surface area larger by a factor of four. Tripling the length makes the surface area larger by a factor of nine; the volume increases by a factor of twenty-seven. Buckminster Fuller would have described the larger tetrahedron as being divided in frequency 3. The factor for area and volume compared with line lengths is usually called squared and cubed, but it would be equally appropriate to call them triangled and tetrahedroned.

Cubes can fill space without gaps. So, too, can a combination of regular tetrahedra and octahedra. You can make a nest of octahedra if each set of four smaller octahedra is folded from squares that have half the edge length of the larger octahedron. (C)

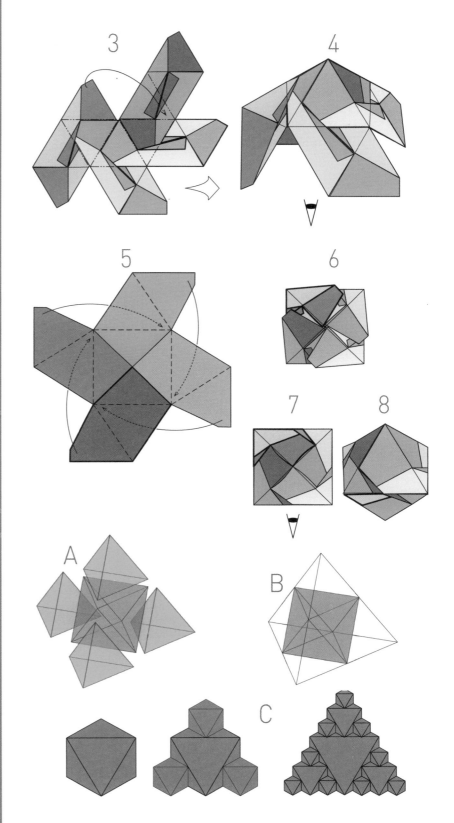

ICOSAHEDRON ASSEMBLY ◆◆◆◆

1 Make five units. Then make five more that are mirror images of the first ones.

2 Join the first five units. This is like the octahedron assembly but with an extra unit. Use paper clips to hold the units together.

3 Turn over.

4 Insert the fifth unit into the first to form half of the icosahedron. The flaps are on the outside of the icosahedron.

Add the mirror image modules. Use more paperclips as needed. Tuck the flaps into the pockets at top of the icosahedron.

5 Model complete. Remove the paper clips. This model is secure but not very strong—this is caused by the large dihedral angle.

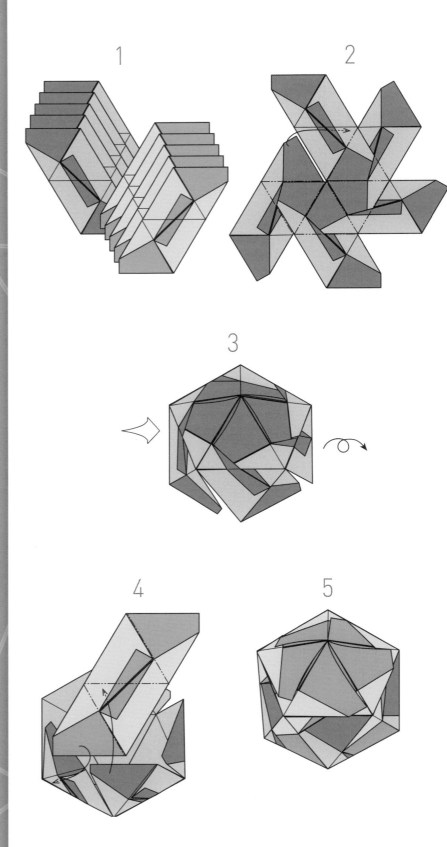

1

2

3

4

5

STELLA OCTANGULA ASSEMBLY ◈◈◈

1 Assemble twelve units. Make the horizontal fold a valley fold on each unit.

2 Join three units. Use paper clips to hold the units together.

3 Add units to make the tetrahedral corners complete. Use paper clips to hold the units together. (3a)

Add more units to the sides. You can avoid using more paper clips by putting the remaining units in place. The flaps will hold the units in place. Tuck the flaps in to secure the model. The model is quite strong. (3b)

For an illustration of a completed stella octangula, see A on page 74.

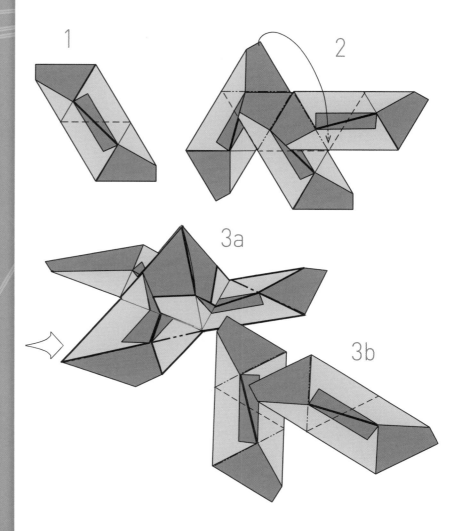

1

2

3a

3b

THE REGULAR TETRAHEDRON AND THE STELLA OCTANGULA

The stella octangula (see A, on right) is a compound of two regular tetrahedra (B, right). It is also the only stellation of the octahedron (C, right). To stellate a polyhedron, extend the faces into planes: where the planes meet, it creates the edges of a new polyhedron. Sometimes it is not possible to stellate a polyhedron (e.g., a stellated cube does not exist, since the planes intersect at lines that do not converge).

A stella octangula will sit inside a cube (B): its eight vertices coincide with the eight vertices of a cube. The edges of the stella octangula form the diagonals of the square faces of the cube.

TRIGONAL TRAPEZOHEDRON ASSEMBLY ✪

This shape is also known as a trigonal deltohedron. It is a rhombohedron (meaning a parallelepiped with edges of equal length). It is also a zonohedron (meaning a convex polyhedron with faces that are parallelograms).

1 Make three units but omit the horizontal valley fold in unit step 1. Then make three more that are mirror images of the first.

2 Join the first three units.

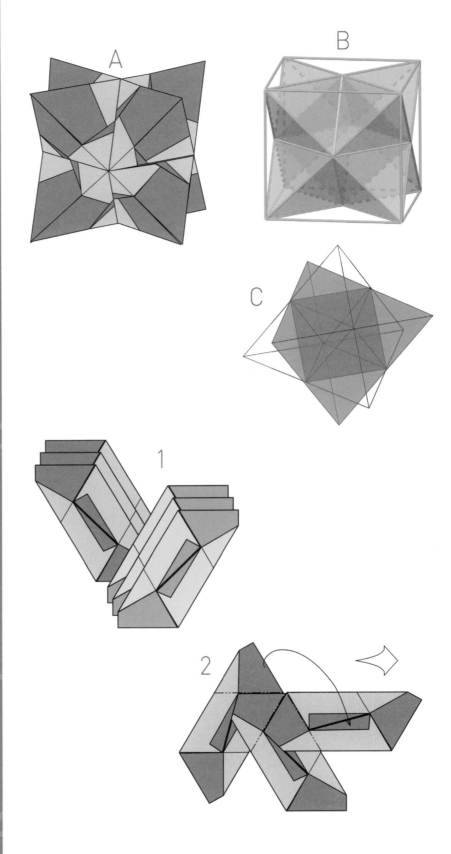

3 Add the other three units to complete the model.

4 The shape is a compound of a regular octahedron and two regular tetrahedra. What other shapes can you create?

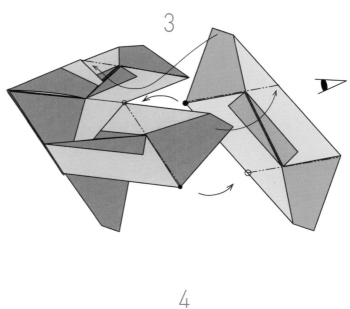

3

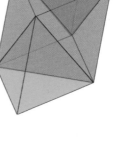

4

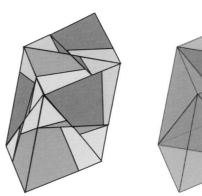

SIX-PART STELLATED RHOMBIC DODECAHEDRON ◈◈◈◈
BY DAVID MITCHELL

Paper requirements: six silver rectangles A6
or larger, in three colors
Finished model ratio: 0.8

Dave Mitchell created this classic work in 1989, and it is
one of his best. The unit and precreasing use the inherent
geometry of silver rectangles. Also, the final move to
make the flat form into the final 3-D unit is surprising and
satisfying. Take particular care to follow the turnover
instructions. You can use mono paper even though the
diagrams use duo paper.

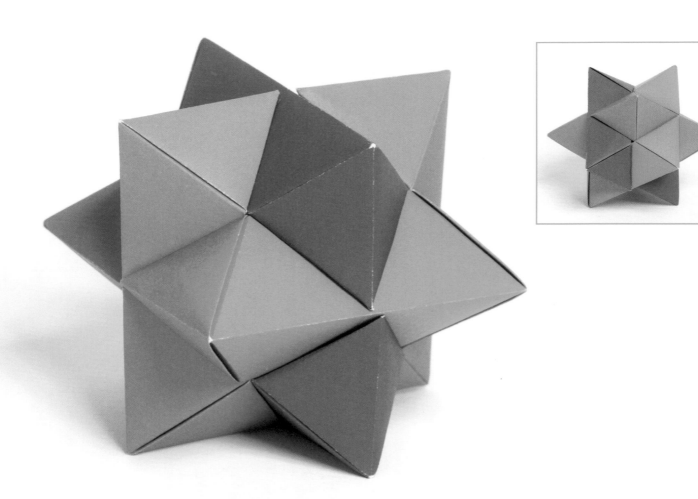

MODULE ◈◈◈◈

1 Fold the long edges together and unfold. Then fold the long edges to the middle and unfold. Turn over.

2 Fold the short edges together and unfold. Then fold the long edges to the middle and unfold. Fold the left edge to the right.

3 Fold a single layer of paper along the diagonal. Use the location points to help you: fold the upper quarter mark on the right to the lower quarter mark on the left.

4 Turn over.

5 Fold to match the flap behind.

6 Unfold the flaps. Turn over.

7 Repeat steps 3 to 5. Unfold completely.

8 Fold the short edges to the middle.

9 Fold the flaps along the diagonal of the rectangle.

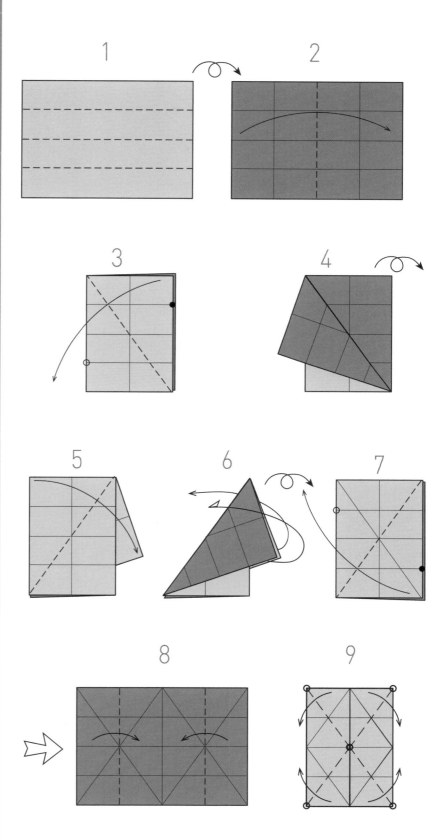

10 Unfold completely.

11 Turn over.

12 Fold the top edge down to the bottom edge to fold in half.

13 Use the existing creases to fold the corners to the center. If you turn the paper over, it will look exactly the same at the back as at the front.

14 Open up the top layer.

15 Fold on the horizontal valley fold.

16 Squash the flaps at the left and right ends of the valley fold.

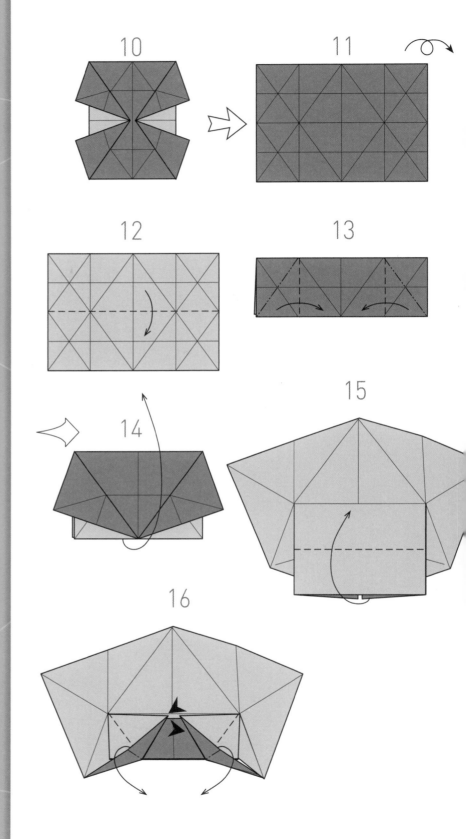

17 Re-form the folds of the upper layer. (17a)

Turn over. Repeat steps 15 and 16a but do not undo any folds. (17b)

18 Bring the bottom edge upward. The sides will open on the left and right: squash these flaps.

19 Firmly crease on the left and right edges of the irregular hexagon.

20 Lift out the flaps from the center. The unit becomes 3-D or equivalent.

21 Unit complete. (20a)

22 Turn over. (20b)
You need six units completed before assembling. (20c)

ASSEMBLY ◈◈◈◈

1 When all six modules are ready—note that these modules do not have flaps that tuck into pockets. Instead, you need to wrap the modules around each other to hold each in place. Assembly can be awkward at first. Hold three pieces in the correct position in the palm of one hand and use the other hand to insert the other modules, one at a time.

The units are almost like the wooden pieces of a similar burr puzzle, which has a specific way of being put together and being pulled apart. However, the paper units can bend, unlike the wooden pieces, which means you do not have to use the assembly method of the wooden puzzle.

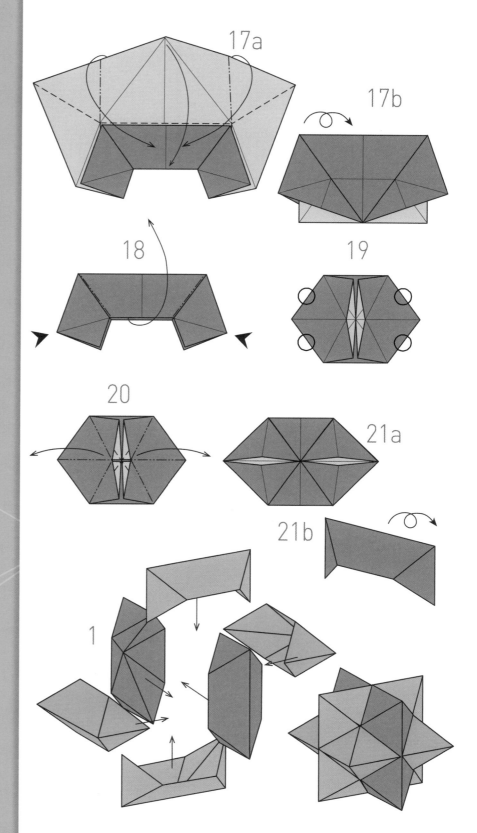

DODECAHEDRON NO. 14 (EASY MODULE)
BY SILVANA BETTI MAMINO

Paper requirements: Use thirty silver rectangles
(e.g., A7 or larger)
Finished model ratio: 2.3

This simple module by Silvana Betti Mamino elegantly
creates the angles and lengths needed for a good
approximation of a regular dodecahedron. A common
problem when making polyhedra is to color it so that only
different colors touch each other. For the thirty edges of a
dodecahedron, you can use either five or six colors.

MODULE 🔹

1 Fold the long edges together and unfold. Fold the sides to the middle.

2 Turn over.

3 Fold the bottom edge to the top edge and unfold.

4 Fold the bottom right corner to the midpoint of the left edge. Rotate 180° and repeat.

5 Turn over.

6 Unit complete

ASSEMBLY 🔹🔹

1 Tuck the tip of the second unit into the pocket of the first unit.

2 Tuck the tip of the third unit into the pocket of the second unit.

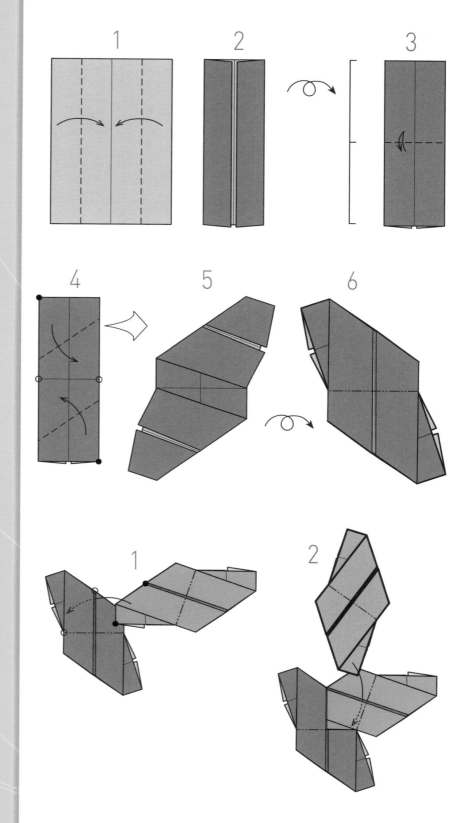

3 After adding the fifth unit, pull the first unit toward you, so that is on top of the fifth unit. You can now tuck the tip of the first unit into the pocket of the fifth unit.

4 Add the sixth unit to a vertex. The model will become 3-D. Keep adding more units. Pay attention to the pattern of colors if you want to avoid the same colors touching each other. This can be a satisfying puzzle. However, the color of each edge of the dodecahedron is partially hidden, so extra effort is needed. The five- and six-color versions are now explained with wire-frame models that let you see through the faces of the dodecahedron.

FIVE COLORS

A regular dodecahedron can be contained within a cube, with six of its edges each lying on a different face of the cube. Five cubes account for all edges; if each cube is one of five colors, the edges lying on its faces should be that color. (4a–c)

1 Start with five units joined as a pentagon.

2 For the next five units, the color of the unit at a vertex is that of the unit opposite the vertex.

3 For the next ten units, the color of the unit at a vertex is that of the unit opposite the vertex. Two units each are used to form five new vertices.

4 For the next five units, the color of the unit at a vertex is that of the unit opposite the vertex.

5 The colors of the final set of five are simpler to identify: use the color not in the pentagons of the upper bowl.

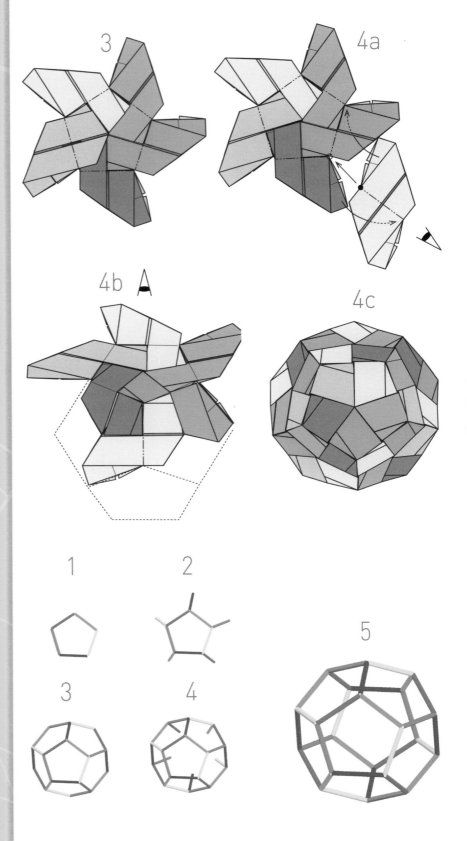

SIX COLORS

A regular dodecahedron can be thought of as two connected bowls. The rim around a bowl has ten edges. One color runs around the rim in one direction on five of the edges.

1 Start with five units joined as a pentagon.

2 For the next five units, the color of the unit at a vertex is shifted by one from that on the pentagon.

3 The next ten units make the rim of the bowl. For five of the units, use the sixth color for units in the counterclockwise direction. For the other five units, shift by one from those on the base in the opposite direction: or use the color that is not already in each pentagon.

4 You can now see that the bands of the same color run on the rims of incomplete bowls. Carry the pattern on.

5 Repeat for the last five units, or complete each pentagon using the color that is missing.

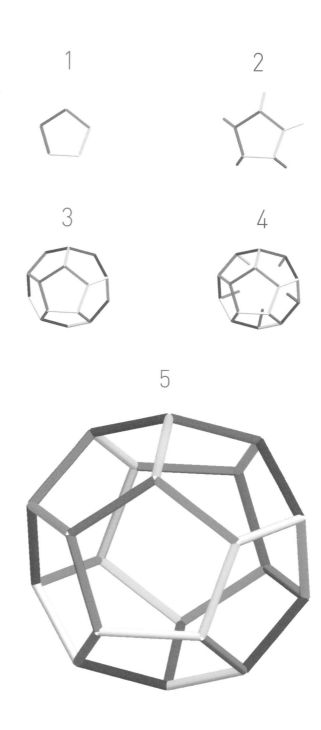

83

ACTION MODELS

These models move, spin, or change shape in an appealing way.

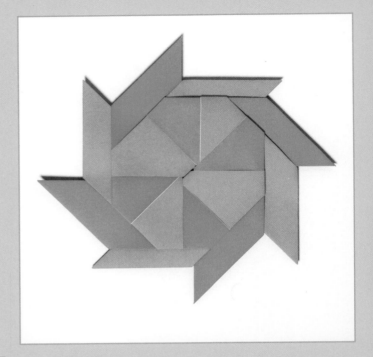

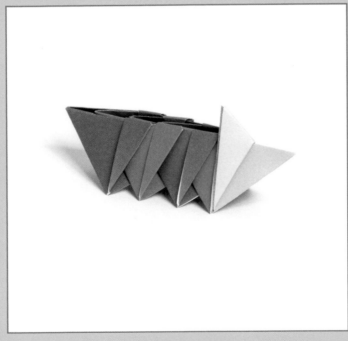

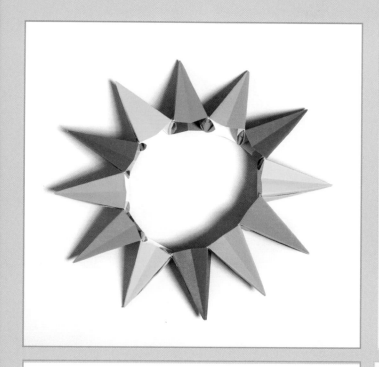

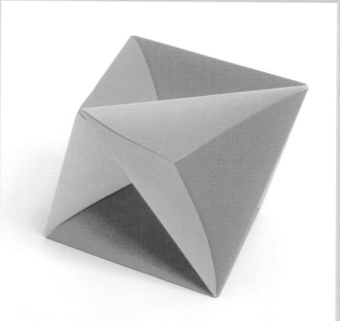

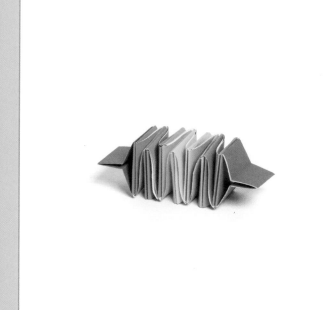

CATERPILLAR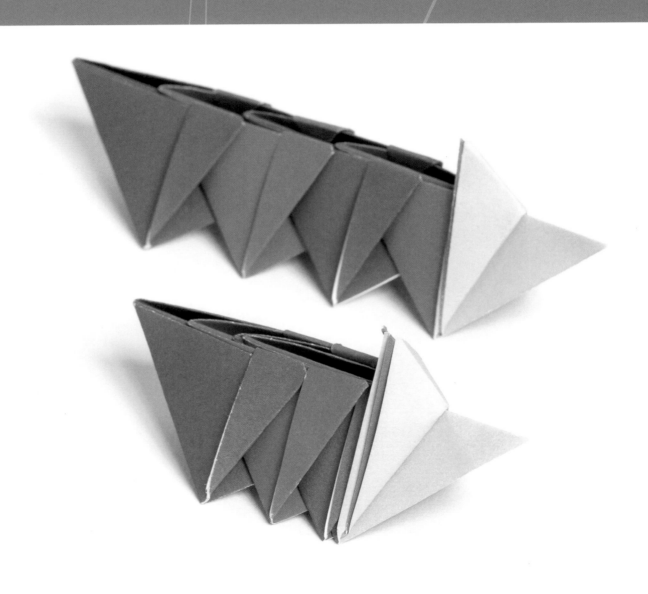

Paper requirements: four or more, each about 2.9 to 3.9
in. (7.5–10 cm)
Finished model ratio: 1.5

MODULE ⬡

1 Fold the lower corner to the top corner to fold the diagonal.

2 Fold the left corner to the right corner to fold in half.

3 Fold the right flap to the top. Repeat behind. Rotate 90° clockwise.

4 Fold the right flap to the left and unfold.

5 Fold the lower right edge to the crease made in the previous step.

6 Turn over from side to side.

7 Fold the left flap to match the flap behind.

8 Unit complete. Turn over.

9 Make a total of at least four units.

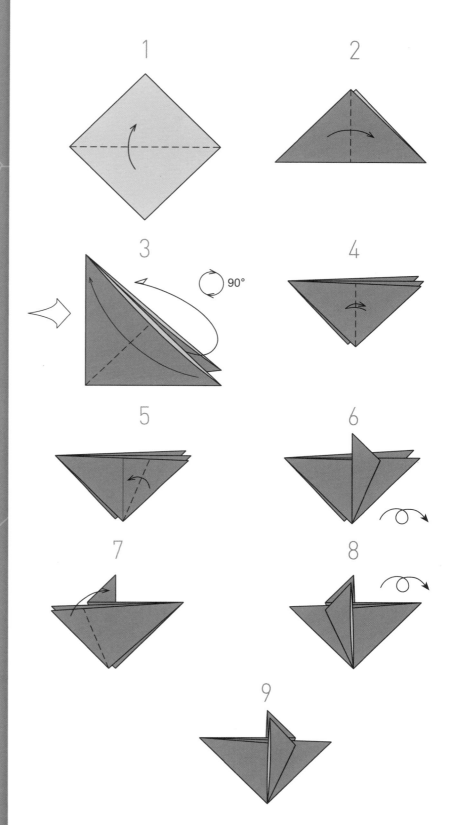

ASSEMBLY ⬡

1 The first unit is the tail end, which will be on the left. Place the second unit on top of the first unit.

2 Tuck the tips of the first unit into the second: the folds need to be firm, but not too tight.

3 Add more units.

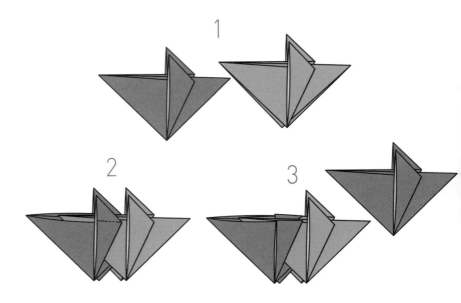

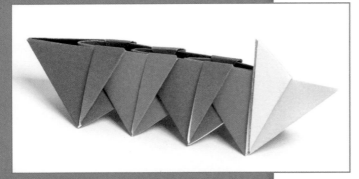

4 The last unit is the head. To secure the units, outside-reverse-fold a single layer of the head.

5 To slide the caterpillar, hold the tail and head ends with your left and right hands. (5a) Push and pull your hands together and apart to make the caterpillar wriggle. (5b)

You may need to adjust the joining folds in step 2. Either loosen them if the units will not slide, or tighten them if they come apart.

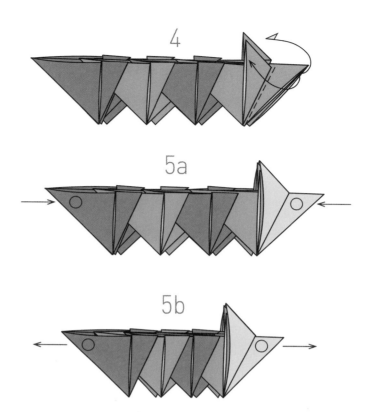

4

5a

5b

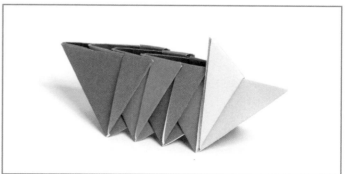

MAGIC STAR (PINWHEEL-RING-PINWHEEL) ◈◈◈
BY ROBERT NEALE

Paper requirements: eight squares, at least 3 in. (75 mm), in two or four colors
Finished model ratio: 1.4

This is a classic model by Robert Neale. Whenever adding a unit or tucking a tip is difficult, slide the existing units to make the space you need. Note the model's rotational symmetry.

MODULE 🎲

1 Fold in half.

2 Fold the corner.

3 Fold the corner flaps.

4 Unfold and rotate the paper so that the center line is vertical.

5 Use the existing creases to fold two corners to the center.

6 Make both partial diagonals valley folds. Use these creases to make an inside reverse fold as you close the paper in half.

7 Reverse fold in progress. (7a, 7b)

8 One unit complete. You need eight units; two or four colors work well.

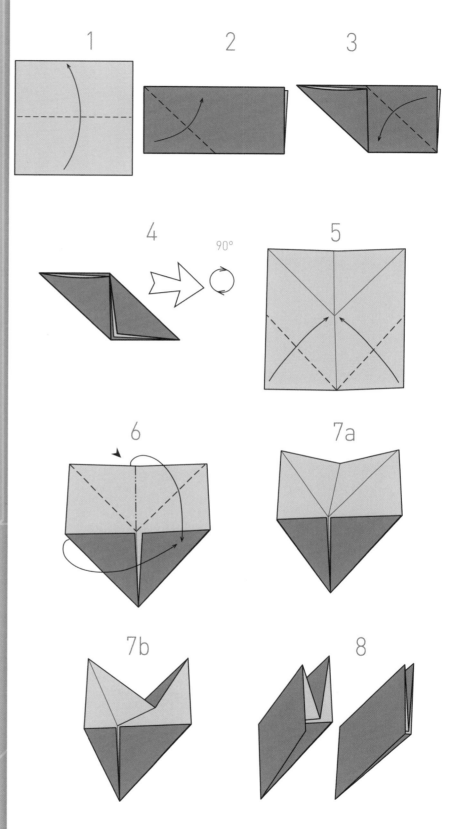

ASSEMBLY ●●●

Whenever adding a unit or tucking a tip is difficult, slide the existing units to make the space you need. To make adding the last unit easier, remove the first unit and add this as your new last unit. To make this helix into a ring, flip the start of the ring toward you and tuck it into the arms of the last unit. Carefully bend the ring to do this.

1 Slip the second unit into the arms of the first unit. The circled points will be the center of the ring.

2 Fold the tips of the first unit into the second. Leave a small gap so that the units slide easily.

3 Continue adding units in a clockwise direction: slip the third unit into the arms of the second unit.

ACTION

1 Slide the units by pushing them toward, or pulling away from, the center. (1a, 1b)

2 The ring will not close if you push the units too far: slide the ring open and try again. If the sliding is blocked, check that the tips folded in assembly step 2 are not trapped.

3 Pushing and pulling the units by different amounts creates a variety of shapes. What shapes can the hole be? (3a, 3b)

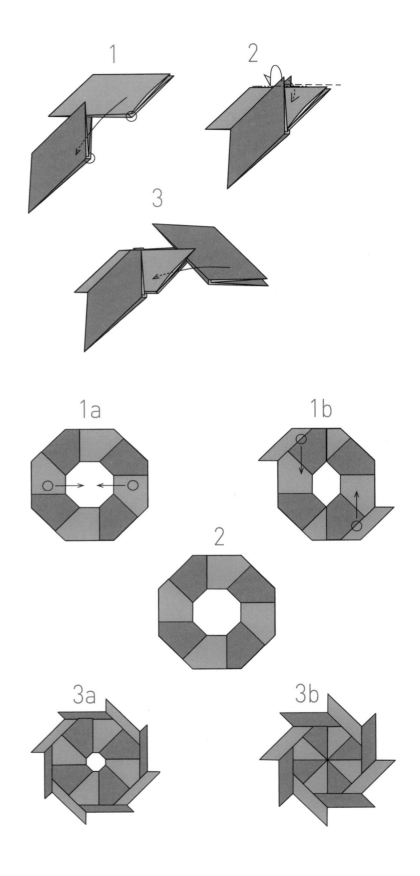

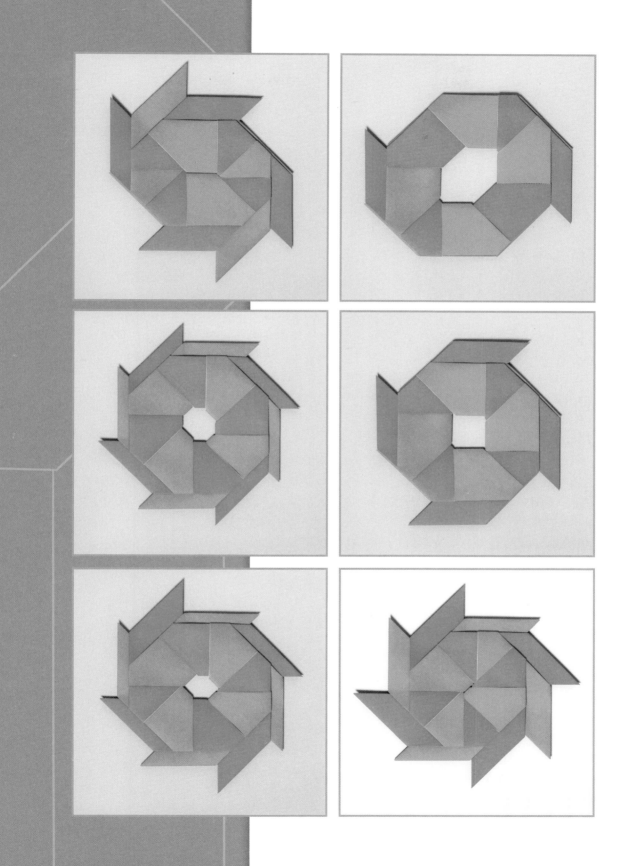

SKELETAL OCTAHEDRON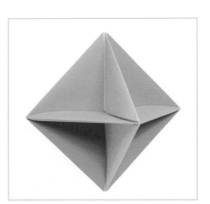
BY ROBERT NEALE

Paper requirements: six squares, at least 2.9 in. (75 mm), in three colors
Finished model ratio: 1.0

This is another classic by Robert Neale. The shape can be interpreted as three intersecting squares. It is also the skeleton of a regular octahedron because the outer edges can be filled with eight equilateral triangles. For your first attempt, you can use paper clips during assembly; alternatively, ask a friend to help if you need it.

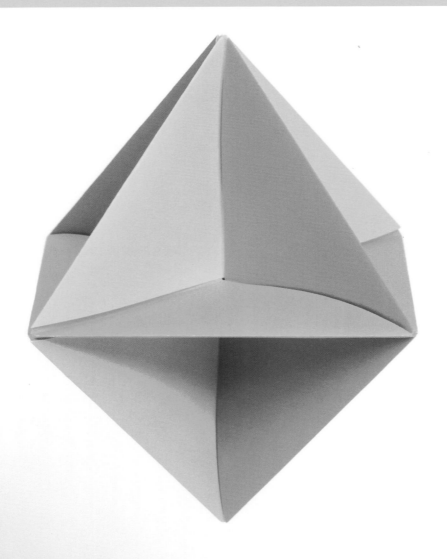

MODULE ◈◈

1 Fold opposite edges together and unfold. Fold the other edges together and unfold. Turn over.

2 Fold a diagonal and unfold. Fold the other diagonal and unfold.

3 Using the existing creases, push in the center and squeeze the paper into a 3-D star shape.

ASSEMBLY ◈◈◈

Each unit will have two flaps and two pockets. Each star point can be either a flap or a pocket. On each unit, choose two opposite points to be flaps, and then the other two will be pockets.

1 Tuck the flap of the first unit into the pocket of the second unit.

2 Two units joined. Add a third unit so that the second unit goes into it, and it goes into the first unit.

3 Notice how one flap of each unit goes into the next in a clockwise direction. You can push these three units tightly together. However, note that the diagrams show a loose assembly so that you can see how the flaps are arranged.

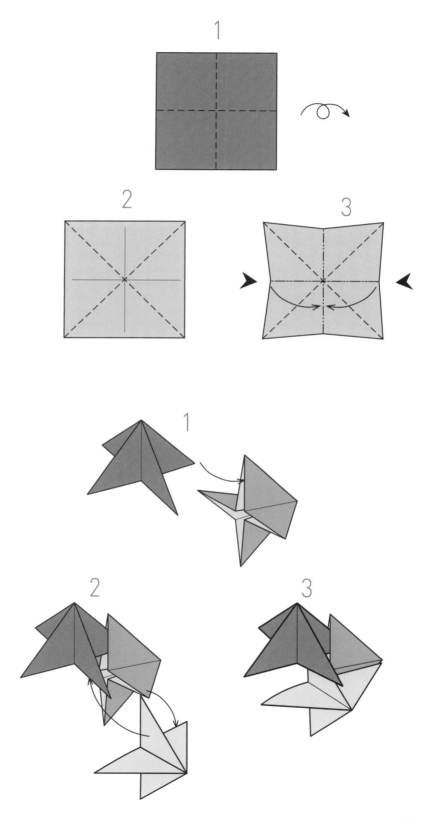

4 Add the fourth unit.

5 Add the fifth unit.

6 Add the sixth unit.

7 Gently squeeze the units together for a secure assembly. It is strong enough to be thrown about without falling apart.

ACTION

To make the model spin, cup it in your hands by gently and securely holding the vertices in your palms: blow to spin. It can also be hung as an ornament that sways and spins.

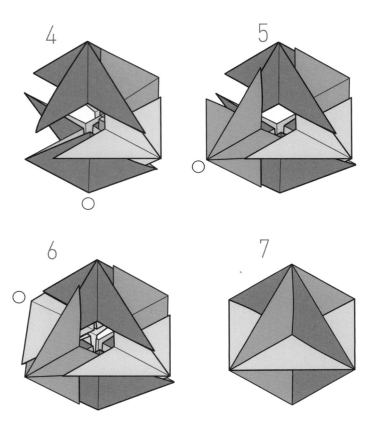

TWELVE-PIECE CAROUSEL ◆◆◆

This is a twelve-piece version of Carousel. Using more units makes the rotation smoother. In module step 4, you can use Fujimoto's method of dividing an angle into equal parts. First, fold the left edge with your best estimate and unfold. Fold the right edge to the crease you've just made. Unfold. Now fold the left edge to the crease just made—if your first estimate was good, this fold will coincide with your first estimate. If not, continue until the error becomes negligible.

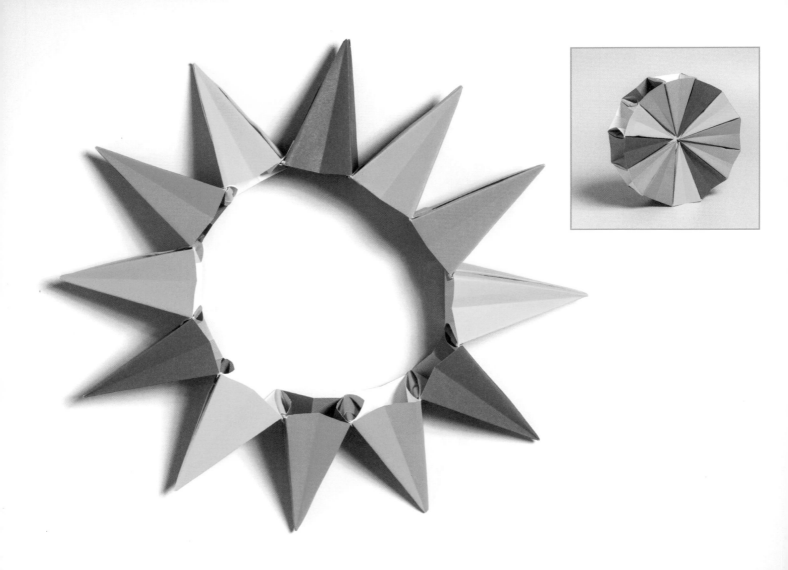

MODULE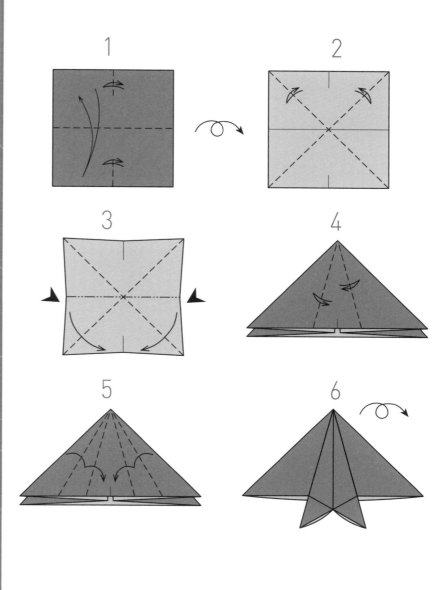

1 Fold the bottom edge to the top and unfold. Pinch the midpoints of the top and bottom edges. Turn over.

2 Fold and unfold each diagonal.

3 Use the existing creases to make a waterbomb base (p. 16). Fold the top edge down and inside-reverse-fold the left and right sides.

4 Divide the right angle into three equal angles. You can do this by eye with good accuracy.

5 Fold left and right flaps over and over to the center.

6 Like this. Turn over.

7 Repeat steps 4 and 5.

8 Fold all four flaps up. The fold lines align with the original edges of the square.

9 Fold each flap inward, using the folded layer behind as a guide. You need twelve units in total. Two, three, or four colors work well.

10 Unit complete

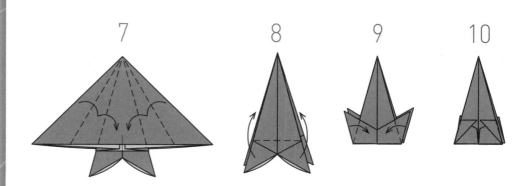

99

ASSEMBLY ◆◆◆

1 Take two units. To avoid the flaps interfering with each other, unfold the rear flaps. Arrange the front flaps as shown. Place the second unit on top of the first unit.

2 Wrap the flaps of the first unit around and inside the flaps of the second unit. The ends of the flaps tuck inside the second unit's pocket.

3 Valley-fold the left unit onto the right unit. You can now add more units as in step 1.

ACTION
Rotate the points of the units around the circumference of the circle formed by the edges of the paper.

1

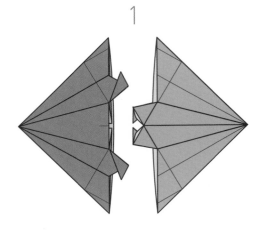

2

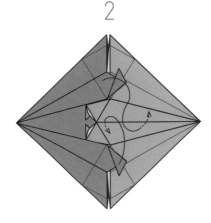

3

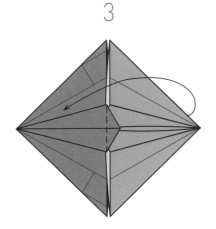

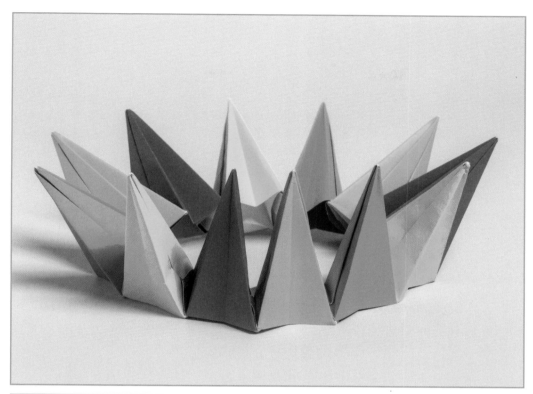

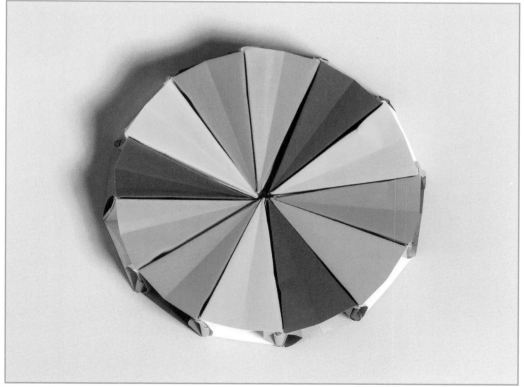

SURPRISE!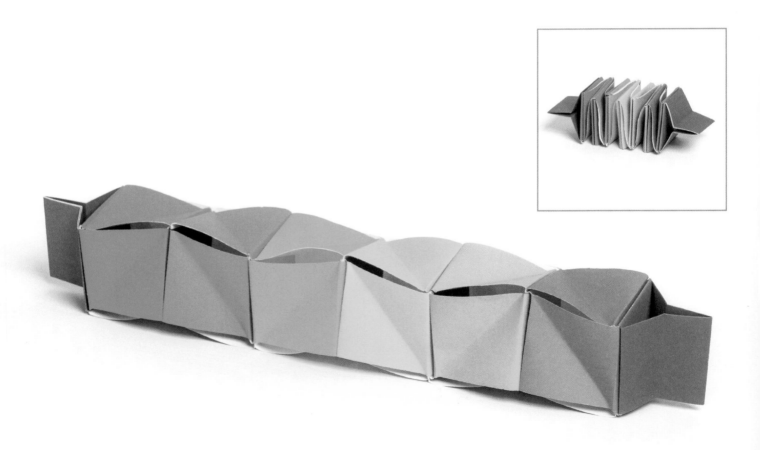
BY HEINZ STROBL

Paper requirements: For a Surprise! consisting of four cubes, you will need twenty-six 3:1 rectangles and two 4:1 rectangles for handles.

This fun action model looks complicated but is made from simple units. You will probably spend more time preparing the paper and joining the units than folding them.

There are four kinds of units: handles, interiror cube faces and two kinds of exterior cube faces.

Each exterior cube piece has a diagonal crease that makes the cubes expand and collapse. The orientation of the diagonal, when viewed as a valley fold, can be called either S or Z. You can make a longer model like the one in this photograph if you make more units.

The first two squares provide eight 3:1 "C" strips and two 4:1 strips for handles.

.

The next two squares provide the eight 3:1 "Z" pieces.
The remaining two 4:1 strips are cut to 3:1 for the two other "C" pieces that are needed.
Discard the unit squares or keep them for another project.

The final two squares give the eight "S" pieces. The remaining two 4:1 strips can be discarded from this project. However, you can use them to make another Surprise! or to make one with more cubes.

CUTTING PLAN USING SQUARES

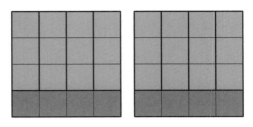

All of the paper strips you need can be cut from six squares. For example, you can use six squares of 6 in. (15 cm) origami paper. Be sure to correctly orient the diagonal of the central squares of the "S" and "Z" pieces.

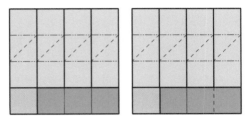

THESE ARE THE "Z" PIECES

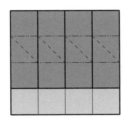 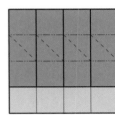

THESE ARE THE "S" PIECES

CODE		QUANTITY	RECTANGLE	COLOR	DESCRIPTION
	C	10	3:1	Doesn't matter—these are hidden inside the finished model	Two "C" pieces make an "O" pocket piece; total of five pockets
	Z	8	3:1	Color #1	Forms the sides of two cubes
	S	8	3:1	Color #2	Forms the sides of two cubes. Note that "S" and "Z" pieces are mirror images.
	H	2	4:1	Color #3	Handles (H)

CUTTING PLAN USING A4 RECTANGLES

A4 paper is usually the same color on both sides, which means that you can easily convert between "S" and "Z" pieces by changing mountain folds to valleys and vice versa.

1 Divide the long edge into eight equal units.

2 Locate the diagonals of two squares that have length: three units.

3 Crease through the top of the squares of length: three units.

4 Use the diagonals to divide the edge into three units.

5 Above the squares, divide into two units, with a bit left over.

Note: Use cutting plan #1 for most of your A4 sheets. Use plan #2 when you need to make handles.

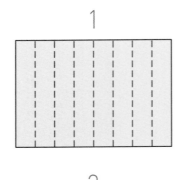

1

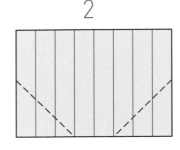

2

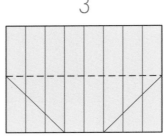

3

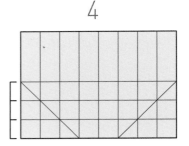

4

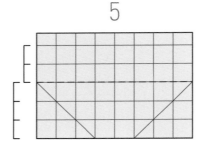

5

CUTTING PLAN #1

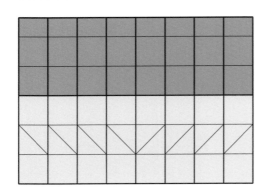

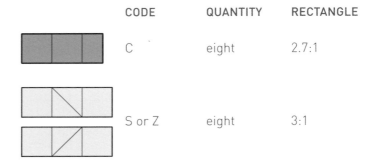

CODE	QUANTITY	RECTANGLE
C	eight	2.7:1
S or Z	eight	3:1

CUTTING PLAN #2

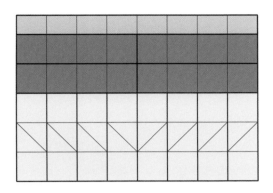

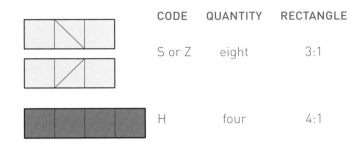

CODE	QUANTITY	RECTANGLE
S or Z	eight	3:1
H	four	4:1

Note that you can use "C" pieces as "S" or "Z" pieces. Also, you can convert "S" pieces to "Z" and vice versa by turning over and reversing the creases (i.e., change mountain folds to valleys, and change valleys to mountains).

MAKING AN "O" PIECE

1 Take 2 "C" pieces. Fold the first strip in thirds. It does not matter in which order you fold the ends.

2 Take the second strip and, using mountain folds, tuck the ends into the first folded strip. The piece can be slightly larger than the unit square so that it easily accepts "S" and "Z" pieces.

3 The ends of both strips are inside the pocket; the center squares of both strips are on the outside. You need five "O" pieces.

The "Z" pieces

1 Note that the diagonal of the middle square runs from bottom left to top right.

2 One "Z" piece finished. Repeat with the remaining strips.

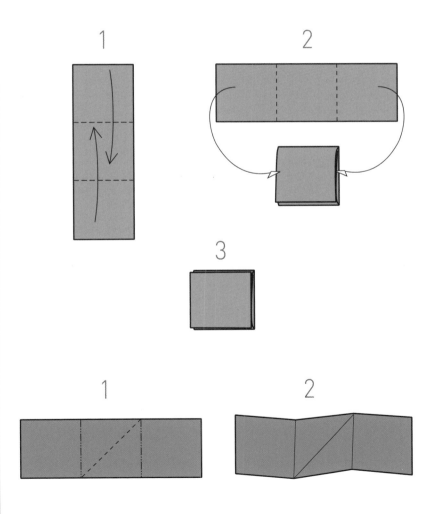

The "S" pieces

1 A mirror image of the "Z" piece. The diagonal of the middle square runs from top left to bottom right.

2 One "S" piece finished. Repeat with the remaining strips.

The Handles

1 Fold each of the 4:1 strips with these pleats:

2 3-D view

ASSEMBLY ◈

1 Take two "O" pieces and four "Z" pieces. Tuck the ends of each "Z' piece into each of the four pockets of one "O" piece. The diagonal valley folds are on the outside of the cube so that it can twist and collapse flat.

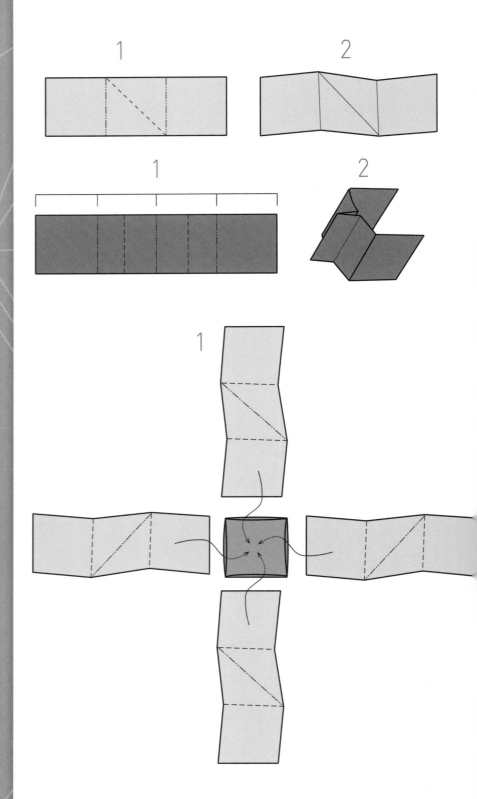

2 Take the second "O" piece and insert the free ends of the "Z" pieces in it.

3 3-D view with one "Z" piece inserted. Continue tucking in the other free ends.

4 One cube formed with all of the ends tucked in

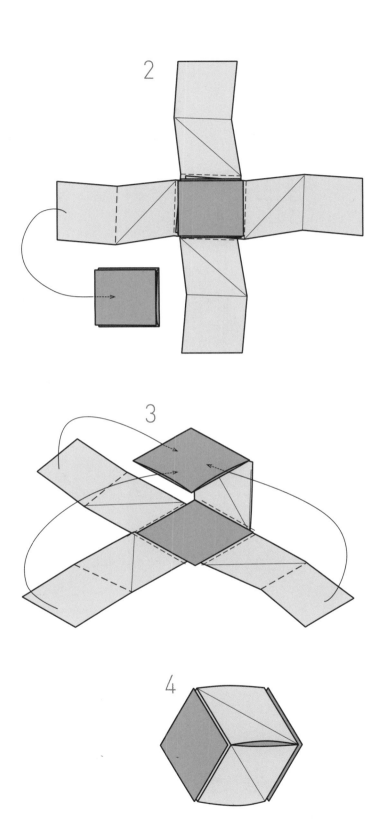

5 Continue building more cubes, taking care to alternate cubes of "S" pieces with cubes made of "Z" pieces.

6 You might find assembly easier if you collapse your cubes before you add another one.

7 Finish the model by inserting a handle at each end.

ACTION

1 To collapse the model, hold the handles and push them toward each other.

2 To expand the model, hold the handles and pull them away from each other. Whether expanding or collapsing the model, you do not need to twist your hands as you pull or push.

5

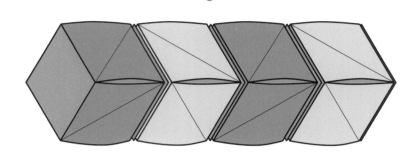

6

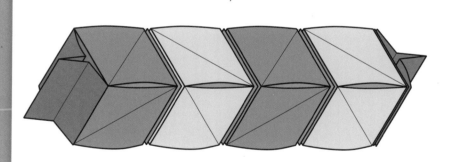

7

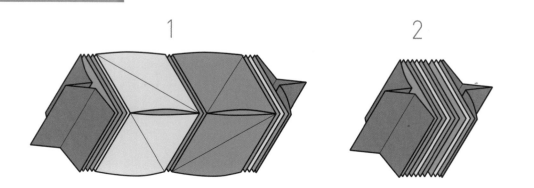

1

2

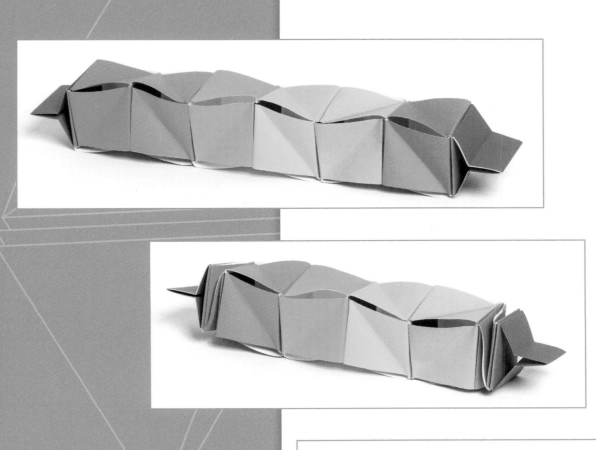

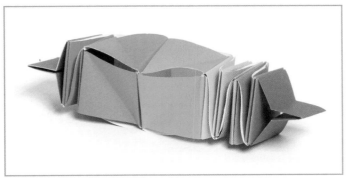

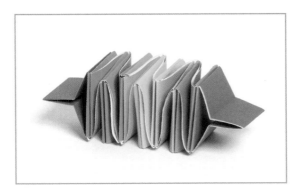

JITTERBUG ◈◈◈◈

Paper requirements: Twelve squares
Finished model ratio: 1.0

Buckminister Fuller gave the name Jitterbug to this transformation. I first came across the Jitterbug in Amy C. Edmondson's *A Fuller Explanation* (Edmondson 87). Since I didn't have dowels and four-way rubber connectors, I made several cuboctahedra that worked as Jitterbugs but were not very reversible. Some were from paper, and others from drinking straws and elastic thread. My first unit, Triangle Unit, was partly successful as a Jitterbug. A better result came from using three units per triangular face (or one unit per vertex), which was published in 2000.

This improved version is slightly harder to assemble but has a stronger lock. The sequence is pleasingly rhythmical, and all steps have location points. The pleats in step 18 form the spring that make the model return to its cuboctahedral shape.

MODULE ◈◈◈◈

1 Make two folds in half. Do not crease the middle for the vertical fold. Turn over.

2 Fold the left side to the center.

3 Fold the bottom half behind.

4 Fold the bottom right corner to lie on the left edge, while the fold starts from the original center of the square.

5 This creates a 60° angle. Unfold completely.

6 Fold the right edge to the center.

7 Fold the bottom half behind.

8 Repeat step 4 and unfold, leaving the right flap folded.

9 Fold the left edge to the center and then rotate the model 90°.

10 Fold the points shown with filled circles to the center. Note the filled circles are the ends of the creases, not the corners.

11 Unfold.

12 Reverse fold. You will need to extend the existing creases slightly. (Enlarged)

13 Reinforce three creases.

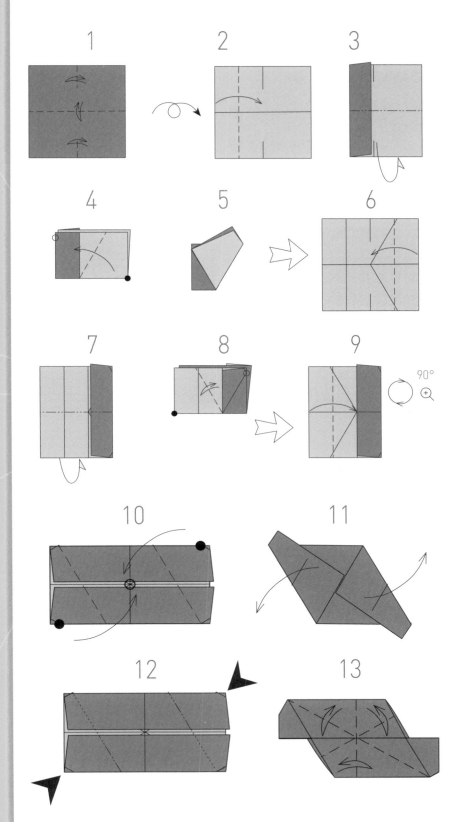

14 Fold and unfold the ends. These creases make the third sides of partial equilateral triangles. Turn the paper over and rotate it 90° clockwise.

15 Fold in half, using the given location points. Unfold.

16 Fold in half, using the given location points.

17 Unfold.

18 Reinforce the creases and make a total of twelve units: three colors work well.

ASSEMBLY

1 Join three units to make a triangle. Use the creases from step 14 to lock the units.

2 Continue adding units to make more triangles. If you are using three colors, note that the order of colors on each face is not always the same.

3 Remember to make square "holes" with four triangles. As you make the cuboctahedron, the vertices have colors that form three rings.

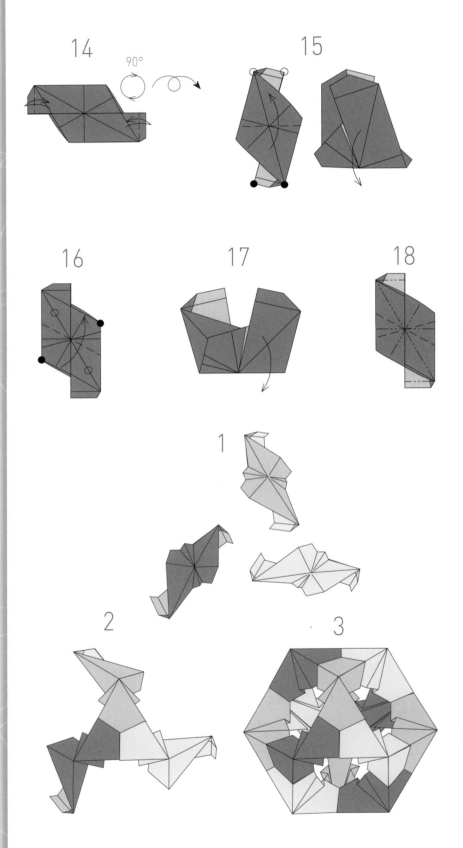

4 Push near and far faces together; faces will twist as they approach...

5 the circumference will buckle, making an icosahedral configuration.

6 Continue pushing to form an octahedron.

ACTION

Pressing the opposite faces of Jitterbug (below) transforms it from a truncated cuboctahedron to an octahedron—let go, and it springs back to its original shape.

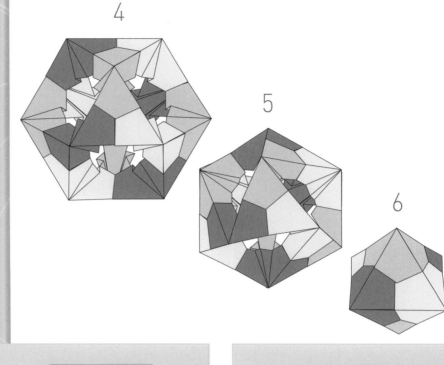

Going Further

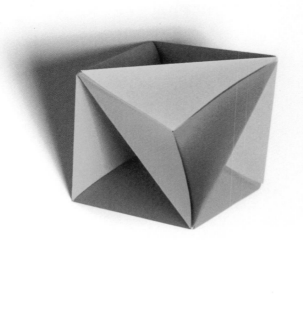

CREATING MODULAR ORIGAMI

I hope that you have enjoyed making the projects in this book. If you have made all of the models, then congratulations—you are a dedicated and skilled folder! However, there can be more to origami than following instructions in a book.

As you folded the projects, did you wonder how the creators came up with these models? Or did you consider what would happen if you varied some of the folds? What else could you make?

This section gives you some ideas for creating your own modular origami. It also gives you some ideas for further reading.

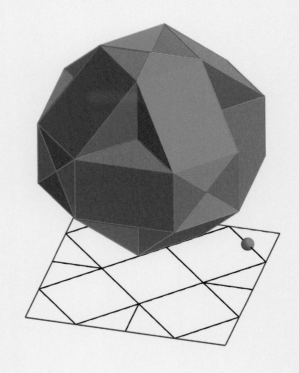

YOUR OWN MODULAR ORIGAMI

The *Skeletal Octahedron* is ripe for variations. For example, if each diagonal is replaced with a pair of parallel folds, then the module will enclose some space (right, above). Depending on the gap between the folds, the result is like a rhombicuboctahedron. The limit of this variation would be a cube made from blintz squares, but there would be no flaps and pockets.

Another variation is to add reverse folds to make pyramids appear (right, below).

GENERALIZING A MODULE TO OTHER POLYGONS OR RECTANGLES

Another way to vary a unit is to generalize the geometry. For example, the square used for the *Pinwheel Cube* (right) could be changed to a regular hexagon to make a triangular unit.

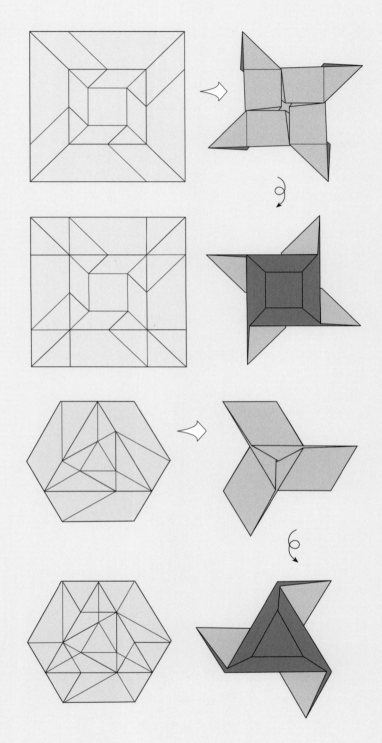

WHAT IF?

A powerful technique is to ask yourself, "What if ...?" For example, what if I wanted to make a Magic Star with a different number of units—say, six or four? What about odd numbers such as five?

REUSING CREASE PATTERNS

This can be a way of using pseudo-random provocation to upset established patterns of thinking. Take a unit and unfold it: How can you use these creases to make something else? The benefit of this method is that you are not starting with a blank sheet of paper.

SHAPE AND SURPLUS

When you make modules, you usually make pockets and flaps to use during assembly. However, to make a flap you need excess paper that is reduced by folding. For example, for the *Caterpillar* we want a square folded along the diagonal with extra flaps. The original square will lack the flaps unless we fold extra paper. Step 4 of the *Caterpillar* is a square with extra paper that is used to make the connecting flaps; it also has pockets for the flaps.

In other words, to shape the paper you usually need to create surplus paper beforehand. This is John Smith's theory of "Shape and Surplus."

INHERENT GEOMETRY

We saw earlier how to generalize geometry from—say, a square to a hexagon. Another technique for stimulating ideas is to work with the geometry inherent in particular oblongs. For example, the silver rectangle is related to the cube and tetrahedron. It also makes good approximations to the angles of a regular pentagon.

The bronze rectangle is related to the regular hexagon and equilateral triangle. This means that deltahedra are natural subjects.

MAKING A SPECIFIC MODEL

There are two general approaches for creating origami. These work for both geometric and figurative subjects.

- Exploration: play and doodle with paper until something promising appears.

- Deliberate: begin with a target subject and then find ways to make it.

The two approaches can complement each other. For example, while working in the second approach, you may find something promising but unrelated to your target subject: keep this to one side and work on it later. You may find something that helps the second approach while you were doodling or working on something else: this can be a case of a prepared mind finding something by serendipity.

The deliberate approach may seem impossible to beginners. However, with more experience of folding you begin to see common techniques and ideas that you can borrow. For example, to make a modular origami cuboctahedron, you can start by choosing to make a face, edge, or vertex module. For a face module, you can make either square or triangular faces, or both. If you choose a square face, then you want to find ways of joining the vertices of the square. Using squares, you will need to build some surplus: How could you do that? Some ways may be easy but inefficient, so you will need to choose. Perhaps you want to try triangles instead. As you can see, the deliberate approach can be exploratory.

REVERSE ENGINEERING

See if you can work out how to make an existing model by just looking at the final result. You may find that your version is different from the original.

MODULAR ORIGAMI EXAMPLES

The card cube exploits some of the symmetries of the cube. Instead of cladding the flaps, can we make pockets for the flaps by using the cube units themselves? Or can we transfer the assembly method of the card cube to another unit?

Let's start with a square folded on quarter lines. We could make a pocket by folding back the raw edges at the center. However, we'd need to shorten the flaps so that they will fit the pocket. Folding the flap makes it thicker, which in turn makes it harder to insert into the pocket.

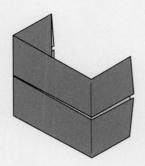

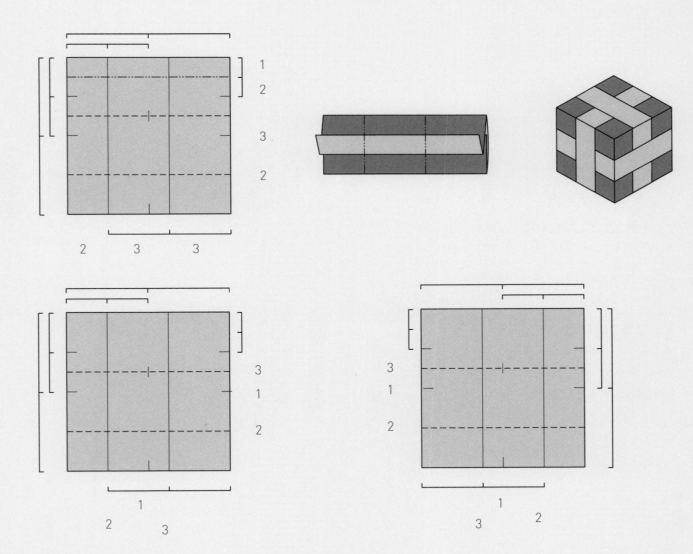

119

How can we adjust the creases so that the flaps do not need to be shortened? We also want the creases to be easy to locate (e.g., using eighths instead of twelfths). One way would be to allocate the paper in an asymmetrical manner (i.e., the lengths of the flaps are unequal). Also, let one pocket be deeper than the other pocket (previous page, middle row). When assembling this, it may be surprising that mirror image modules are needed (previous page, bottom row).

Another way would be to pleat the unit to create a pocket. However, this makes the unit longer so that flaps are now bigger. Why not make the pleat using the quarter line and three-eighths? This belt cube has been independently created by me and others (below, top row).

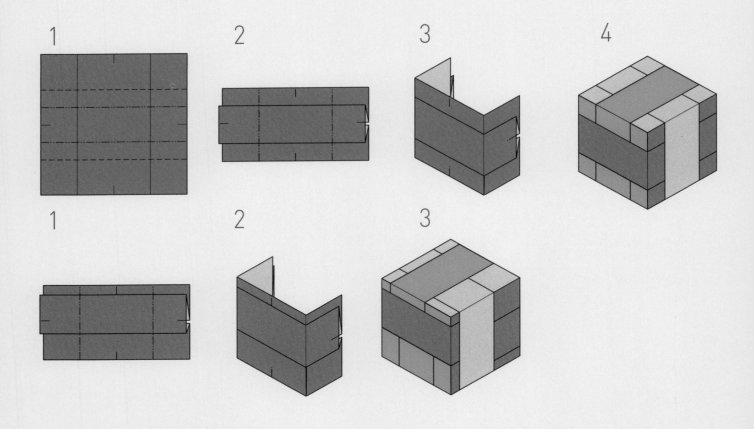

We can now generalize this from a square to an oblong: divide the long edge into quarters and then locate a 2:1 rectangle on the long edge. This gives us the location creases needed for the module (below).

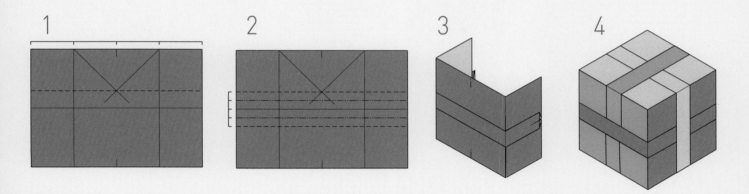

We can "chamfer" the corner to make the flaps easier to insert: this also creates a different pattern on the cube faces (below).

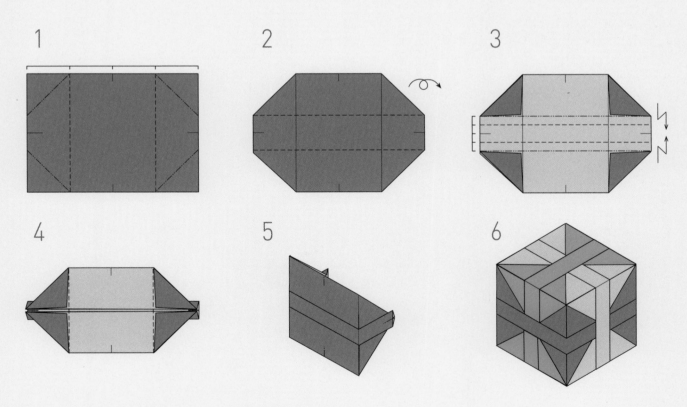

We notice that as long as the quarter lines meet, the
bulge of paper can be asymmetrically flattened.

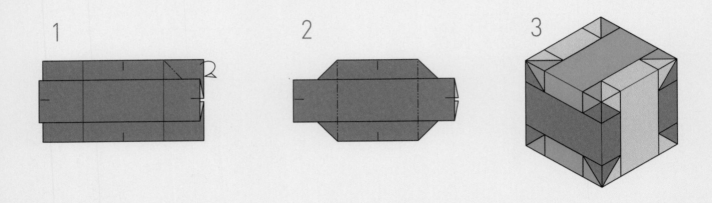

Another variation of the belt cube stems from the insight
that units can be folded into boxes and still be assembled
in a similar manner: this is Dave Mitchell's *Omicron*
(below). Further experimentation gives a unit that makes
a pseudo-rhombicuboctahedron.

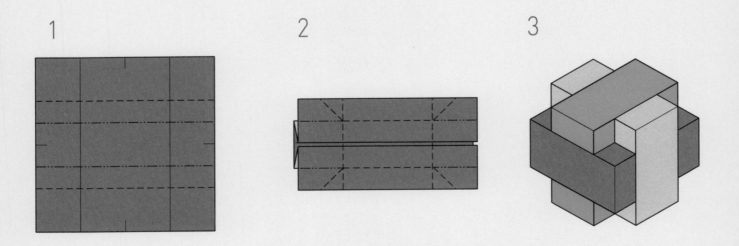

From the card cube we seem to have endless possibilities.
Who'd have thought that the apparently austere restriction
of only folding paper would produce such a variety of
forms and creativity?

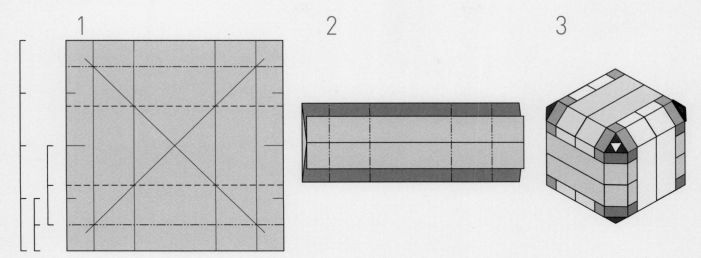

FURTHER READING

Origami

The Sonobé unit has been called the point of origin of modular origami in terms of its popularity and influence (even though it is not the earliest known unit). Kunihiko Kasahara explored the unit and variations (*Kasahara and Takahama 88, pp. 41–42*): a 900-unit sphere can be made, as well as a bird and horse made from 38 and 208 units, respectively. Meenakshi Mukerji varied the Sonobé unit for different structural and visual effects (*Mukerji 08*, pp. 63–81; Mukerji 07, pp. 1–38).

Most of the books mentioned here are dedicated to modular origami. However, a few general origami books have exceptional modular origami or encourage the reader to explore and create (e.g., Brill 96; Kasahara and Takahama 88; Kasahara 88). Brill's book features a wide range of intermediate to complex geometrical, animal, and miscellaneous works (*Brill 96*). Jun Maekawa explores all kinds of origami (*Maekawa 08*), and Nakano includes a few glued modulars that may spark your creativity (*Nakano 85*). Maekawa includes several modular works using 1:√2 paper (*Maekawa 13*).

Sometimes known as the "queen of modular origami," Tomoko Fusé is a key creator and author who is famous for her modular origami boxes (*Fusé 18*), polyhedra (*Fusé 22*), and many other creations (*Fusé 91*; Fusé 07).

For more modular origami polyhedra, including some of the star polyhedra (Kepler-Poinsot), try your hand at Kasahara's polyhedra (*Kasahara 88*, pp. 199–248). Fusé's book uses oblongs as well as squares (*Fusé 22*). Miyuki Kawamura uses squares for her polyhedra (*Kawamura 02*).

Some authors have independently published work books of modular origami (*Garibi 20*; Weinstein 21; Lawson 11). Titles using the phrase "kusadama origami" typically feature thirty-piece 3-D modular stars (e.g., *Lukasheva 15* and *Hwang 21*).

For simple modular work, try the two books of Alexander Heinz (Heinz 22a; Heinz 22b). For challenging modular work, try the compound polyhedra of Fergus Currie (*Currie 21*) and the interwoven wireframes of Byriah Loper (*Loper 16*). For a variety of simple and complex work, Thoki Yenn's book explores dissections of the cube (*Yenn 87*). Dave Mitchell's book features the renowned creator's work (*Mitchell 20*). Maria Sinsaskaya wrote a book of flat and 3-D modular work (Sinayskaya 16). Bennett Arnstein and Rona Gurkewitz have coauthored a number of reasonably priced books (*Gurkewitz and Arnstein 12a and Gurkewitz and Arnstein 12b; Simon et al. 12*).

Some books with the words "3-D origami" or "modular origami" in the title belong to a distinct genre of origami (*Carlessi 16*). The models require dozens—if not hundreds or thousands—of a single unit that is typically glued together. This is sometimes known as "Golden Venture" origami. The *Golden Venture* was a cargo ship that carried Chinese migrants to the USA in the early 1990s. During their imprisonment, some migrants made sculptures using scrap materials. These sculptures were gifts for helpers and were also used to raise funds. Some of these sculptures were made from a simple unit that is slotted together and is usually glued.

Most modular origami uses straight folds on rectangular paper. For nonrectangular paper, try regular pentagons (*Mukerji 10*, pp. 41–60). For curved folds, try the books by Krystyna Burczyk (e.g., *Burczyk and Burczyk 08*).

If you enjoyed Heinz Strobl's work, try Faye Goldman's book of fifteen snapology projects (*Goldman 14*).

For more planar models such as WXYZ, see Petty 13 or Mukerji 08. For more modular origami stars, try Lam 21. For more action-oriented modular origami, try Lam 18.

Geometry

If you are bitten by the polyhedral bug, then you will want some sources for reference and ideas. Cundy and Rollett's classic *Mathematical Models* describes, analyzes, and organizes the regular and semiregular polyhedra (Cundy and Rollett 81).

Peter Cromwell wrote an accessible summary of polyhedra, their properties, and the relationships between them (*Cromwell 04*), as well as a more in-depth and technical work (*Cromwell 97*). Other books include a guide of instructions for making many complicated polyhedra (*Wenninger 71*). For more complex and unusual polyhedra (e.g. featuring tunnels), try *Stewart 80*, which was privately published.

David Wells's *Curious and Interesting Geometry* (*Wells 91*) gathers diverse geometrical theorems, oddities, and facts.

The *Jitterbug* is in *A Fuller Explanation* (Edmondson 87), an accessible introduction to Buckminster Fuller's geometric and mathematical work.

Robert Lang described how he devised polypolyhedra (*Lang 03*).

Symmetrical sticks arranged around the cube, rhombic dodecahedron, and triacontahedron appear in Coffin's book along with other puzzles (*Coffin 91*).

Origami and Mathematics Education

Several books use origami for teaching and learning mathematics. These can be divided by level (school or college/university) and type (descriptions of tasks or descriptions with specific pedagogic advice).

School-level books are typically at secondary school level (eleven to sixteen years of age). Two publications of tasks by the National Council of Teachers of Mathematics have a similar selection of classic material (Olson 75 and Johnson 99). *Geometric Exercises in Paper Folding* is a little dated and hard to understand but is of historical interest (*Sundara Row 66*). Kazuo Haga presents several elegant investigations in *Origamics* (*Haga et al. 08*).

Learning Mathematics with Origami is aimed at primary and secondary school teachers (*Lam and Pope 16*). As well as giving practical advice on using origami for learning mathematics, it promotes opportunities for learners to think creatively, justify decisions, deepen understanding, take responsibility for their own learning, and work collaboratively with others.

Online Resources

Websites come and go, so only a few are listed here:

http://www.modulandia.it features the work of Silvana Betti Mamino and others.

http://www.origamiheaven.com This is Dave Mitchell's comprehensive website of his own origami creations, research, and history.

http://www.knotology.eu Heinz Strobl's website presents ideas about his knotologie and snapologie.

https://www.langorigami.com/article/polypolyhedra Here Robert Lang writes and illustrates his exploration of "compounds of multiple linked polyhedral skeletons with uniform nonintersecting edges."

http://www.foldworks.net This is the author's website featuring diagrams and articles about mathematical origami.

https://en.wikipedia.org/wiki/Uniform_polyhedron The online encyclopedia has many relevant entries: this is one example.

Origami Societies

There are some long-standing origami societies devoted to the advancement of origami. You can buy paper and books, subscribe to their newsletters, meet other enthusiasts, and more. Their websites link to societies in other countries.

British Origami Society
www.britishorigami.org

Centro Diffusione Origami
https://origami-cdo.it

Origami USA
https://origamiusa.org

BIBLIOGRAPHY

Brackets show how book is referenced in text.

Brill, David. *Brilliant Origami: A Collection of Original Designs.* Japan Publications, 1996. (Brill 96)

Burczyk, Krystyna, and Wojciech Burczyk. *Kręciołkowe kusudamy (Twirl kusudamas) 1.* Wydawnictwo i Poligrafia Kurii Prowincjalnej Zakonu Pijarów, 2008. (Burczyk and Burczyk 08)

Carlessi, Maria Angela. *3D Origami.* Search Press, 2016. (Carlessi 16)

Coffin, Stewart T. *The Puzzling World of Polyhedral Dissections,* New ed. Oxford Paperbacks, 1991. (Coffin 91)

Cromwell, Peter R. *Polyhedra.* Cambridge University Press, 1997. (Cromwell 97)

Cromwell, Peter R. *Shapes in Space: Convex Polyhedra with Regular Faces.* Association of Teachers of Mathematics, 2004. (Cromwell 04)

Cundy, H. Martyn, and A. R. Rollett. *Mathematical Models, 3rd ed.* Tarquin, 1981. (Cundy and Rollett 81)

Currie, Fergus. *Compound Polyhedra: Modular Origam.* Tarquin, 2021. (Currie 21)

Edmondson, Amy C. A Fuller *Explanation: The Synergetic Geometry of R. Buckminster Fuller.* Design science collection, Birkhäuser, 1987. (Edmondson 87)

Fusé, Tomoko. *Unit Origami: Multidimensional Transformations.* Japan Publications, 1991. (Fusé 91)

Fusé, Tomoko. *Origami Rings and Wreaths; A Kaleidoscope of 28 Decorative Origami Creations.* Japan Publications, 2007. (Fusé 07)

Fusé, Tomoko. *Tomoko Fuse's Origami Boxes: Beautiful Paper Gift Boxes from Japan's Leading Origami Master.* Illustrated edition. Tuttle, 2018. (Fusé 18)

Fusé, Tomoko. *The Complete Book of Origami Polyhedra: 64 Ingenious Geometric Paper Models.* Tuttle, 2022. (Fusé 22)

Garibi, Ilan. *Origami Modulars for Everyone: Original Designs by Ilan Garibi.* Independently published, 2020. (Garibi 20)

Goldman, Faye. *Geometric Origami.* Thunder Bay, 2014. (Goldman 14)

Gurkewitz, Rona, and Bennett Arnstein. *3-D Geometric Origami.* Dover, 2012. (Gurkewitz and Arnstein 12a)

Gurkewitz, Rona, and Bennett Arnstein. *Beginner's Book of Modular Origami Polyhedra: The Platonic Solids.* Dover, 2012. (Gurkewitz and Arnstein 12b)

Haga, Kazuo, Josefina Fonacier, and Masami Isoda. *Origamics: Mathematical Explorations through Paper Folding.* World Scientific, 2008. (Haga et al. 08)

Heinz, Alexander. *Folding Polyhedra: Kit #1 Squares.* Schiffer, 2022. (Heinz 22a)

Heinz, Alexander. *Folding Polyhedra: Kit #2 Triangles.* Schiffer, 2022. (Heinz 22b)

Hwang, Joseph. *The Art of Modular Origami.* Independently published, 2021. (Hwang 21)

Johnson, Donovan A. *Paper Folding for the Mathematics Class.* National Council of Teachers of Mathematics, 1999. (Johnson 99)

Kasahara, Kunihiko, and Toshie Takahama. *Origami for the Connoisseur.* Japan Publications, 1988. (Kasahara and Takahama 88)

Kasahara, Kunihiko. *Origami Omnibus: Paper-Folding for Everybody.* Japan Publications, 1988. (Kasahara 88)

Kawamura, Miyuki. *Polyhedron Origami for Beginners.* Japan Publications, 2002. (Kawamura 02)

Lam, Tung Ken, and Sue Pope. *Learning Mathematics with Origami.* Association of Teachers of Mathematics, 2016. (Lam and Pope 16)

Lam, Tung Ken. *Action Modular Origami to Intrigue and Delight.* Tarquin, 2018. (Lam 18)

Lam, Tung Ken. *Star Origami: The Starrygami™ Galaxy of Modular Origami Stars, Rings and Wreaths.* A. K. Peters / CRC Press, 2021. (Lam 21)

Lang, Robert. *"Polypolyhedra" in Origami 3: Third International Meeting of Origami Science, Math, and Education.* Edited by Thomas Hull. A. K. Peters, 2003. (Lang 03)

Lawson, Denver, and Paula Versnick, comp. *Unusual Modulars.* Orihouse, 2011. (Lawson 11)

Loper, Byriah. *Mind-Blowing Modular Origami: The Art of Polyhedral Paper Folding: Use Origami Math to Fold Complex, Innovative Geometric Origami Models.* Tuttle, 2016. (Loper 16)

Lukasheva, Ekaterina. *Modern kusudama origami: Designs for modular origami lovers.* CreateSpace, 2015. (Lukasheva 15)

Maekawa, Jun. *Genuine Origami: 43 Mathematically Based Models, from Simple to Complex.* Japan Publications, 2008. (Maekawa 08)

Maekawa, Jun. *Genuine Japanese Origami Book 2: 34 Mathematical Models Based Upon Square Root of 2.* Dover, 2013. (Maekawa 13)

Mitchell, David. *Mathematical Origami: Geometrical Shapes by Paper Folding.* 2nd ed. Tarquin, 2020. (Mitchell 20)

Mukerji, Meenakshi. *Marvelous Modular Origami.* A. K. Peters, 2007. (Mukerji 07)

Mukerji, Meenakshi. *Ornamental Origami: Exploring 3D Geometric Designs.* A. K. Peters / CRC Press, 2008. (Mukerji 08)

Mukerji, Meenakshi. *Origami Inspirations.* A. K. Peters / CRC Press, 2010. (Mukerji 10)

Nakano, Dokuohtei, and Eric Kenneway, trans. *Easy Origami.* Beaver, 1985. (Nakano 85)

Olson, A. T. *Mathematics through Paper Folding.* National Council of Teachers of Mathematics, 1975. (Olson 75)

Petty, David. *Planar Modular Origami.* British Origami Society, 2013. (Petty 13)

Simon, Lewis, Bennett Arnstein, and Rona Gurkewitz. *Modular Origami Polyhedra: Rev. and enlarged ed.* Dover, 2012. (Simon et al. 12)

Sinayskaya, Maria. *Zen Origami: 20 Modular Forms for Meditation and Calm.* Race Point, 2016. (Sinayskaya 16)

Stewart, B. M. *Adventures among the Toroids: A Study of Quasi-Convex, Aplanar, Tunneled Orientable Polyhedra of Positive Genus Having Regular Faces with Disjoint Interiors.* 2nd ed. B. M. Stewart, 1980. (Stewart 80)

Row, T. Sundara. *Geometric Exercises in Paper Folding.* Dover, 1966. (Sundara Row 66)

Weinstein, Michael. *Modular Origami Airplanes.* Independently published, 2021. (Weinstein 21)

Wells, David G. *The Penguin Dictionary of Curious and Interesting Geometry.* Penguin, 1991. (Wells 91)

Wenninger, Magnus J. *Polyhedron Models.* Cambridge University Press, 1971. (Wenninger 71) Yenn, Thoki. Orikata. British Origami Society, 1987. (Yenn 87)

ACKNOWLEDGMENTS

I'd like to thank Steve and Sarah at BlueRed Press, Richard James for the fantastic photography, and Philip Catchpole for the splendid book design. I'm grateful to Peter Symoms-Buchan and Mike Naughton for their help in checking the projects.

Special thanks to the creators who graciously allowed their origami to be included in this book: Silvana Betti Mamino, Dave Mitchell, Robert Neale, and Heinz Strobl. Thanks also to Enrica Gray and the offices of the CDO for their help. I believe that this book is improved by their contribution.

Please note that it is possible that some of the work featured in this book may have been independently created by other people.

AUTHOR BIOGRAPHY

Tung Ken Lam is an origami creator, author, and qualified mathematics teacher. His modular creations are known around the world as fine examples of original and economical folding.

He has taught and presented his origami work across Europe, Asia, and the USA. Tung Ken has run many events for teachers, learners, and the general public. He has been a trustee of the British Origami Society and edited its magazine, *British Origami*.

He accepts commissions for origami projects and creates original origami to order. Clients have included Bletchley Park Trust, the Bodleian Library, University of Oxford, Honda, EuroStemCell (formerly the Scottish Centre for Regenerative Medicine), and Samsung.

His other books include *Action Modular Origami to Intrigue and Delight* (Tarquin, 2018), *Star Origami* (A. K. Peters / CRC Press, 2021), and *Origami: From Surfact to Form* (Wooden Books, 2022). He is the coauthor of *Learning Mathematics with Origami* (Association of Teachers of Mathematics, 2016).

Maritime Activities
of the
Somerset & Dorset Railway

Chris Handley

Millstream Books

*Timber from Scandinavia was a staple traffic handled by the Somerset & Dorset Railway at its harbour at Highbridge and in this 1897 picture the German-owned, Russian-flagged barque **Jupiter** (1864/610g) has just off-loaded her cargo. With more than a little interest in the camera by some of her crew members and with flags hoisted, the ship, under the command of Captain E. Krautmann, is preparing to sail. (Randell Collection/Somerset & Dorset Railway Trust (S&DRT))*

Contents

*The Somerset & Dorset Joint Railway's ketch **Julia** sits at Stert Point in the mouth of the River Parrett in the latter days of the 19th century with the town of Burnham and the 457ft.(141m) island of Brent Knoll on the Somerset Levels clearly visible. Although she has all her sails set the **Julia** has dropped anchor and has a line ashore whilst crew members talk to a mate in the ship's tender. As this is one of a sequence of official railway views, the crew are probably about to swing the ship around to oblige the cameraman on an ideal day when there was little or no wind. (National Railway Museum – DY8520)*

Acknowledgements

My interest was first kindled in this subject as long ago as the 1960s when Grahame Farr, an acknowledged authority on ships and shipping interests in the Bristol Channel, generously gave me much useful information on the ships. Considerable help was also given to me at this time by another well-known North Somerset and S&D historian, Robin Atthill who, in turn, was greatly helped by both Farr and Burnham residents Captain James Dew and Glyn Luxon. To all these gentlemen, now sadly departed, I am eternally grateful.

Like all books of this nature the work has really been a collaborative effort, helped along by many who have freely given of their time and for which I am greatly privileged. I owe a particular debt of gratitude to Jem Harrison for allowing me to make use of much material on the Burnham and Highbridge areas first researched by him; to Dr. Peter Cattermole for the considerable amount of time and effort he has devoted to supporting me with this project and to Duncan Harper for making available material in his collection.

There are, of course, very many others who have either contributed both as individuals, as members of related organisations, or have pointed me in the right direction; I would particularly like to express my thanks to Dr. Robin Craig, John Childs, Colin Green, Alan Hammond, Philip Thomas, Kevin O'Donoghue, Harold Appleyard, Roy Fenton, Rod Fitzhugh, Tony Blackler, John Luxon, Jason Baker, Peter Stuckey, Russ Garner, Martin Benn and Louis Loughran.

Principal amongst the organisations which deserve special mention is the Somerset & Dorset Railway Trust which holds one of the largest collections of information and photographs on this famous railway. I must record my thanks to the Chairman and officers who have freely allowed me access to this unique material over the years.

Many of those who staff our national and local institutions have given me far more help that I could have dared hope for; I would therefore like to take the opportunity to thank the staff of the National Maritime Museum, Greenwich; Ed Bartholomew of the National Railway Museum, York; Somerset Record Office; David Bromwich of the Somerset Studies Library, Taunton; Southampton City Library (Specialist Collections); the Public Record Office, Kew; the British Library; Flintshire Record Office; Andy King of the Bristol Industrial Museum; Bridgwater Library; Burnham Library; and the House of Lords Record Office for their help with my searches and enquiries.

The majority of photographs in this book are credited where possible to their source of origin. Many are from my own collection which have come from a wide variety of sources over many years and it has not always been possible to trace and acknowledge ownership. To the owners of those I have been unable to credit successfully I beg indulgence.

Finally, I must thank my publisher, Tim Graham, for having the faith to bring this book into print and last, but certainly not least, the most important member of the team, my wife Margaret who has allowed me to indulge in the subject for very much longer than I ought to have done.

Cover illustrations:
*front: The Somerset & Dorset Railway's steamer **Julia**, built in 1904, awaits a refit at Highbridge New Wharf sometime after the First World War.*
*rear: The first **Julia**, a wooden ketch built in 1863, anchored off Stert Point at the mouth of the River Parrett.*

First published in 2001 by Millstream Books, 18 The Tyning, Widcombe, Bath BA2 6AL

Set in Times New Roman and printed in Great Britain by The Amadeus Press, Cleckheaton, West Yorkshire

© Chris Handley 2001

ISBN 0 948975 63 6

A catalogue record for this book is available from the British Library

Introduction

Our Victorian forefathers were very quick to see the advantages of an integrated transport system so when railways became a viable proposition and were able to offer a cheap and reliable service it was a natural outcome to extend the scope of their operation into both road and sea travel. Following its opening in 1854 the Somerset Central Railway quickly exploited sea travel, firstly through its newly acquired wharf at Highbridge, then later through nearby Burnham where a regular ferry service to and from Cardiff was developed. Extending southwards and joining with the Dorset Central Railway in 1862, the Somerset & Dorset Railway (S&DR) set its sights on a channel-to-channel service connecting Cardiff with Cherbourg.

Meanwhile the little harbour of Highbridge was developed as a railhead for coastal and foreign trade; a place where the S&DR might entice ships from all parts of the near continent to trade conveniently with its railway. Soon the railway company was a ship owner in its own right, operating both passenger and cargo vessels; bringing its own rails and coal from South Wales.

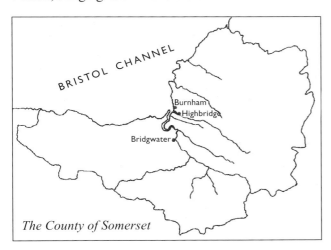

The County of Somerset

Very mixed fortunes lay ahead as befits anything to do with this famous railway and the troubled times hit by the company were reflected in the shipping operations yet at its peak during the mid-1880s the Joint Committee of the S&D Joint Railway (as it had become in 1876) operated a mixed passenger/cargo fleet of six vessels. By 1888 the ferry services had failed and the railway withdrew from passenger operations but the fortunes of the small cargo fleet flourished into the 20th century. By the 1930s even these ships were withdrawn although the small railway

harbour at Highbridge survived in commercial operation until the end of the 1940s.

Typical of so many smaller railway operations throughout the United Kingdom, the exploits of the Somerset & Dorset's maritime interests and a full description of their small fleet of ships has taken a back seat for far too long in favour of the better-known antics of the railway itself which is surely one of the best documented in the country. Yet the story of their ships and maritime affairs was a full and exciting part of this railway's history; a story which includes paddle steamers, screw steamships and ketches in a fascinating montage where rail met sea.

I have a tremendous admiration and respect for the seamen of the Somerset & Dorset who took their frail vessels out, often in atrocious weather, to keep the ferry service operating or to ensure the all-important cargo service met the railway's requirements. The Bristol Channel and Severn estuary must be one of the most difficult and challenging stretches of navigation in which to operate small coasting ships, particularly those totally under sail. The massive tidal drop, the difficult races, the impossible little harbours up winding rivers and, of course, all that mud served to test the seamanship qualities of all who plied their trade in this area to the utmost limit. Although the stories of those who engaged in this have been well told by many others it is, nonetheless, fascinating to see just where the ships of the S&D fleet got to! Lydney for coal – quite the most difficult harbour to enter when under sail in the upper reaches of the Severn estuary; Bridgwater where pilotage was compulsory to navigate the twisting River Parrett; tiny little Porthgain, a mere crack of an inlet that formed a small harbour beneath steep hills out in West Wales, Fremington on the River Taw which involved negotiating the infamous Bideford Bar; or they would happily 'round the Lands' and make for Porthoustock, Penzance or even the Fal if cargoes offered.

It was a brave enterprise and one so typical of the optimism which befitted the Somerset & Dorset Railway. Indeed the S&D men and women afloat – and there were well over 200 of them over the years, not to mention all those who gave their support on shore – were very much a part of that wonderful extended family for which the railway was so renowned. It is only right that their part in the story should be given the prominence it deserves.

1 In the Beginning

There are few such places in the world where the tidal fall can be so great as in the Bristol Channel yet along the difficult shores of this major sea lane our master mariners and traders have pursued their legitimate business over hundreds of years despite the inevitable difficulties presented to them, and they have done this with typical verve and optimism in vessels which today would be discarded without any thought as being far too small and frail to attempt such voyages.

Somerset, like so many other counties, has played its part in the development of trade and many a minor 'pill' or creek has played host to the odd ketch-rigged sailing vessel or Severn trow[1] as it discharged its cargo shoreside amid totally primitive conditions. Inevitably several of the larger rivers and creeks would be developed into flourishing ports to serve wider interest and one such was the pivotal town of Bridgwater. Situated a dozen or so miles up the River Parrett, it was a less than easy place to get to by sailing craft which had to navigate a narrow and twisting estuary in an area where tidal limitations were uppermost amongst the problems. Indeed it could take as many as three days to achieve this tortuous trip. Nevertheless the port, which was established as long ago as the 14th century, survived to grow into a busy facility which would continue to trade until well after the Second World War, even becoming a port of registry, centre of a small but significant shipbuilding and repair industry and controlling a large part of the adjacent coastline.

Inland, Bridgwater served a predominantly agricultural community which had developed largely upon the difficult Somerset Levels and Moors, an interesting tract of land mainly reclaimed from the sea over hundreds of years and still very susceptible to flooding. The Parrett and its tributaries provide much of the drainage capacity helped by numerous man-made drains.

Amidst grandiose schemes to allow access to Bridgwater and its dock by seagoing vessels via a canal system, little more than piecemeal improvements to the dangerous river navigation itself were ever undertaken and this was a source of much discontent at times, its meanderings spilling out into Bridgwater Bay close to the small town of Burnham. Hereabouts was the estuary of another of the several rivers which drain the northern levels, the Brue, which itself was navigable for a mile or so upstream to a small pill at Highbridge.[2]

At Burnham, on the eastern shore of Bridgwater Bay, the church of St. Andrew, situated towards the north of the present town centre, marks the hub of the original little settlement and cluster of cottages. Although much of the present building dates from the 14th and 15th centuries there are records showing that a place of worship stood on this spot some considerable time before this. The 16th and 17th centuries saw a number of land improvements and drainage schemes carried out and this increased the amount of usable land in the area but it was not until the 1830s that the little village spread southwards into a small resort and spa when several local businessmen, the Rev. David Davies and, later, landowner George Reed amongst them, invested in housing, hotels, guest houses and other town services.

Highbridge is said to have existed before 1324 but there is no obvious evidence to show that this pill (known as the River Brent until the 18th century) actually connected to any watercourse further inland. Originally the Brue watercourse, in all probability, flowed out via the River Axe, taking a route north from Glastonbury to join the Axe near Panborough and it is suspected that the present watercourse was man-made for much of the distance west of Meare to Highbridge sometime around the 13th century.[3]

The whole of the 250-square-mile area of the Somerset Levels and Moors was at one time under the sea and over many thousands of years has been subjected to alternating periods of inundation and drying out. Each successive inundation brought more clay and silt which was deposited mainly along the coastal belt reaching as far as six miles inland in places, leaving freshwater bogs to develop further to the east where generations of plant life built up a generous layer of organic material to form the giant peat bogland which still characterises much of the wetland areas particularly to the north of the Polden hills, a long finger of higher ground which protrudes out into this vast sea. The Levels are, on average, about 16 to 20ft.(5-6m) above sea level whereas the peat Moors average only about 10ft.(3m). Extensive field work over more recent years has proved that man inhabited these inland wet areas from about 3000BC forming farming communities and lake villages with crude trackways over the swampy ground often joining the many 'islands' of slightly higher ground. The last significant inundation of sea water in the area occurred around AD250 during the Roman occupation which deposited the final layer of clay along the coastal belt and it is this that was later to be used extensively in the tile and brick manufacturing industry around Bridgwater and Highbridge.

Although there is plenty of evidence that the Romans were active in this part of Somerset it seems that they did not waste their time trying to tame the wetland areas; indeed there is little evidence that any real progress was made in trying to utilise this area more profitably until the mediaeval monasteries were established and became involved. From that time onwards much of the land came into the ownership of either the established church (the Bishopric of Bath and Wells) or monastic settlements at Glastonbury.

By the 13th century some serious efforts by the estates concerned had been made to try to drain and improve the land for agricultural use. To stop inundation by salt water extensive sea walls were built along the coastline over a period of many years. At many of the tidal estuaries manually controlled sluice gates were constructed to prevent sea water entering when the tide rose while allowing fresh water to drain through them as it receded. To allow freshwater to drain off the levels many watercourses were dug. A tidal sluice (known locally as a 'clyce' or 'clyse') had been constructed by 1485 probably just to the west of the 'High Bridge' on the River Brue which by this time of course flowed westward.

The clyce worked adequately to prevent high tides flooding inland but if it was not operated correctly it would also prevent freshwater escaping and in these circumstances it could exacerbate the flood problem.

Despite continued work to improve the drainage of the area the Levels had not been freed from flooding by the end of the 18th century and this led to a number of Local Enclosure and Drainage Acts being passed requiring a more systematic approach to the problems. These led to the construction of a comprehensive drainage system centred around hundreds of miles of ditches to take water off the low-lying fields thus created. The water was taken away by much larger channels known as rhynes (pronounced 'reens') which in turn fed the main arterial 'drains'. Combined with better sea defences and newer clyces, the area was finally made productive although even today vast tracks of land are still liable to go under water following particularly wet winters.

Getting the surplus water to the sea was not easy and several pumping stations were eventually built to aid this, the problem being compounded by the extremely high tides experienced in the Bristol Channel which can rise to 40ft.(12.3m) and occasionally signi-

ficantly higher, given the wrong weather conditions. With this sort of rise a breach in the sea defences could still flood vast areas as it did in 1811 when the floods reached Glastonbury and again much more recently on Sunday 13 December 1981 when a tempestuous storm coinciding with a high tide burst through the sea defence walls at Burnham and along the Parrett estuary to cause considerable flooding and damage.

Like all such places in this part of the Channel the Brue navigation suffered not only from the extremes of tides but also from the massive amounts of silt which constantly deposited itself in the form of a thick grey-black slippery mud, a feature of all the rivers and many beaches on the upper reaches of the Channel. Inadequate operation of the clyce could also silt up the doors which relied on a good flow of water through them to stop the mud deposits from building up. However, the river had been used for a good many years as a navigation, an old maritime map of 1723 marking a Mr. Garchel's warehouse at the pill in 'High Bridge'.

Responsibility for land drainage eventually passed to the Commissioners of Sewers culminating in the Brue Drainage Act of 1801 when the time had come to replace the original mediaeval clyce by a completely new drainage cut and tidal sluice just to the south of the original. Dug by French prisoners of war, the 'New Cut' – a wider, straight channel – and sluice, once in operation in 1803, soon caused the original Brue Channel and clyce to silt up. The real solution would have been to lower the outfall by deepening and widening the Brue through the clay belt which bordered the coast. Such action was eventually avoided by the opening of the Glastonbury Canal in 1833 which gave the Brue a second outfall utilising the original river channel which had, in the meantime, accumulated some 20ft.(6.15m) of silt in 30 years.

For those whose business was coastal trading the mud and tidal limitations were a necessary evil which just had to be taken in their stride: it certainly didn't put our forefathers off the prospects of opening up the hinterland for the purposes of trading or, indeed, seeking solutions to time-honoured problems, and one of those problems was getting around Lands End. It had been claimed in the early 18th century that as many as 200 men were lost annually at sea in ships trading to and from the Bristol Channel, South Coast and the near continent. By the mid-1700s the technology certainly existed to cut a ship canal across the south-western peninsula and thereafter a number of schemes were put forward which would not only open up large inland areas to waterborne transport but also get around the dangerous sea journey. As was often the case, scheme after scheme came and went, often foundering through lack of finance, lack of support or outright opposition until, in 1825, an Act was passed to construct the English and Bristol Channels Ship Canal. By this time the enthusiasm to build such a mighty waterway was dwindling and this early attempt to construct a channel-to-channel link was eventually lost. It was to be the construction of the Bristol & Exeter Railway in later years which would finally complete this link but not, of course, without costly transhipment between ship and rail, so ships continued to trade all the way via Lands End; the interior of Somerset saw only piecemeal improvements to navigation, mostly involving the Rivers Parrett and Tone.

During the 1820s a group of local dignitaries and entrepreneurs in and around the Glastonbury and central Somerset area, hampered by the difficult communications that they were experiencing, came to the conclusion that a canal should be built from Glastonbury and it is really here that this particular maritime story begins. In the years following, there was a lot of discussion as to the best route to be taken culminating in a public meeting in 1825 when a local surveyor, Richard Hamnett, was engaged to look at the options. In 1826 he suggested two alternatives: one, along the River Brue was rejected, whilst the other proposed making existing drainage navigable but included two locks on a canal section. Also included in this scheme was a branch canal to Street and a floating basin at Highbridge. He believed that the canal could be constructed for less than £10,000.

There were a number of criticisms of this scheme so a second survey was carried out by John Beauchamp but at a revised cost of a little over £15,000. The plan eventually chosen was in fact quite close to that of Hamnett's. The navigation was to start at a sea lock below where the Brue entered the tideway at Highbridge where a floating harbour would be formed together with wharf space. Beyond this the original Brue channel, which had been by-passed by the 1803-built Brue drainage straight cut and tidal sluice, would be reopened to give vessels access into the river itself. The Brue would then be utilised past Bason Bridge to a point then known as Cripp's House but later as Cripp's Corner. At this point a new 1¾-mile canal cut would be constructed southwards towards the existing South Drain which it would join at Gold Corner. The drain would then be utilised for almost six miles to a point near Ashcott Corner. At this point the drain turned sharply towards the south whilst the canal was to turn north-east. The final section took the canal back on to a south-easterly then easterly course to follow the Cuckoo Ditch as it approached the River Brue.

This was to be crossed by a lock to river level followed immediately by another lock to take the cut into Glastonbury. A final tight 90° bend brought the canal into the terminal basin close to the mill stream.

At a meeting at Glastonbury in late February 1827 Mr. E.T. Percy, an engineer, spoke in favour of the project and with subscriptions already being received it was decided to go ahead with a Bill. By the time this had reached Parliament no less than £15,250 had been raised, mainly from within the county. One or two smaller contributions had been received from South Wales whilst Newport coal shippers and the promoters behind the Monmouthshire Canal showed their support.

The Act 'for improving and supporting the Navigation of the River Brue from the mouth thereof, at its junction with the River Parrett, to Cripp's House, and for making and constructing a canal from thence to the town of Glastonbury, the county of Somerset' received Royal Assent on 28th May 1827. The new Glastonbury Navigation & Canal Company was empowered to raise £18,000 in shares, or, rather unusually, by promissory notes or borrowing from the Exchequer Bill Loan Commissioners, and a further £5,000 on mortgage of the undertaking, if necessary. Significantly as the drainage of the lowlands on the banks of the Brue was the responsibility of the Commissioners of Sewers, the new company had to invest £1,000 to be at the disposal of the Commissioners for their use in effecting repairs or making alterations in the drainage as a result of the construction of the canal.

Shortly after the Act had been obtained it quickly became clear that the plan was actually impracticable. The company therefore contacted the eminent canal engineer John Rennie to consider what might be the best course of action. His recommendations were of great importance to the project: he first considered three possible sizes of waterway; one 10ft.(3.1m) deep to take full seagoing vessels such as large sloops and small brigs of 120-140 tons; one 8ft.(2.5m) deep to take 40-60 ton estuarial vessels then trading in the Bristol Channel; or a 5ft.(1.54m) deep barge canal. The latter would necessitate transhipment of goods at Highbridge whilst the former, he considered, was probably beyond the needs of Glastonbury, so he recommended the second alternative, at an estimated cost of £28,720 and with locks 64ft. long by 18ft. wide (19.7m x 5.5m). The cut was to be 44ft.(13.5m) wide at the top and the two Brue locks originally anticipated were to be replaced by an 18ft.(5.5m) wide three-arch aqueduct with a syphon for the river. There would be another single-arched syphon aqueduct over the South Drain and a single lock near Shapwick.

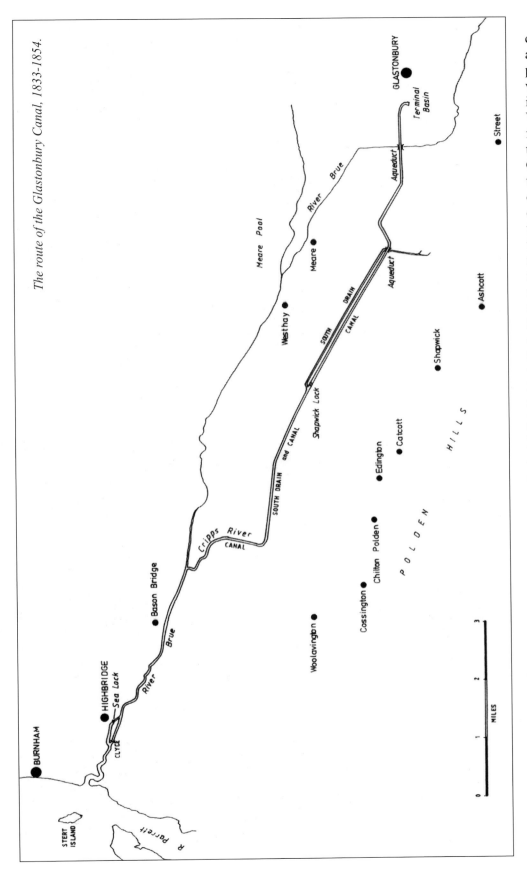

The route of the Glastonbury Canal, 1833-1854.

There were some clear advantages for acceptance of the new plan particularly as it would allow vessels to import such cargoes as Welsh coal and manufactured goods from the north directly to Glastonbury without transhipment. In view of the immense amount of waterborne trading that was carried out on the long-established network of navigable rivers and canals bordering the rivers Severn and Wye and the increasing suitability of the up-river trows to venture as far south-west as Bridgwater, Rennie had clearly identified the best possible compromise. His recommendations were accepted but the unhappy proprietors were left with a greatly increased cost estimate.

Unfortunately his plan was not to be completed quite as originally envisaged, partly due to the need to find economies. The canal above Shapwick lock (which was built immediately to the south and parallel to the South Drain) was cut to only 6ft.(1.54m) deep whilst the very sharp turn just short of Glastonbury basin was built as originally planned, despite Rennie's recommendation that it should be eased. The sea lock was relocated back to the upper end of the old Brue channel and some 200 yards (185m) to the west of its upper junction with the Brue Drainage channel of 1803. This meant that the proposed floating basin was not built and all the wharfage was below the lock and therefore tidal. Although it is not clear why this latter change came about, one can only speculate that the coasting traders objected to paying a lock charge to reach Highbridge.

The total length of the navigation from the confluence of the Rivers Brue and Parrett to Glastonbury was 14 miles, 1 furlong and 7 chains (23.1km). Of this the first 7 furlongs, 6 chains was from the Brue estuary to the tide-lock at Highbridge which replaced the old mediaeval clyce. From this lock the original short silted channel of the Brue to the new Brue Drainage channel was re-excavated. The lock was constructed so that the top of the gates would be level with the highest known smooth tide which rose some 40ft.(12.3m) at that point. The surface of the canal was 10ft.(3.1m) below the top of the gates with a 10ft.(3.1m) water depth. In effect this sea lock acted much like a tidal sluice but it was to be the cause of inestimable trouble in the future.

The rise at Shapwick lock (ST411419) was 3ft.2in.(1m), and some three miles to the east the canal crossed the South Drain on a small iron aqueduct as envisaged by Rennie. Between Ashcott and Glastonbury the canal crossed the Brue at what became known as Aqueduct Crossing, again as intended. Swing bridges were added where drove roads crossed the navigation.

The final cost of construction was probably in the region of £30,000, rather more than the £23,000 stipulated by the Act. The Brue aqueduct alone is said to have cost £3,000. Some of the debts may never have been paid: Rennie, who had not only carried out the final survey but provided specifications for the locks, aqueducts and a bridge, was still owed £367 out of his total bill for £567 in spite of frequently reminding the company, and that was in 1837.

On 15 August 1833 the canal was finally opened from Glastonbury to the tidal pill just below the sea lock at Highbridge. On the great day, the company's barge **Goodland** and the yacht **Water Witch** left Glastonbury with local dignitaries and a band of musicians bound for Highbridge. Following this the obvious need for a transfer point between seagoing vessels and canal boats caused the pill at Highbridge to be developed into what was then known as the New Wharf.

Despite the high hopes of the promoters and an initial flurry of trading activity in the immediate years after 1833, the Glastonbury Canal was actually destined to lead only a mediocre existence; indeed as a navigation it was really remarkably unsuccessful and it never earned more than about £300 per annum. Although initially it was useful as an additional drain, the penning of water to maintain sufficient depth for navigation caused the peat moors to become waterlogged, thus frustrating its drainage function. Lack of dredging, a rising bed due to waterlogged peat and insufficient tidal scouring due to the coastal, clay belt landowners demanding gates to be shut to pen enough water for their stock purposes, all made navigation difficult and totally unpredictable. One has to speculate on just how many through shipping movements were made and from what locations on the River Severn and Bristol Channel they came from: how much South Wales coal or manufactured goods from Birmingham and the north actually penetrated to Glastonbury or reached this part of Somerset in any greater quantity is certainly open to question.

Not surprisingly the canal was destined to have only a very short working life and with the continual development of the railway system and, in particular, the opening of the Bristol & Exeter Railway through Highbridge in the early 1840s there was a certain inevitability that a railway would eventually be driven across the flat terrain traversed by the canal. As a precautionary move, and to ensure that they should have a stake in any future rail development of this part of Somerset the Bristol & Exeter Railway (B&ER) purchased the canal company in 1848 for £7,000 but not without misgivings from some of their shareholders. In 1850 the lock gates were re-opened and the penning of water discontinued. Much of the canal, although remaining a notional navigation, thus more-or-less reverted to its previous function as part of the drainage system.

A serious plan to replace the canal by a railway was promoted by the local business community shortly afterwards. This envisaged building a broad-gauge line a little over 12 miles in length largely along the canal towpath connecting with the B&ER at Highbridge and also the New Wharf, whilst it would terminate in a station on a site close to the canal terminal basin at Glastonbury. Interestingly one of those who was prominently involved in this was James Clark, one of the founders of the well-known boot and shoe manufacturers, C. & J. Clark of Street.

Incorporated under an Act of 17 June 1852, the Somerset Central Railway (SCR) relied very much on the help and co-operation of the B&ER if its plans were to be fulfilled and part of the agreement envisaged the transfer of the canal into SCR ownership at a cost of £8,000, an event which took place on 16 September 1852.[4] The B&ER was paid shares to this value and

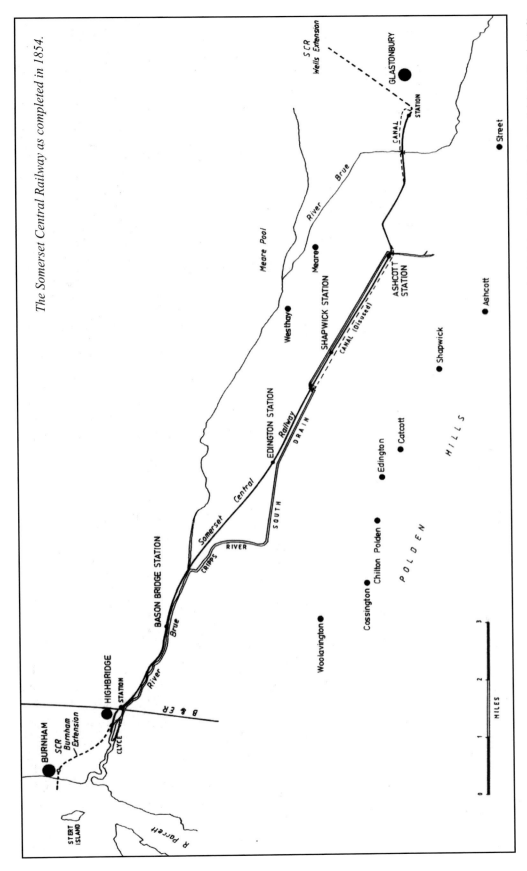

The Somerset Central Railway as completed in 1854.

also gained an all-important option to work the new line for a period of seven years following its completion. The contract was let to Messrs. J. & C. Rigby of Westminster and Charles Gregory was appointed as the line's engineer. The first sod was cut by the chairman on 18 April 1853 with construction proceeding rapidly despite difficulties being experienced in building the line over the unstable turf bog east of Shapwick, and it is recorded that by February 1854 the track between the Bristol & Exeter line and the New Wharf had been laid.

The canal continued to trade until such time as it became impossible to carry on. Indeed, during this period it was probably busier than it had ever been since it was used by the contractors to carry construction material for the new railway. Final closure as a navigation took place on 1 July 1854. The new broad-gauge railway opened some six weeks later, on 17 August, with public services commencing on 28 August. The Bristol & Exeter Railway provided all the locomotives and rolling stock and integrated the new services into their own timetable.

There are few traces of the Glastonbury Canal to be seen today but the line of the former navigation can still be traced near Glastonbury by a modern-day drainage ditch which appears at a lower level. Taken on 28 March 1965 the modified abutments of the former aqueduct over the River Brue were still visible at a point where the canal's replacement, the Somerset Central Railway, ran slightly to the south. It crossed the Brue by an adjacent bridge together with a level crossing over the road from which this photo was taken known as Aqueduct Crossing. (R. Atthill/S&DRT)

By this time the small town and harbour of High-bridge had grown into a thriving little port[5] and as a direct result of the facilities provided, a local brick and tile manufacturing industry had developed whilst at the Wharf an increasing amount of imported timber was being handled. In anticipation of the opening of the new railway the harbour tolls were generally reduced to encourage trade with a special low tariff for all coals destined to be carried over the line.

Following the opening of the new line the ultimate, if modest, ambitions of the promoters had been achieved. The area at New Wharf, like the canal, had also come into the ownership of the SCR and shortly after 1860 the whole wharf area was greatly improved by the construction of a much longer and more substantial quay with better siding facilities.

A government survey of the Bristol Channel had identified Highbridge as a potential packet port and dock developments at both Cardiff and Newport on the other side encouraged the prospects of a substantial development of trade with South Wales. Additionally coastwise trade to other Somerset, North Devon and even Cornish ports was also envisaged. The Somerset Central not surprisingly attached great importance to its new outlet and although the actual line was being worked by the B&ER the SCR retained sole rights to revenue from the harbour.

That a ferry service might also be run between Highbridge and South Wales had been anticipated and as soon as the railway opened an attempt was made to start one. In July 1855 the wooden paddle tug **Rapid** (53grt)[6] was placed on the service and advertised as 'the new fast packet steamer sailing from the New Wharf, Highbridge'. Just how long the vessel ran is not known but it is doubtful if a regular service was maintained and it must have been painfully obvious to railway company and ship operator alike that the Wharf, although adequate for cargo operations, was rather less so for passenger services because of its severe tidal limitations and silting problems.

The head of the tidal pill at Highbridge photographed around the turn of the 20th century shows the original New Wharf on the left together with its fixed timber crane. Ships had been trading up to this point for as long as there had been local coastal trading vessels but it took the arrival of the Somerset Central Railway in the 1850s to provide the impetus for development of port facilities in this area as successors to the Glastonbury Canal. Vast quantities of timber were originally handled across this quay although in this view two smack-rigged coastal cargo vessels, the furthest being a Severn trow, are moored there. Providing a sufficient depth of water at the quay for larger vessels was always a problem to the S&D because of the constant silting problems. (Randell Collection/S&DRT)

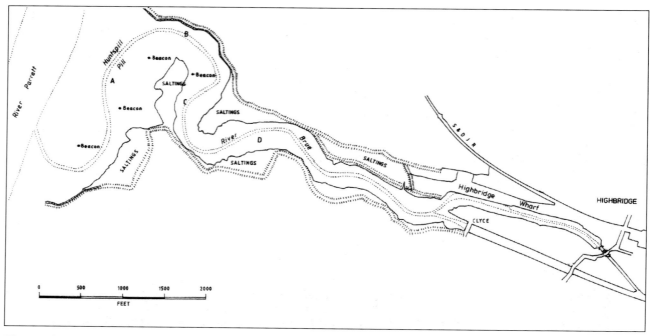

The winding course of the estuarial River Brue reveals the difficulties faced by Bristol Channel mariners and many a foreign sailor as they set sail up the meandering course to Highbridge. Vessels entered the deep water channel from the Parrett via a marker buoy at the river outflow at Huntspill Pill, otherwise known as the Sea Reach (A on the map). A severe 180-degree turn saw ships negotiating firstly the Burnham Bars (B), followed by the Little Hope Reach (C) before regaining an easterly course into Great Hope Reach (D) whence it was reasonably easy until the approach into the harbour and wharf area itself.

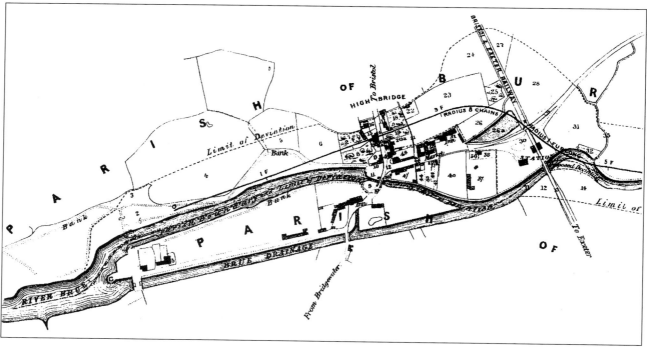

Part of the Parliamentary Plan of the Highbridge area which accompanied the Somerset Central Railway Act of 17 June 1852. The proposed extension of the railway to the west of the Bristol & Exeter main line reveals the position of the branch to the New Wharf which was situated at the eastern end of the harbour area close to the sea lock. The initial railway developments were in the area of the orchard marked 8 on the north bank and did not extend westwards to include the final furlong so authorised until the 1860s. Note the original alignment of the protective flood bank on that side.

14

Perhaps it is no coincidence that in the same year, 1855, the Somerset Central decided to seek Parliamentary powers to construct a short seaward extension of the railway to Burnham, a mile-and-a-half further west, then a small but developing holiday town. Here, said the SCR, the line would terminate on a pier from where they could run packet steamers at all states of the tide. The idea seemed simple and obvious enough; Burnham would deal with the passenger trade whilst the Wharf at Highbridge would continue to look after the cargo operation. A further Act was obtained on 30 July 1855 to authorise construction of the line (together with the proposed extension from Glastonbury to Wells in the opposite direction).

The actual pier was planned to be constructed towards the southern end of the little town's promenade at a point where the main shipping channel into the Parrett ran within about 300 yards (277m) of the shore. A pier of conventional Victorian

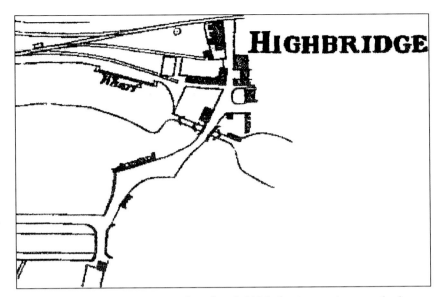

Taken from a Parliamentary plan dated 1859 the interesting sea lock gate arrangement into the Glastonbury Canal can clearly be seen with two gates designed to act against the sea. The height of the sea at high tide could be as much as 10 feet (3.1m) above that of the river level which meant that ships would have to be locked down into the old Brue cut. Conversely when the tide was low and below that of the river the eastern lock would prevent water escaping unless its sluices were opened.

design was proposed but what was actually built was to end up rather different – all was not to be plain sailing!

Notes:

1. A trow is a small sailing cargo vessel indigenous to the River Severn, found in two forms: a larger version used in the Severn estuary and upper reaches of the Bristol Channel and a smaller one used exclusively on the river above Gloucester as far as the head of navigation near Welshpool. The larger trows were flat-bottomed, but with distinctive deep transom sterns, originally square rigged but later more often fore and aft smack or ketch rigged. They habitually traded out of Bristol, Bridgwater and South Wales ports to Gloucester.

2. The tidal part of the River Brue between its estuary and High-bridge is commonly known by local mariners and inhabitants as the Highbridge River or Pill although a glance at the 1966 reprint of the OS 1:25,000 map will reveal that it changed names to become the Huntspill Pill only to become the Brue Pill on the 1989 reprint! More properly the 1886 survey and 1903 and 1929 revisions of the OS 1:2,500 scale maps describe the watercourse as the River Brue, Huntspill Pill being confined to that part of the river which forms the actual estuary.

3. Ken Fletcher, *The Somerset Levels and Moors*, p.32.

4. The canal was purchased from the Bristol & Exeter Railway except for the short 200-yard (112m) channel at Highbridge which came under the control of the Commissioners of Sewers. Technically this latter portion remained open as a sluicing cut until formally abandoned in 1936.

5. The area at Highbridge was always referred to in all official correspondence and documents by the SCR, S&DR and S&DJR as 'Highbridge Harbour' and not 'Wharf', the latter term being reserved more rightly as a description for the quays.

6. The *Rapid* was built at South Shields in 1838. After several owners and a major rebuild, she was purchased by Hercules Towell of Bridgwater in December 1852, and remained at this port until her sale in June 1876. Although a paddle tug, it was common in this period for such vessels to be employed on local passenger and excursion work whenever business offered.

2 Channel-to-Channel

Although the local business community might have been pleased with their efforts to provide a rail connection into the hinterland of Somerset there remained the fact that it served no great pocket of industry nor centre of population. Glastonbury could boast rather less than 4,000 inhabitants at this time with Street very much smaller, whilst Highbridge was nothing more than a small village at the head of navigation of the Brue. Ideally the railway would have made for Bridgwater but this involved crossing the Polden Hills and at the time the easiest and cheapest option was to follow the near level terrain out to the coast.

During a special general meeting of the SCR in October 1855, the directors, whilst alluding to the success of Highbridge as a port, made a significant statement which recognised that the catchment area around Glastonbury, Street and Wells alone was unlikely to provide enough trade:

> The connection of the Bristol and English Channels has for many years been considered to be of great importance particularly with a view to the more rapid conveyance of the produce of South Wales to the ports of the South Coast of England.

By this time therefore it had become quite clear that the directors of the SCR had greater plans and were looking much further afield. There were two obvious options available to them; either to extend eastwards from Wells to join the Wilts, Somerset & Weymouth Railway (later Great Western Railway) at Frome or instead take a route further to the south to make a junction with the same railway at Wyke Champflower near Bruton. Whilst both would have accessed the south coast at Southampton the latter alternative had a specific objective to connect with a proposed line from Poole which can only refer to the building of the Dorset Central Railway (DCR).

The Dorset Central originally proposed a railway to run from a connection with the existing London & South Western Railway standard-gauge line at Wimborne through Blandford to Wyke Champflower, where it too proposed to join the Wilts, Somerset & Weymouth Railway. A strange coincidence indeed until it is realised that the embryonic Dorset Central shared a secretary, engineer, solicitors and London offices with the Somerset Central. Clearly the two railways shared a common ancestry; only the gauge of the two lines was different.

With decisions made on the way ahead, the Somerset Central had already applied for an Act to extend towards Bruton and this was authorised on 21 July 1856, just a week before the Dorset Central Railway gained its initial Act to construct a 10½ mile line up the Stour Valley from Wimborne to Blandford on 29 July 1856. By 10 August 1857 the DCR was already seeking Parliamentary approval for a further extension northwards to meet the SCR at Wyke Champflower. The problem of the difference in gauge had already been addressed by the SCR who had resolved at a meeting in February 1857 to lay standard-gauge rails in anticipation of the link-up, despite misgivings by the B&ER. Everything was now set to create a unified standard-gauge trunk line some 70 miles in length which would connect the Bristol and English Channels.

Meanwhile the construction of both the Burnham and Wells extensions was well under way, Rigby again being contracted. The short Burnham extension, just 1 mile 50 chains in length, was ready by August 1857 but the Wells extension, now clearly to be a dead-end branch much to the chagrin of the people of that city, took a little longer, being opened formally on Thursday 3 March 1859. Both extensions were initially worked by the Bristol & Exeter Railway.

Work commenced on the DCR in mid-November 1856 and the line as far as Blandford was ready for opening on 1 November 1860. Like the SCR, the DCR was worked by its large and supportive neighbour, the London & South Western Railway (LSWR). Meanwhile, following the completion of the Wells branch, Rigby, who had won the contract to extend the SCR to Bruton, had started work. With the B&ER's lease due to expire on 28 August 1861 and with no intention of renewing it the SCR was also faced with providing its own standard-gauge locomotives, rolling stock and a locomotive works at Highbridge together with a station, it having hitherto used the B&ER's. Following parliamentary opposition the SCR was forced to lay mixed-gauge rails on its new extension and this, combined with bad weather, delayed its completion.

By February 1861 the SCR directors were already talking of the mutual advantages of the two companies being worked as one. In the interim, a proposal by the SCR to undertake the working of the DCR was approved

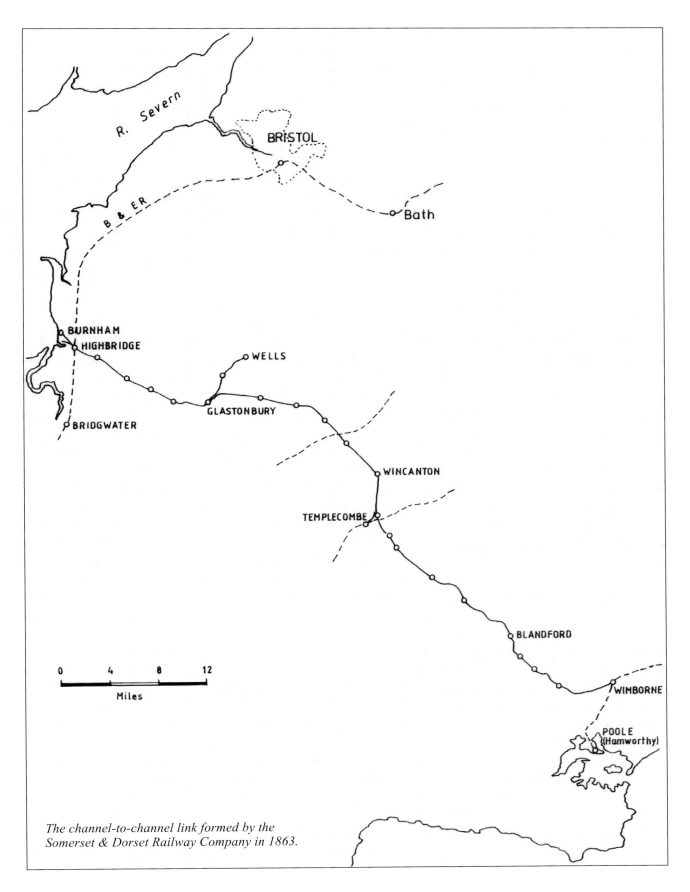

*The channel-to-channel link formed by the
Somerset & Dorset Railway Company in 1863.*

This unidentified three-masted barque makes an interesting sight at Highbridge sandwiched between two local ketch-rigged trading vessels. Getting such large sailing vessels as this up and down the tortuous River Brue was no mean feat but was probably accomplished with the aid of a Bridgwater tug. (Craig/Farr collection)

at a meeting held on 29 June. In November, the isolated DCR section between Templecombe and Bruton was completed but could not be opened to traffic until 18 January 1862 when the SCR line between Glastonbury and Bruton was ready so the formal opening of standard-gauge services from Burnham and Highbridge to Templecombe was delayed until 3 February. Approval for a Bill of Amalgamation was given in May 1862 and this received the Royal Assent on 7 August. On 1 September 1862 the SCR and DCR amalgamated to form the Somerset & Dorset Railway Company.

On this momentous day the new through link was anything but complete and construction work was still in hand on the missing 16-mile Templecombe-Blandford section. This was finally opened on 31 August 1863. The piecemeal way in which the line had been planned and built did not always lend itself to easy operation and a reversal at Templecombe, where a junction was made with the Salisbury & Yeovil line and station, was always to remain a nightmare. Another reversal was required at Wimborne on the Southampton & Dorchester line where trains entered LSWR territory

if they were to continue to the ultimate destination of Poole, or to be precise, Hamworthy. Notwithstanding that, the new S&DR had managed to produce its much wanted channel-to-channel route.

It is, perhaps, worth pausing at this point to realise what the potential outcome of this could have been. There were, of course, no regular passenger or cargo services by sea between Burnham or Bridgwater and Poole, nor indeed from Cardiff, but the distance was approximately 360 miles. The opening of this new railway cut the distance between Burnham and Poole to just 65 miles. The distance from Cardiff to Burnham by sea is about 18 miles so potentially it brought some South Wales ports to within 85 miles of the South Coast and thereby services to the continent. This was the attraction and vision the directors had seen and wished to develop but there had been a formidable cost to the new S&DR in setting it up. The directors had completed the link but could they afford to run the necessary services and, more importantly, realise the potential in terms of trade on which they had pinned all their hopes and ambitions?

3 The Battle of Burnham Pier

In the prospectus that preceded the Act of 30 July 1855 authorising the short Burnham extension it was stated that it was expected to be remunerative owing to strong local support and its favourable position for development of steamer communications with South Wales. Most importantly the pier was planned to accommodate small vessels at nearly all states of the tide and ocean steamers at half-flood. Natural protection, it was claimed, would be afforded by Stert Island on the south-west and Gore Sands to the north-west.

There was considerable opposition to the Act and a number of problems regarding both the financial arrangements and the letting of contracts. The strongest opposition came from Bridgwater Corporation over the question of the proposed pier. They saw any port developments within their jurisdiction as potentially threatening to their own trade but in this particular situation they held a key card as they had control over the navigational safety of the River Parrett including the area of the proposed new pier.[1]

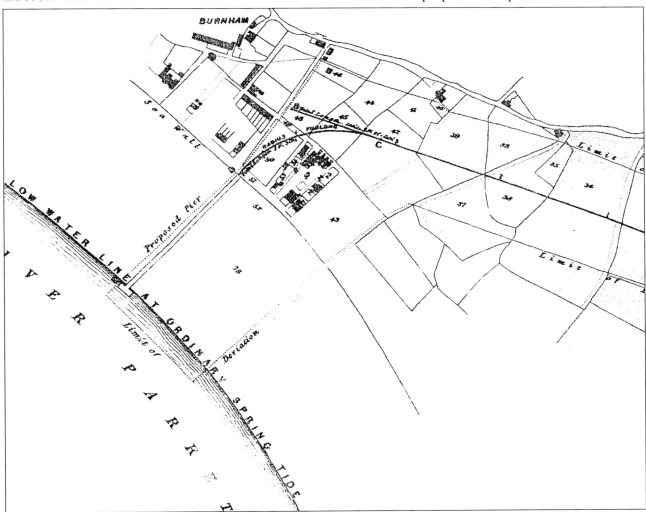

The proposed pier at Burnham. This extract from the Parliamentary plan which accompanied the SCR Act of 30 July 1855 clearly shows the original intentions at Burnham. The main line was to terminate in a station almost parallel to the shore with a short 1 furlong 3 chain long branch making a junction at C and curving sharply around to the esplanade on a rising 1 in 136 gradient. The metalled esplanade terminated by the adjacent Reed Arms Hotel *so the railway was scheduled to cross no more than a rough path on the level. Although not shown, tracks would have continued straight onto the horizontal pier structure, the level gradient of which is so marked on the section relating to the pier.*

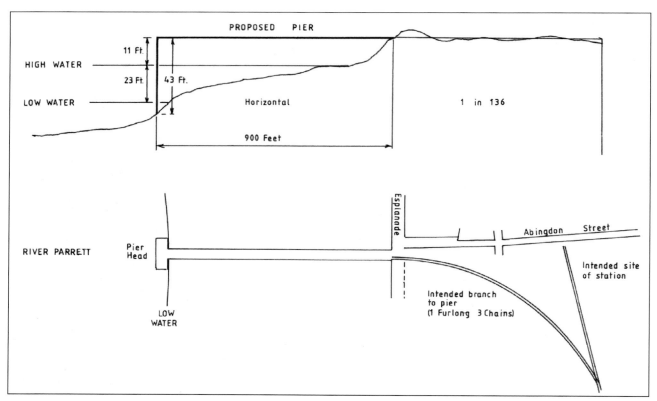

The proposed 900ft-long pier at Burnham as shown in the Parliamentary Plan was a substantial structure which would have allowed steamers to berth at the pier head in all but the very lowest tides. The High and Low Water marks are those at ordinary spring tides. The plan also shows the intended branch; although stopping short of the pier it would in practice have been extended along its length. The acquisition of extra land (through the auspices of George Reed) allowed the realignment of the railway. The separate pier branch was abandoned but eventually built as an extension to the main line although the final position of the station was not much altered from the original.

From evidence put before the House of Commons Special Committee hearing the SCR Bill a number of interesting points come to light. In the proposed area of the new pier there was already an old Admiralty causeway. Officially it was designated as stepping stones, but in fact they were a load of irregular rocks which the SCR's engineer, Charles Gregory, referred to as a dilapidated causeway. The pier as planned (and indeed as shown on the Parliamentary plan) was to have been 900 feet in length from the esplanade to a little beyond the low water mark. This would take advantage of the fact that Burnham had greater facilities for the access of vessels, even under severe weather conditions, than any other part of the Bristol Channel, where a convenient access could be made by railway. It was made clear that Burnham would be complementary to Highbridge where the SCR still intended to land heavy goods. It was pointed out that light goods and passengers could be dealt with at Burnham under this proposal within 1½ hours of the tide beginning to flow. The distance between Burnham and Highbridge via the River Brue was 2½ miles, and

that represented between two to three hours owing to tidal limitations. Such time saving that Burnham would offer had an even greater significance when it was considered that it would be possible to travel from Cardiff to Bristol via Burnham, the SCR and B&ER quicker than going direct by ship because Bristol was only accessible at certain states of the tide. As for Bridgwater, it was stated that it was 13 miles from Burnham, up the twisted Parrett, a stretch of water that had witnessed numerous accidents to shipping, especially in the vicinity of Combwich. Clearly the railway was a better option and clearly that was going to upset the establishment in Bridgwater!

Competition was not, Parliament felt, a valid reason for stopping the construction of the SCR's extension despite Bridgwater's procrastinations, but the erection of a safety hazard might be. The Admiralty felt that Bridgwater Corporation was justified in considering the pier a hazard to navigation and sent Captain Aldridge to investigate the situation. As a result of his report the SCR were limited to a pier 100 feet from high-water mark and from thence a causeway 18-20ft. wide by

Burnham pier opened, along with the SCR's extension from Highbridge, on 3 May 1858. In this early view which must date from shortly after this, a group of people are standing by a barrier which straddled the entrance and consisted of two uprights with a crossbar secured by a chain. Lengths of rail can just be made out alongside the line centre right although the permanent railway fence has not yet been erected. However the 1 in 23 slope of the new structure is plainly visible. Not everyone welcomed the arrival of the ships, some fearing that it would take trade away from the emergent little town, but according to the Wells Journal *urban amenities in the town certainly did not encourage visitors to stay. Drainage was lacking, some streets were ankle deep in sand, there was little taste in buildings, an utter absence of all amusements and parts of the Esplanade were unfit for ladies to walk on. The young lady with her child in this view didn't seem over worried by all this though! The hotel was built by George Reed in 1848 and was conveniently placed for custom from both trains and ships in the absence of other shelter at this exposed point. Following a period of closure it re-opened in 1884 as* The Queen's Hotel *but time did not obliterate the carved legend* The Reed Arms *which still exists high up on the building, commemorating the foremost citizen of Burnham who would, no doubt, be pleased to know that it still remains a hotel as he intended.*
(G. Luxon collection via Robin Atthill collection/S&DRT)

2ft. high leading down to low-water mark. As such, vessels would only be able to lie off the causeway at the end when the tide was out. Gregory tried several times to get the Admiralty to change their minds but in vain. However, he did get an intimation that they would not object to a 12ft.-deep cut being made alongside the causeway so that ships could be warped up to it as the tide rose. This trench would be kept clear of mud and silt by a flushing system thereby allowing passengers and parcels to be landed at any state of the tide.

At the Committee Hearing, Mr. Montague-Smith, counsel for Bridgwater Corporation, asked Gregory if he had told anyone in Bridgwater of his plan to cut a trench. Gregory replied that he had not, because he did not intend to 'give weapons to the enemy to fight us with', but went on to say that he

did, however, consult them about the causeway, and while they 'thought that this would be perfectly useless to us' they were as smooth and indulgent as possible, but the moment one of their own party, a gentleman whom I think I see in this room, said 'they can make a good deal of use of this causeway by making a cut at the side', I saw the eyes of the Worshipful Mayor light up with intelligence and he at once communicated to the Town Clerk, and from that moment they have been against us.

More dialogue followed in which Montague-Smith hinted that Gregory was dishonest not to tell Bridgwater Corporation of his plans for a trench. Montague-Smith's attack then veered to the causeway as a navigational

*An interesting view of the pier and dredged 'gut' seen at low tide with, in the foreground, the sluice-gate necessary to control the adjacent sluicing pond. When opened, the impounded water was allowed to flow under some pressure into the berth in order to scour away any excess mud. This was helped by men with scrapers who would pull the mud and sand from beside the pier into the stream. The rails on the 1 in 23 gradient are clearly visible, wagons being controlled by a wire rope attached through a ring at the landward end of the pier. Sully & Company's 71-ton paddle tug **Petrel** (built 1863) lies at anchor at the end of the gut in the deep-water channel of the River Parrett awaiting high tide to tow several loaded ketches up the river to Bridgwater.* (Rod Fitzhugh collection)

hazard. It transpired that Gregory had met the Mayor, Town Clerk and others at Burnham where they suggested that if he reduced the height of the causeway by 2 feet there would not be so much objection and if the idea of a causeway was dropped altogether there would be no objection! Arguments followed about the differences 2 feet would make: passengers would have a muddy and wet surface on which to alight if the causeway was level with the mud, whereas the extra 2 feet would allow the tide to wash it clean. Montague-Smith tried to show that a 2ft.-high ledge of rock would constitute a real danger to shipping. Gregory replied that this 'ledge of rock' would be smooth (which was more than could be said for the existing stepping stones) and that the sides would be sheathed in Camp Sheeting. Montague-Smith asked Gregory if he thought that the Camp Sheeting would protect a ship that ran against it but the engineer, on his toes, replied that his object was to protect the stones!

Amongst other points raised it was claimed that ships loading and unloading at the causeway would be an obstruction to other shipping going up to Bridgwater. Whereas Gregory claimed that he had never seen ships using that part of the river, the Bridgwater interests claimed that they often did. However vessels going up to Highbridge would have to pass the new causeway and the SCR were hardly likely to erect a hazard for themselves. Gregory stated that the SCR was more interested in 'supporting the completeness and efficiency of the port of Highbridge than we are in the extension to Burnham'. Then he digressed; 'I shall never forget that one of the Corporation of Bridgwater said when opposing a previous Bill – he said: "Gentlemen you must oppose this ...".' That was as far as Gregory got because Montague-Smith raised an objection that was sustained. Nevertheless, with Mr. Slade, the SCR's counsel, now doing the questioning, Gregory managed to score several more points. On expressing the hope that the time would come when there would be more trade flowing through Highbridge than through Bridgwater, Slade asked:

Do you suppose that your pier and causeway will at all interfere with the legitimate enterprise of Bridgwater?

To which Gregory replied,

I do not think it will hurt that trade, legitimate or illegitimate.

It was only when Slade was questioning Gregory that the true identity of the Mayor of Bridgwater was revealed and the nature of his interests. The Mayor was John Browne who carried on a very large trade at Dunball, 'a rival port lately established', and he and others had laid down 'a small railway of their own' there. Browne, who was present at the hearing, then interrupted with 'I have no more interest in Dunball than you have'. This would seem to be rather less than honest since Browne was responsible for building the first wharf at Dunball in 1841 specifically to import coal, a trade in which he was heavily engaged and which continued into the 1920s and beyond.

The inquiry brought to light some interesting speculations about the operation of the pier and causeway. Gregory envisaged that at low water, to save passengers a long walk to the esplanade or station, they would be conveyed by rail in coaches hauled by ropes. Alternatively they could ride in their carriages (taken to mean road vehicles) or they could walk. Even if the Admiralty did not sanction the cut Gregory had plans to overcome the resultant obstacles. He explained that passengers could still be landed in boats without the cut or,

supposing there should be any impossibility which we do not foresee in the making of this cut, rails might be laid down upon the hard or causeway and upon these rails there might be a travelling platform which would be loaded so as not to float. This platform might be worked up and down the railway by a rope and upon that platform passengers might be landed from steamers at all states of the tide.

In the end parliament agreed to the Burnham extension and to the provision of a causeway. Bridgwater's opposition was to no avail and it invoked criticism from its own townsfolk.[2]

With the way ahead now clear, thoughts could turn to the construction of the short railway extension and pier, the cost of the latter being estimated at £6,600. The station was originally planned to be a terminus slightly further inland with a short branch of 1 furlong 3 chains running via a 10-chain curve to connect with the pier. In the event the position of the station was changed so that it was at right angles to the esplanade itself, the rails merely being extended beyond the platform and directly on to the pier.

Raising funds was not so easy although this was mainly because of troubles on the Wells part of the extension. There were also complications regarding letting the contract, Messrs. Rigby and Waring Brothers both tendering. In the end Rigby's won but not before a change in the contract, namely that there would be no changes to the original plans that would cause them expense and that they would not be liable for defects arising from the Engineer's mistakes. This seems to suggest that they were not entirely happy with Gregory's plans for the pier. As work progressed on the branch Rigby's intimated that they could not guarantee to stick to the pier estimate. But at this time funds did not actually exist for its completion and the SCR sought to borrow £4,000 as it was considered essential that the causeway was completed before the equinoctial gales.

By August 1857 the railway had been inspected but the Admiralty withheld their approval until the cut was made alongside the pier although the foundation stone of the latter was not actually laid until 5 September by George Reed, described as the 'foremost' citizen of Burnham, and one of the SCR's directors.

In the end what was constructed was a 900ft. causeway which sloped from the esplanade at approximately 1 in 23 to terminate just at the low-water mark. Although always referred to as a pier, this was not strictly the case since it hardly fell into the same category as the many ornate edifices that so marked the Victorian period. It was simply a functional, if not very convenient slipway.

The cut, once produced on the south side, soon filled up with mud so Gregory experimented with a sluicing pond. The experiment was successful so the Board granted an extra £100 for the construction of another larger sluicing pond.

Calamity struck in November when there was a 12-foot slip in the causeway retaining wall. It was feared that reconstruction might be necessary, particularly as there were indications that the design was at fault. Rigby's offered to add fender piles and railings in front of the wall, tied by iron rods to piles at the back, within the original contract price, provided Gregory found savings that would not impair the causeway's efficiency or stability. The Board agreed. Had they not, Rigby's would have raised the question of faulty design. Under Rigby's pressure Gregory consented to the substitution of Stert Island ballast for concrete under the pitching, although he held Rigby's responsible if

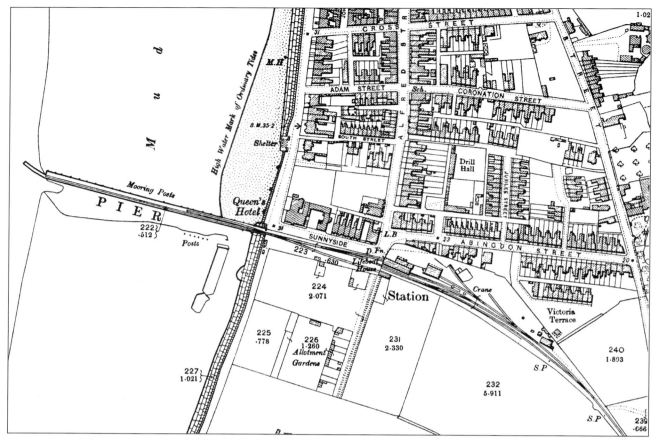

The town of Burnham in 1903 showing the final position of the railway station, goods yard and the pier. Note also the connecting siding into the lifeboat house. The 1848-built Reed Arms *had become the* Queen's Hotel *by the 1880s but curiously Pier Street had become Sunnyside by this time. (OS 25.15, 2nd edition 1903, by permission of the British Library)*

this did not work. He recommended that owing to the expense of the works and as Rigby's had not estimated for the laying of rails on the pier, they should be allowed the benefits of the saving. The Board did not agree. The dispute over repair costs grew until arbitration was resorted to, resulting in a 50-50 sharing of the costs. When questioned about the fault the Board defended Gregory and his design by saying that no-one could have foreseen the 'recurrent disturbances attending the action of tides, storms and tempests'.[3] The pier was finally opened on Monday 3 May 1858.

The railway from the station was extended on to the sloping pier, the first short part of which was of wooden construction on piles. The rails were positioned on the cut (south) side and extended right to the end without any substantial stop blocks. A short siding at the top end left the 'main' line on the wooden section and ran parallel and to the north of it. Right at the seaward end, which submerged as the tide flowed, a tall marker post was erected, effectively providing a hazard to navigation!

Notes:

1. Both Burnham pier and the harbour at Highbridge (together with Dunball and Combwich) came under the maritime jurisdiction of the Port of Bridgwater which was under the control of Bridgwater Corporation and who in turn acted through their Port & Navigation Committee. The bounds or limits of the port extended along a lengthy part of the Somerset coastline including Bridgwater Bay whilst the port responsibilities extended not only to ensuring safe navigation but also to providing customs facilities and acting as a port of registry for ships.

2. Mainly from the House of Commons Special Committee Hearing into the SCR Bill, courtesy Jem Harrison.

3. Information from Jem Harrison, S&DRT *Bulletin* No.57 dated July/Aug 1973.

4 From Cardiff to Cherbourg – The Ferry Services

On 3 May 1858 arrangements were made to bring the first steamer, the Cardiff Steam Navigation Company's *Iron Duke* (1857/121grt), alongside the pier at Burnham at about 10.00am. Like all such events in the Victorian period the day was not allowed to pass without due celebration, with a procession of SCR directors, school children, the brass band of the B&ER Carriage & Wagon Works and a host of banners and slogans wishing the railway well. The customary collation followed. Among the speeches was a toast to Bridgwater Corporation who 'opposed the works and spent a few thousand pounds doing so'. This had not dissuaded a Bridgwater citizen from being the first to use the pier, en route to Port Talbot.

The day was also characterised by the appearance of excursion trains which brought many people to Burnham for the day whilst the *Iron Duke* disgorged many more, some of whom availed themselves of the new train service to visit other parts of the country.

Unfortunately the SCR's dealings with Bridgwater Corporation were not yet over because the pier had not, at this time, been equipped with the proper moorings, the Bridgwater Navigation Committee (being part of the Corporation) being responsible for providing them. The SCR felt that the Committee was dragging its feet over this matter and threatened 'ulterior measures' unless immediate action was taken. Protecting the Corporation, the Navigation Committee refused to sanction the works or admit that it was done in accordance with the 1855 Act. Gregory's estimate of seven floating chains costing £70, the Committee suggested, should be laid by the SCR and the cost defrayed by the tolls (normally due to the Navigation Committee). The official excuse was that the chance trade that Burnham might get would not make it worth Bridgwater Council's effort. The real reason was that Bridgwater did not wish to be associated or liable in any way for the pier. By July however, the Navigation Committee had bowed to reason and agreed to provide seven mooring buoys and two posts.

Regular steam communication commenced on 24 May 1858 when the *Taliesin* (1842/158grt) left Cardiff at 5.30am arriving at 8.00am in good time to connect with the B&ER up and down trains at 9.00am. Despite unfavourable weather, and the lack of moorings, 80 passengers landed at Burnham thus opening up a hopefully valuable service. Passengers could avail themselves of this daily service for as little as 3/- (15p) return. The Somerset Central Railway had no powers to operate ships of its own so it relied on others to maintain the new service, railway companies being prohibited by the Railways Act from owning ships at this time. The Cardiff Steam Navigation Company seemed quite happy to oblige but in order to do so they had to divert the *Taliesin* from its former Cardiff-Bristol run.

At the next general meeting of the SCR shareholders they were informed that:

> the great convenience thereby afforded for speedy communication between the West of England and South Wales, and for the transmission of the agricultural produce of Somersetshire to that great market, has secured for it a large traffic.

By July it was estimated that the steam packet alone would yield £100 per annum in tolls. In August a Liverpool to Bristol steamer substituted Burnham for the latter port because of the more favourable tide.

Not everything was going according to plan though; it was soon realised that the B&ER had not made any arrangements for the transfer of goods accumulating at Highbridge to the pier for transit to South Wales. Nor did everyone welcome the ships. Many feared they would take would-be visitors away from Burnham. However Burnham's 'foremost citizen', George Reed, had development plans for the town and optimism was expressed by several companies who were reported to be looking forward to the increased trade from the steamer service.

The first possible record of the pier being used solely for freight occurred as early as November 1858 when an application was received from Captain Henry Jones, master of the steamship *Marley Hill* (1854/508grt), which had just arrived with a cargo of railway sleepers and which he wished to discharge at Burnham rather than Highbridge, 'the river not being navigable for a vessel of her length'. At 164ft.(50.5m) this ship was considerably shorter than many vessels which navigated the Brue. Unfortunately no records survive to tell us if this was allowed.[1]

Cardiff Steam Navigation Company

Table of Fares – Cardiff-Burnham Ferry Service 1858

PS Taliesin

Fore Cabin	3/- return
After Cabin	4/6 return
4-wheel Carriages	20/-
2-horse Phaetons	15/-
1-horse Phaetons	10/-
4-wheel drawn by 1 horse	12/-
Horse & Rider (after cabin)	7/-
Horse & Rider (fore cabin)	6/-
Cattle	4/-
Horses	5/-
Sheep	8d
Lambs	6d
Pigs	9d
Dogs and calves	1/-

The ferries on this route were able to take road vehicles as well as passengers and general cargo but the cost of the convenience of shipping animals by the ferry service in 1858 should be compared with the considerably cheaper costs using the cargo services from Highbridge circa 1856 – see Chapter 6.

Examples of Passenger Fares

Cardiff-Burnham Ferry Service

PS Ruby	**1860**	Single	Return
Saloon		3/-	4/6
Fore Cabin		2/-	3/-

PS The Lady Mary or **Wye**	**July 1882**		
After Cabin		3/6	6/-
Fore Cabin		2/6	4/6

Excursion Fares

In 1882 the Cardiff steamer **The Lady Mary** or **Wye** ran excursions including through fares from Cardiff to Glastonbury and Wells for 3/-

On 27 July 1885 trains from Templecombe and Shepton Mallet were run to connect with the **Sherbro** which sailed from Cardiff at the early hour of 7.30am. The cost, return, was:

Saloon	3/6
Bridge	4/6

The SCR had, in what was to characterise the optimism shown by the company over the years to come, aimed high but in reality it must have been with some disappointment that the directors viewed their new pier; hardly the grand 'all-states-of-the-tide' structure originally featured in the Parliamentary Plan. All too soon the limitations of an open slip built with a 1 in 23 gradient, exposed to the weather, liable to the extreme tidal limitations of the Parrett estuary and constant silting, became evident.

The reason why the Cardiff Steam Navigation Company terminated its sailings of *Taliesin* is uncertain (although it has been claimed that it was because of mis-management) but the service didn't last long and George Reed, together with the SCR, soon found themselves without their coveted ferry. Sadly this was to become an all too familiar situation. At the end of February 1860, James W. Pockett, a Swansea ship-owner, visited Burnham to make arrangements to run a new ferry service to and from Swansea and in April he put his iron paddler *Prince of Wales* (1842/187grt) on the service advertising a passage of about four hours, out one day and back the next, with two round trips each week. The service ran only to the end of the season and had ceased by September, never to reappear.

Again it is not clear why this service failed but operating from the open pier may have had something to do with it because on 6 August 1860 the directors of the SCR incorporated, under a separate Act, the Burnham Tidal Harbour Company (BTH Co.). Its purpose was to put in place a scheme for a major development which would transform Burnham by giving it a proper rail-connected 'quay or landing place' in lieu of the original pier that, it was now acknowledged, suffered from such difficult tidal limitations, whilst converting the River Brue into a tidal harbour. Importantly the new Act also stated that it would be

> expedient that the Company be authorized to provide and use Steam and other vessels in the Bristol Channel, and to agree with the Mayor, Aldermen, and Burgesses of the Borough of Bridgwater with respect to Rates and Dues payable to the Corporation of the Company's Vessels.

Powers were also conferred on the company to connect its operation by rail with the SCR. The Bill was promoted by George Reed, Henry Danby Seymour and Sir Edward Baker Baker, Bt., all well known in SCR circles.

The independence of the BTH Co. was only nominal, sharing the same headquarters and officers as the SCR in Glastonbury including Robert Arthur Read as secretary. Its first directors were the three above-mentioned gentlemen together with the Rt. Hon. Charles Ponsonby Lord De Mauley. The company's original capital was fixed at some £37,000 and both the SCR and B&ER were authorised to subscribe up to £20,000 between them. Significantly the Burnham company was allowed to enter into agreements with both these railways and also the Dorset Central Railway. By an additional Act (incorporated on the same day as that of the BTH Co.) the SCR was further authorised to issue preference shares at 6% to cover its subscriptions of £12,000 to the Burnham company, in addition to appointing a director to the latter's board, and to work its railways when completed. Clearly the SCR saw the BTH Co. only as a tool to further its ambitions and create the harbour development at Burnham that George Reed so desperately aspired to.

Engineered by John Hawkshaw, the new company was granted powers to create a substantial development at Burnham and Highbridge in two distinct parts, the latter involving considerable civil engineering works to the River Brue. The principal features of the Act so authorised were as follows:

1. the embanking, widening, deepening, and improving of part of the River Brue lying north-westward of a point where the Somerset Central Railway crosses the turnpike road from Bridgwater to Bristol, and the converting of that part of the River Brue into a tidal harbour;
2. the improving, dredging, and preserving of that part of the River Brue so as to convert it into a tidal harbour, and the preventing of any obstruction or impediment therein or in the entrance thereto;
3. a river wall or quay, timber stage or landing place, with all proper works and conveniences connected therewith, on the south-eastern bank of the River Parrett near to the jetty at Burnham belonging to the Somerset Central Railway Company: provided that the company shall not make any part of the river wall or quay, timber stage or landing place, so that the frontage line thereof shall project into the River Parrett more than eighty feet riverward of the proposed termination of the line of railway or siding No.1 shown on the deposited plan, or so that any part thereof shall extend towards the mouth of the River Brue more than forty feet from the line of that railway as shown thereon by the black continuous line;
4. the improving, dredging, and preserving of so much of the River Parrett as lies contiguous and is

necessary to facilitate the access or approach to the river wall or quay, and to the entrance to the harbour respectively;

5. the making, repairing, and maintenance of all proper stations, sidings, shipping places, wharves, staithes, jetties, landing places, timber staging, cranes, drops, approaches, dolphins, guide piles, buoys, moorings, mooring posts, and other works and conveniences in connection with and for the better user and occupation of the harbour, river wall, or quay, and works, and of the River Brue and the entrance thereto, including, if thought expedient, the laying down, maintaining, and using of lines of railway as sidings in connection with the Somerset Central Railway as shown in the deposited plans, and those sidings to be either on the broad gauge or on the narrow gauge, or on both gauges, as the Company think fit: provided that the point at which the siding marked No.2 on the deposited plan shall join the Somerset Central Railway at such a point within the Limits of Deviation as shown on those plans, and not on the main line of the Somerset Central Railway.

The Burnham Tidal Harbour works from the Parliamentary Plan dated November 1859 which accompanied the Act of 1860. Examination reveals that the work was in two parts. Firstly there was to be a completely new L-shaped jetty or quay which was to be constructed just a little to the south of the existing pier at Burnham and which would be rail served by 'Railway No.1' from a junction with the SCR at 'A', the outer end of which would lie in the deep-water channel of the Parrett whilst the inner side would form part of a protected harbour area. Secondly the entire length of the Brue was to be widened, straightened and dredged considerably by the provision of a new embankment on the north side leading into the area of the existing wharf at Highbridge, this being referred to as the 'tidal harbour'. This would also be rail served ('Railway No.2' – junction with the SCR at point 'D'). A considerable area within the 'Limit of Deviation' for this railway would be reclaimed for subsequent development and expansion of the harbour and facilities and from references in the third Burnham Tidal Harbour Act of 1870 it was probably intended to construct a closed dock in this area. Provision was also made in the Act for the company to take small amounts of additional land if required. The winding course of the estuarial River Brue reveals the difficulties faced by Bristol Channel mariners and many a foreign sailor as they set sail up the meandering course to Highbridge.

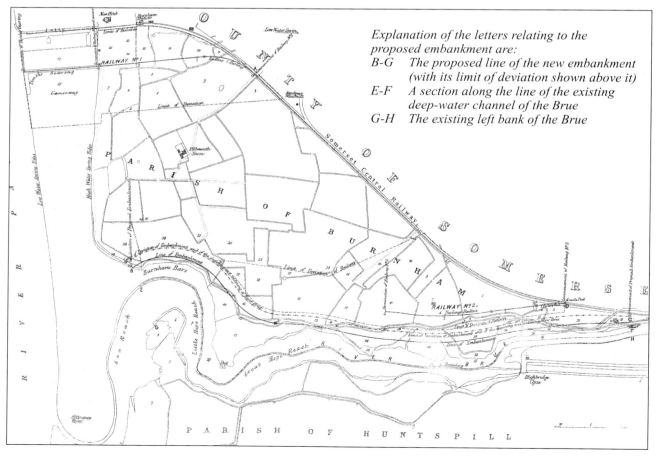

Explanation of the letters relating to the proposed embankment are:

B-G   The proposed line of the new embankment (with its limit of deviation shown above it)

E-F   A section along the line of the existing deep-water channel of the Brue

G-H   The existing left bank of the Brue

The consequences of the work in the Brue would have resulted in a considerably wider, straighter and deeper course of the river between its mouth and the existing wharves at Highbridge. However, what is not made clear in this particular Act but which is referred to in a third Act passed on 1 August 1870 for the purposes of extending the construction time, was the building and maintaining of a dock or docks at Highbridge and the diversion of water from the Rivers Brue and Parrett into the intended docks, and into the intended altered and diverted channel. This may have meant enclosing the existing harbour area at Highbridge to form a floating harbour much as was originally intended by the Glastonbury Canal but it is also noted that a considerable area within the 'Limits of Deviation' for 'Railway No.2' would be reclaimed for subsequent development and may well have been the intended site of a new enclosed dock. In addition to the works stipulated above the BTH Co. was also to become a local pilotage authority.

Despite the new company's formation very little followed. The ability of the SCR to operate its own ships via the company rather than having to rely on others to provide a ferry service was, however, valuable. The BTH Co. also opened a shipping office at 5 Stuart Street, Bute Docks, Cardiff, which served as an agency for the SCR/DCR and the B&ER. The stationmaster at Burnham (Mr. C. Hayman in the mid-1860s) was additionally appointed as managing agent for the new company in the town.

Whilst the Bill for the BTH Co. was being considered by Parliament George Reed was anxious to restart the Burnham-Cardiff ferry service so together with his two associates, Henry Seymour MP, and Sir Edward Baker Baker Bt., they set out to purchase a vessel. They found the iron paddler *Ruby* which had been built for service in the Firth of Clyde as a packet steamer in 1854 and purchased her in January 1860. The *Ruby* made her first run under new ownership on 11 February taking just 1 hour 16 minutes to reach Cardiff and returning in 1 hour 7 minutes, a creditable effort and considerably faster than the 2-hour passage of the smaller *Taliesin*. As the ship was not fully utilised throughout the week the owners attempted to use her on excursion work during July with some success despite poor passenger loadings on Sundays.

During the following four years the *Ruby* maintained the Burnham-Cardiff ferry quite successfully and it was during this period, in 1862, that the SCR and DCR amalgamated to form the S&DR.[2] Then on 18 August 1863 there was a major set-back. When the ship was approaching Burnham the wind slewed her stern around and she settled across the cut with her bows

on the pier and her stern on the mud bank beyond. Although all the passengers were landed without incident, efforts to lighten the ship were to no avail and as the tide fell she quickly broke her back. Following temporary repairs she was towed to Bristol six days later. During the course of these repairs, on 15 October 1863, the ownership of the vessel was transferred from Reed and his compatriots to the BTH Co. to become the first to be registered to the new company. However she was never to sail under their flag because on 20 April 1864 she was sold.

Once again the ferry service was in trouble and the S&DR had to resort to chartering to keep it going. The Cardiff Bute Dock Towing Company's tug *Pilot* (1857/109grt), was quickly pressed into service and advertised as a 'fine fast sailing steamship'. On one of its first runs she is said to have embarked over 350 employees of a large Ebbw Vale smelting works at Newbridge for an excursion.

The loss of the *Ruby* came at an embarrassing time for the newly created S&DR; just under five weeks before this, on 10 September 1863, the new through route between Burnham and Poole had opened and no time was lost to search for a suitable replacement. Late that month the BTH Co. purchased the iron paddler *Defiance* of 150 tons gross, and this vessel replaced the *Pilot*, going on to run the ferry service successfully for a number of years along with excursions.

Strangely when the *Ruby* was finally sold in April 1864 another ship, the *Heather Bell* of 152 tons gross, was purchased and registered to the BTH Co. at the same time leading to speculation that a part-exchange deal of some sort was set up. Thus from that April the Cardiff-Burnham ferry became a two-ship operation and with the benefit of the new found flexibility they were able to provide at least one crossing each day but sometimes if tides and weather permitted, two. At long last, it seemed, the ferry service in the Bristol Channel was settling down so it was now time for the company to turn its attention to the English Channel, for the S&D's aim had never really been just to provide a channel-to-channel rail connection. In the summer of 1864 Robert Read, the long-serving secretary of the railway, entered into talks with the management of the Chemin de Fer de l'Ouest (the Western Railway) of France which, amongst other routes, operated trains between Paris, Caen and Cherbourg. His purpose was to discuss the forthcoming plan to introduce a ferry service from Poole which Read wanted to promote with both faster train services and reduced fares on the French side. Around April 1865 Read also went up to Glasgow to examine the iron paddle steamer *Albion* (1860/306grt), initially with a view to chartering

Robert Arthur Read, the loyal, energetic and long-suffering secretary to the company. He came from the Bristol & Exeter Railway to succeed the first secretary of the Somerset Central Railway in 1853 and held a similar position with the Dorset Central Railway from 1856 and with the Burnham Tidal Harbour Company from its inauguration in 1860. He continued in this capacity following the amalgamation of the two constituents into the Somerset & Dorset Railway Company in 1862. At the same time he also became the General Manager, styled Managing Director from 1872 to 1874, from which time he gave up his position of secretary. Following the lease of the line in 1875 by the Midland and London & South Western Railways jointly, Read was appointed Secretary and General Manager for the Joint Committee, a position he held until a well-deserved retirement in 1891.   (Robin Atthill collection/S&DRT)

the ship for the Poole-Cherbourg service from the well-known shipbroker, Captain Peter Henderson, who had acquired the vessel from its previous owners on 5 April 1865. It seems that the *Albion* had already been identified in February as possibly suitable for the new service since there is a reference in one of the S&D minutes about the proposed 'purchase' of the ship. Read optimistically hoped that it might be possible to get the ship south in time to start the new service on 1 May. It was also hoped that a special crossing could be arranged beforehand with the intention of issuing an invitation to the Mayor and Town Council of Poole. There was a good reason for

this because the Poole Harbour Trustees had gone to considerable expense to extend their quay in the expectation that the S&D would contribute a share towards the cost of this but the company had declined. Whether there was ever any time to run this trip is not now known but the ship did enter service during that month.

Although it had been the original intention for the S&D to purchase the *Albion,* in the event the ship remained on charter and there is every reason to believe that the ferry service to Cherbourg was run successfully for the remainder of the 1865 summer at least and through the next winter also.

During early 1865 the BTH Co. took one of its few positive moves by ordering a purpose-built vessel for the Burnham-Cardiff run. This was the first new ship for the S&D and it was to be engined specifically as a screw steamship for the company rather than as a paddler. Another Act was also obtained on 29 June 1865 to extend the construction time for the tidal harbour by a further five years. New capital was authorised (£225,000 in shares and £75,000 on mortgage) for its construction.

Like so many grandiose schemes nothing seems to have been done towards achieving this goal although it is known that a great deal of preliminary planning was carried out. It may have been because of the severe engineering difficulties involved in making Burnham independent of tidal considerations but it is more likely that other events were getting in the way.

By 1866 it had become very obvious that the S&DR was in severe financial difficulties. Although traffic receipts were comfortably exceeding working expenses, the company had never really been able to solve its motive power and rolling stock requirements following the take-over of services from the B&ER. There was a great inability to move all the freight traffic that offered itself and the consequent loss of traffic only served to compound the financial problems facing the company. Having ordered the new ship through the BTH Co. it became increasingly obvious that the company could not afford to pay for it. The company's salvation was Burnham's George Reed who could yet again see his dreams disappearing so he effectively purchased the vessel on their behalf. As a result it was initially registered in his name alone and, perhaps in gratitude or maybe at his request, the S&DR named her *George Reed*. As an iron screw packet of 170 tons gross, she was delivered from her Cubitt Town, London builders in August 1866 and placed into service immediately. She was described as being a good sea-boat, very fast and equipped with excellent passenger accommodation.

PS Albion

This vessel was chartered to the S&DR for the Poole-Cherbourg ferry service from 1865 to 1867, being in the ownership of Captain P.L. Henderson from 5 April 1865 until 4 February 1867. She was first registered on 15 November 1860 at Glasgow (Port No.94/60).

Official Number:	28895
Type:	Single-deck Paddle Steamer
Construction:	Iron
Build:	Clencher
Tonnage:	306.71 gross, 160.07 net
Completed:	1860 by Tod & McGregor, Glasgow
Engines:	2 x 150HP Steeple single-cylinder by builders
Length:	165.1ft.
Beam:	24.2ft.
Depth:	11.8ft.

The ship was schooner rigged with bowsprit, two masts and round stern.

Meanwhile, back on the South Coast, the Poole-Cherbourg service was again maintained through the summer of 1866 by the *Albion*. Typically the ship was scheduled to sail overnight from Poole twice a week on Mondays and Thursdays departing at 11.45pm, having connected with the 8.30pm train from Burnham (8.50pm from Highbridge). The passage time to France was six hours with a connection to Paris scheduled to depart Cherbourg at 7.10am arriving in the capital at 5.00pm but then only if you travelled first-class. Second- and third-class travellers had to wait at Cherbourg for the 9.30am train which did not arrive in Paris until, amazingly, as late as 10.20pm. It would seem that Robert Read was less than successful in persuading the French management to speed up their dismally slow services to Paris!

Very soon after the new service began in 1865 special cheap return tickets were introduced from a range of Somerset & Dorset stations and other starting points, including Cardiff, for travel on Mondays only, allowing visitors a full day in Cherbourg before departing on the 9.00am Wednesday sailing back to Poole.

The full extent to which the S&DR and its predecessors had been undercapitalised came home to roost during the year and the company lapsed into receivership. Finding itself in this plight it was forced to make some severe economies if the railway was to survive at all. In August 1866[3] discussion centred on whether the *Albion* should be laid up for the six winter months or chartered elsewhere. At the general meeting early in February 1867 it was announced that the service had been 'for the present suspended, the operation having hitherto resulted in a loss'. As a result the ship was promptly taken off charter and sold by Captain Henderson to John Pool and partners based at Hayle in Cornwall. Re-registered in Hayle on 25 February 1867 she was subsequently used on the Hayle-Bristol service until railway competition brought this to an end in 1868.

Not surprisingly others had things to say about the short-lived Cherbourg service and in the 1 June 1867 edition of the monthly periodical, *Poole Pilot,* the following appeared:

Will steam communication between Poole and Cherbourg be resumed? A company was being formed to buy the *Spicy* only one foot less in length and beam than *Albion*. Three years before another company had been mooted, but before their prospectus was issued the S&D Railway offered to supply the required accommodation and the result was the placing of *Albion* on the station.[4]

So ended the S&D's dream because the Poole-Cherbourg ferry was never to reappear as part of the railway's through route again; their much vaunted integrated service from South Wales to France was in tatters and they were in no financial state to try and salvage it.

SOMERSET AND DORSET RAILWAY.

NEW & CHEAP ROUTE TO PARIS,

BORDEAUX, & THE SOUTH OF FRANCE.
(Via Poole, Cherbourg and Caen.)

REGULAR SERVICE BY THE FAST AND POWERFUL STEAM SHIP,
"ALBION."

From POOLE to CHERBOURG every MONDAY and THURSDAY, at 11.45 p.m.
From CHERBOURG to POOLE every WEDNESDAY at 9,0 a.m., and FRIDAY, at
10.30 p.m. (Wind and Weather permitting.) SEA PASSAGE SIX HOURS.

Fares and Rates. — Passengers.

TO CHERBOURG.

FROM	SINGLE TICKETS available for FOUR DAYS.		RETURN TICKETS available for ONE MONTH.	
	1st Class.	2nd Class. and after Cabin.	1st Class.	2nd Class. and after Cabin.
	s. d.	s. d.	s. d.	s. d.
London (Waterloo Bridge Station)	27 6	20 0	45 0	32 6
Exeter (Queen Street, Station)	30 0	22 6	45 6	34 0
Birmingham (New Street Station).........	47 6	36 9	71 3	55 3
Worcester (Midland Station)	42 0	32 8	63 0	49 1
Cheltenham ditto	37 0	29 0	56 0	44 1
Gloucester ditto	35 9	28 3	53 8	42 7
Bristol (Bristol and Exeter Station)	28 0	23 0	42 0	34 7
Cardiff (5, Stuart Street, Bute Docks) ...	27 6	23 6	41 6	35 5
Highbridge (Somerset & Dorset Railway)	23 6	19 6	35 6	29 4
	Aft. Cabin	Fore Cabin	Aft. Cabin	Fore Cabin
Poole	15 0	10 0	22 6	15 0

TO CAEN.

FROM	SINGLE TICKETS available for FIVE DAYS.		RETURN TICKETS available for ONE MONTH.	
	1st Class.	2nd Class. and after Cabin.	1st Class.	2nd Class. and after Cabin.
	s. d.	s. d.	s. d.	s. d.
London (Waterloo Bridge Station)	...	...	...	...
Exeter (Queen Street Station)	...	...	...	...
Birmingham (New Street Station)..........	56 7	43 9	89 9	69 5
Worcester (Midland Station)	51 1	39 8	81 6	63 3
Cheltenham ditto	46 1	36 0	74 6	58 3
Gloucester ditto	44 10	35 3	72 2	56 9
Bristol (Bristol and Exeter Station)	37 1	30 0	60 6	48 9
Cardiff (5, Stuart Street, Bute Docks) ...	36 9	30 7	60 0	49 7
Highbridge (Somerset & Dorset Railway)	32 7	26 6	53 9	43 6
Poole..	19 3	17 1	33 6	29 2

TO PARIS.

FROM	SINGLE TICKETS available for FIVE DAYS.		RETURN TICKETS available for ONE MONTH.	
	1st Class.	2nd Class. and after Cabin.	1st Class.	2nd Class. and after Cabin.
	s. d.	s. d.	s. d.	s. d.
London (Waterloo Bridge Station)	...	...	...	...
Exeter (Queen Street Stations)	...	...	...	...
Birmingham (New Street Station)......	53 2	42 5	106 4	84 10
Worcester (Midland Station)	53 4	41 3	104 2	79 2
Cheltenham ditto	50 8	39 11	97 8	74 7
Gloucester ditto	49 8	39 8	95 5	73 2
Bristol (Bristol and Exeter Station)	43 9	35 5	83 9	66 0
Cardiff (5, Stuart Street, Bute Docks) ..	45 4	37 3	83 3	66 1
Highbridge (Somerset & Dorset Railway)	43 0	35 9	81 0	63 0
Poole..	33 3	27 5	61 6	49 10

To Paris.

The last Train (1st and 2nd Class) for the Steamer leaves London (Waterloo Bridge Station), at 5.10 p.m.—Birmingham at 4.45 p.m.—Bristol at 8.0 p.m.—Exeter (Queen Street,) at 5.5 p.m.—Burnham at 8 30 p.m.,—and Highbridge at 8.50 p.m., but passengers may travel by any previous Train.

The Steamer leaves Poole Harbour for Cherbourg every MONDAY and THURSDAY at 11.45 p.m. The Train leaves Cherbourg for Paris (1st Class only) at 7.10 a.m., and arrives in Paris at 5.0 p.m.;—at 9.30 a.m., (1st, 2nd, and 3rd Class) arriving in PARIS at 10.20;—and at 4.45 p.m., (1st, 2nd, and 3rd Class) arriving in PARIS at 4.35 a.m.

Trains leave CHERBOURG for CAEN at 7.10 a.m., 9.30 a.m., and 4.45 p.m.

(For Service between Cardiff, Burnham and Swansea see Advertisement Pages.)

From Paris.

Trains (1st, 2nd, and 3rd Class) leave PARIS (*Rue d'Amsterdam*), at 7.25 a.m., and (1st Class only) at 11.25 a.m., and arrive at CHERBOURG at 9.30 p.m.; and leave PARIS (1st, 2nd, and 3rd Class at 8.0 p.m., and arrive in CHERBOURG at 7.15 a m.

The Steamer leaves CHERBOURG every WEDNESDAY at 9.0 a.m, and FRIDAY at 10.30 p.m. Trains for the West of England CARDIFF, BRISTOL, and the North, leave POOLE at 6.20 a.m., and 5.25 p.m., but passengers may travel by any other train.

Children—Under Three years, free; Three to Seven years, half price; above that age, whole price. Holders of Through Tickets can break the Journey at Bristol, Burnham, Poole, Cherbourg, and Bayeaux for Caen; and at those places, and Caen and Lisieux for Paris. The Tickets include Railway, Pier, and Dock Dues, and Steam Packet Fares, and are not Transferable. The Single Journey Tickets are available for Four Days, and five days respectively, inclusive of the day of issue; the Double Journey Tickets are available for One Month.

TICKETS MAY BE OBTAINED AS FOLLOWS:—
FORWARD JOURNEY.

LONDON	Waterloo Bridge Station.
EXETER	Queen Street, Station.
BIRMINGHAM	
WORCESTER	
CHELTENHAM	} Midland Railway Stations.
GLOUCESTER	
BRISTOL	Bristol and Exeter Railway Station.
CARDIFF or SWANSEA	Burnham Tidal Harbour Office, 5, Stuart Street, Bute Docks, and on Board the Burnham & Cardiff & Swansea Steamers.
HIGHBRIDGE	Somerset and Dorset Railway Station.
POOLE	On Board the Steamer.

HOMEWARD JOURNEY.

PARIS	Railway Station, Rue d'Amsterdam.
CAEN	Railway Station.
CHERBOURG	On Board the Steamer.

BAGGAGE.— The French Customs do not allow merchandise to be landed or shipped as personal baggage.

SPECIAL NOTICE.—All Goods other than personal baggage belonging to Passengers, although not manifested as merchandise, to pay accustomed freight. Passengers are requested to have all the Packages, composing their Luggage distinctly marked with their names and addresses. and to take the whole on board with them. The Company is not liable for any damage or loss of Baggage unless registered.

GOODS for PARIS, CAEN, &c., should be directed in full "PER SOMERSET AND DORSET RAILWAY AND STEAM BOAT, *via* POOLE AND CHERBOURG," and to ensure the lowest possible charges should be addressed to the care of Mr. GIORGI, POOLE.

To prevent delay all Goods should be advised by post, to Mr. GIORGI, POOLE. In the case of Bonded and Exciseable Goods, the Goods without such advice cannot be shipped.

PASSPORT—BRITISH SUBJECTS are allowed to enter, and to travel in France, WITHOUT PASSPORTS *on a simple declaration of their Nationality.*

GENERAL REGULATIONS.—Passengers are requested to be at the Trains and on board the Packets fifteen minutes at least before their departure. Berths are not guaranteed.

Persons purchasing TICKETS elsewhere than through the authorised Agents of the Company will render themselves LIABLE TO PROSECUTION.

The Company is not liable for unavoidable delays, accidents, or sea-risks of any kind whatsoever. The Company do not undertake to carry passengers or Goods by any particular Vessel.

For Particulars apply in Paris, Railway Station,—Rue d'Amsterdam; Caen, Railway Station,—Chemin de fer de l'Ouest; Cherbourg, Railway Station,—Chemin de fer de l'Ouest, and Messrs. Mahieu Freres; Birmingham, Worcester, Cheltenham and Gloucester, Midland Railway Stations.—Swansea, Mr. Pockett, South Dock. - Cardiff, Mr. Thomas, 5, Stuart-street, Bute Docks.—Bristol, Mr. Barton, 16, High Street.—London, Mr. Williams, 53, King William-st., City; Waterloo Bridge Station.—Exeter, Queen-st. Station.—Poole, Mr. Giorgi, Steam Packet Agent.

All information relative to Goods Traffic on application to the Goods Manager, and at the Stations of the Somerset and Dorset Railway Company.

Offices, Glastonbury, April, 1865.   **BY ORDER.**

Bristol and Exeter, and Somerset and Dorset Railways.

ONE CLEAR DAY IN FRANCE.

Cheap Return Tickets to

CHERBOURG,

ON MONDAY, THE 5th OF JUNE,

AND ON EACH

Succeeding MONDAY until further Notice,

(Except Monday the 14th of August),

For which see seperate Advertisement page.

Cheap Return Tickets to Cherbourg

will be issued for the Steamer leaving POOLE QUAY at 11,45 p.m., available for the Return Journey, on the following WEDNESDAY, by the Steamer leaving Cherbourg at 9,0 a.m. (Wind and Weather permitting.) Sea Passage Six Hours.

FARES TO CHERBOURG & BACK:

FROM	1st Class. and After Cabin.		2nd Class.	
	s.	d.	s.	d.
Bristol				
Clevedon } By Bristol and Exeter Railway to Highbridge	15	0	13	0
Weston }				
Cardiff *via* Burnham by Steamer....................................				
Burnham				
Highbridge				
Shapwick				
Glastonbury				
Wells	12	0	10	6
Pylle (for Shepton Mallett)				
Cole (for Bruton and Castle Carey)				
Wincanton				
Temple Combe				
Stalbridge...				
Sturminster Newton	11	0	9	6
Shillingstone				
Blandford				
Poole	7s. 6d.			

Passengers travelling with these Tickets, and leaving the train at any intermediate Station, will be charged the Full Fare to that Station.

The last Train for the Steamer leaves Bristol at 8.0 p.m., Highbridge at 8.50 p.m., but Passengers holding these Tickets may Travel by any Advertised Train.

No Luggage except a Carpet Bag or Portmanteau allowed.

☞ There are several Good Hotels in Cherbourg, where English is spoken.

Offices, Glastonbury, May, 1865.　　　　　　　　　　BY ORDER.

Back at Burnham things were not much better. In July 1867 the **Heather Bell** was sold and this was promptly followed by the purpose-built **George Reed** in August. In view of her ownership it is not totally clear just why this almost new ship should have had such a short life on the station – it may have been financial because George Reed was of course a director of the S&DR and he may have lost much of his personal wealth trying to bail the company out. Liverpool shipbroker Captain Henderson was asked to purchase her and this he did with the help of a mortgage. Effectively he chartered her straight back to the BTH Co. because the ship was left on the station until, in the following March, his mortgagees became restive and ordered him to sell the ship, from which time she left the area.

From March 1868 the S&D could only rely on their sole remaining ship, the **Defiance**, to maintain the ferry service. This vessel was allowed to carry on despite the ruthless actions being taken elsewhere on the railway to turn the ailing company around. The Receivers were finally discharged during 1870 and, freed from restraints, the S&D Board in characteristic style immediately turned their attention to their next ambitious development. One might have been forgiven for believing that their first act would be to consolidate their position so that they could place their existing services on a sounder footing. Instead they boldly announced their intention to seek to build a completely new northward extension of the railway from Evercreech to Bath.

In short they had finally come to the conclusion that trying to develop and expand their shipping services out of the existing ports available to them would simply be too costly. They saw their salvation instead in tapping the lucrative north-south market by connecting with the Midland Railway at Bath and providing a through link to the LSWR in the south without a break in gauge.

Effectively this would isolate Burnham and Highbridge altogether although the company had not quite lost sight of the proposed harbour improvements at Burnham. Having had ten years in which to construct the new facilities and having made no progress whatsoever they did in fact go back to Parliament in 1870 to ask for a third extension of time which was granted for a further period of five years by The Burnham Tidal Harbour Act, 1870.

Burnham Station

Train Arrivals and Departures, 1869

Down	**Burnham dep:**	8.10am	to Poole (arr. 12.00 noon)
		9.00am	to Wells (arr. 10.00am)
		11.35am	to Wells (arr. 12.52pm)
		1.15pm	to Poole (arr. 4.20pm)
		2.10pm	to Highbridge (arr. 2.16pm)
		4.00pm	to Poole (arr. 9.25pm)
		7.50pm	to Highbridge (arr. 7.56pm)
		8.40pm	to Wells (arr. 9.50pm)
Up	**Burnham arr:**	8.00am	from Highbridge
		8.46am	from Wells
		12.00 noon	from Poole
		2.00pm	from Poole
		3.30pm	from Highbridge
		5.25pm	from Poole
		7.12pm	from Highbridge
		8.15pm	from Wells

The passenger service to and from Burnham in 1869 shows three trains serving Poole daily. Obviously it was not possible to take account of the tides as far as the ferry service was concerned. The S&DR ship on station at this time was the paddle steamer **Defiance**.

Somerset and Dorset Railway.

EXTENSION OF RETURN TICKETS
TO
WEYMOUTH.

On and after Monday, 1st of May, and until 31st Oct., 1865,

ORDINARY RETURN TICKETS

Issued at any Station on this Railway to

WEYMOUTH,

WILL BE AVAILABLE FOR ONE WEEK.

By Order, ROBERT A. READ,

Offices, Glastonbury, April, 1865. *Secretary and General Manager.*

CARDIFF to SOUTHAMPTON,
PORTSMOUTH, &c.

Improved and Additional Communication via BURNHAM.

The Splendid, Fast-sailing, Clyde-built Steamers

DEFIANCE AND HEATHER BELL,

E. L. BARRON, Commander. *W. DENSHAM, Commander.*

PLY DAILY BETWEEN BURNHAM & CARDIFF.

CHEAP RETURN TICKETS
Available for One Week.

On and after MONDAY, 1st of May,

And until 31st October, 1865, Cheap Return Tickets will be issued, as under on MONDAYS and SATURDAYS, available for one week.

FARES TO AND FROM	1st Class, 2nd Class, and After Cabin.		3rd Class, and Fore Cabin.
CARDIFF and PORTSMOUTH - -			
GOSPORT - - - - -			
SOUTHAMPTON - - - - -	25s.	20s.	12s. 6d.
LYMINGTON - - - - -			
WEYMOUTH and EXMOUTH - -			

Passengers travelling with these Tickets, and leaving the train at any intermediate Station, will be charged the Full Fare to that Station.

Children under Three Years of age, Free; above Three and under Twelve, Half-fares.

TICKETS NOT TRANSFERABLE.

Passengers by this Route are allowed to BREAK the JOURNEY either at BURNHAM, SALISBURY or WIMBORNE.

For Sailings of STEAMERS between BURNHAM & CARDIFF see Small Bills.

Full information may be obtained on application at the Burnham Tidal Harbour Company's Offices, 5, Stuart Street, Bute Docks, Cardiff, or at the Stations of the London and South-Western Railway. *BY ORDER.*

The Shortest and Cheapest Route to and from the South-east, South and West of England, South Wales, Liverpool, the Channel Islands, Paris, and all Parts of the Continent, via Poole and Cherbourg.

IMPROVED STEAM COMMUNICATION BETWEEN

BURNHAM AND CARDIFF,

☞ Passengers, Parcels and Goods can be Booked Throughout between **Cardiff** and **Poole,** and all stations on the **Somerset and Dorset Railway,** and **Cherbourg, Caen** and **Paris,** and **London, Portsmouth, Gosport, Southampton, Guernsey Jersey, Lymington, Weymouth,** and all the principal Stations on the **London and South Western Railway.**

THIRD CLASS Tickets for **Cardiff** are issued from any Station between **Poole** and **Highbridge,** inclusive, by all Trains arriving at Burnham immediately before the departure of the Steamer; and from Cardiff, available by any train leaving Burnham next after the arrival of the Packet.

THE FINE AND FAST CLYDE-BUILT STEAMERS,

| **Defiance,** |  | **Heather Bell,** |
| E. L. BARRON, *Commander* | | W. DENSHAM, *Commander.* |

Or other suitable Steamers, are intended (Wind and Weather permitting, with or without a pilot, and with liberty to tow,) during the month of

MARCH, 1866,

TO PLY WITH PASSENGERS AND MERCHANDISE, AS FOLLOWS:—

FROM BURNHAM TO CARDIFF.			FROM CARDIFF TO BURNHAM.		
2 Friday	...	8.0 morning.	1 Thursday	...	7.0 morning
5 Monday	...	9.30 "	3 Saturday	...	8.0 "
7 Wednesday	...	10.0 "	6 Tuesday	...	10.15 "
8 Thursday	...	10.30 "	8 Thursday	...	7.30 "
9 Friday	...	11.0 "	9 Friday	...	8.0 "
10 Saturday	...	12.30 afternoon.	10 Saturay	...	9.0 "
12 Monday	...	3.30 "	12 Monday	...	12.0 noon.
14 Wednesday	...	3.30 "	13 Tuesday	...	1.30 afternoon
16 Friday	...	3.30 "	15 Thursday	...	3.30 "
17 Saturday	...	4.0 "	17 Saturday	...	7.30 morning.
20 Tuesday	...	9.30 morning.	19 Monday	...	9.0 "
22 Thursday	...	10.30 "	21 Wednesday	...	10.15 "
23 Friday	...	11.30 "	23 Friday	...	8.30 "
24 Saturday	...	12.30 afternoon.	24 Saturday	...	9.0 "
26 Monday	...	3.30 "	26 Monday	...	12.30 afternoon.
27 Tuesday	...	4.15 "	27 Tuesday	...	1.15 "
29 Thursday	...	3.30 "	28 Wednesday	...	2.15 "
30 Friday		Excursion from Cardiff.	29 Thursday	...	"
31 Saturday	...	4.15 afternoon.	30 Friday	...	Excursion from Cardiff.
			31 Saturday	...	7.30 morning.

FARES:—Saloon and After Cabin, 3s.; Fore Cabin, 2s.

For further particulars as to Trains see pages in centre of Book.

All information as to Freight, &c., may be obtained on application to Mr. BRISCOE, the Burnham Tidal Harbour Office at Glastonbury, at Burnham, or 5, Stuart Street, Bute Docks, Cardiff; Mr. J. SMITH, York House, Bridgwater; Mr. J. W. BARTON, 16, High Street, Bristol; Mr. GIORGI, Steam Packet Agent, Poole; Mr. E. K. CORKE, Steam Packet Superintendent, Southampton; or Mr. WILLIAMS, 53, King William Street, City, London.

By Order,	ROBERT A. READ,
Offices, Glastonbury, March, 1866.	*Secretary and General Manager.*

BURNHAM TIDAL HARBOUR COMPANY,
AND SOMERSET AND DORSET RAILWAY.

SATURDAY TO MONDAY
AT
ILFRACOMBE,
CALLING AT
LYNTON,
LYNMOUTH FOR THE VALLEY OF ROCKS.

On SATURDAY, 18th of MAY,
And until further Notice,
One of the Burnham Tidal Harbour Company's

SPLENDID CLYDE-BUILT PASSENGER SALOON STEAMERS
'DEFIANCE' OR 'HEATHER BELL,' OR 'GEORGE REED,'

Is intended, (wind, weather, and other unforeseen circumstances permitting) to ply between Burnham, Weston-Super-Mare, and Cardiff and Ilfracombe, as follows :

From Burnham.	From Weston.	From Cardiff.	From Ilfracombe
June 1 2.30 p.m.		4.30 p.m.	June 3 3.30. p.m.
June 8 12.30 p.m.		10.0 a.m.	June 10 8.0 a.m.
June 15 9.30 a.m.	7.45 a.m.	7.30 a.m.	June 17 11.30 a.m.
June 22 10.30 a.m.	8.30 a.m.	12.30 p.m.	June 24 7.30 a.m.
June 29 2.30 p.m.		4.30 p.m.	July 1 11.30 a.m.

FARES—After Cabin, 5s.; Fore Cabin, 3s.; To-and-Fro, After Cabin, 7s.6d.; Fore Cabin, 4s.6d.

		Saloon	Fore Cabin
Lynton to Ilfracombe	or vice	2s. 0d.	1s. 0d.
Do. return	versa.	3s. 0d.	2s. 0d.

THROUGH RETURN TICKETS to Ilfracombe, at a Single Fare for the Double Journey, will be issued from all Stations on the Somerset and Dorset Railway, from Poole to Glastonbury inclusive.

☞ Further information may be obtained on application to the Company's Offices, 5 Stuart-street, Bute Docks, Cardiff; Burnham; Glastonbury; at the Stations of the Somerset and Dorset Railway; of Mr. W. Bevan, West House Inn, Lynmouth; and of Mr. John Davey, Lantern Hill, Ilfracombe. By Order,

ROBERT A. READ,
Secretary and General Manager.

Offices, Glastonbury, May, 1867.

In July 1871, after eight years in company service the *Defiance* was put up for sale. She did not immediately find a buyer but when, in October she was finally disposed of to a Bristol metal merchant it marked the end of the S&D's first excursion into ship ownership.

With no vessels on their books and a ferry service to operate Captain Henderson again obliged by chartering the *Diana* to the BTH Co. She was another iron paddler of 160grt, built at Renfrew in 1851. After a very short period on the ferry service Henderson sold her to Manchester owners and she was withdrawn from Burnham.

To replace the *Diana* the company next chartered the *Avalon*. She was a two-funnelled iron paddle steamer of 670 tons gross built in 1865 and was considerably larger than any other ship used on the ferry service. It is not really surprising to learn that she lasted but a month or so and in September 1871 Henderson obtained the rather smaller iron paddler *Flora* of just 119 tons gross which he chartered to the Burnham company. At Burnham this 1852-built vessel settled down on the run but in October 1872 Henderson sold her to F.C. Winby, a Cardiff engineer. Winby kept her on charter but she was sold again in April 1873 to Henry Cousins, also of Cardiff. Yet again her new owner kept her on the station and she maintained the ferry service until in early 1879 she was sold for scrap.

Sometime around 1875 the BTH Co. was formally wound up having achieved very little other than as an operating company for the ships in the early years. Indeed by 1874 the S&DR had opened its northern extension to Bath and the feared neglect of the Burnham service began to happen. So long as the *Flora* had been available the ferry was maintained but once again the Somerset & Dorset Railway directors had bitten off more than they could chew with their new 26-mile extension over the Mendip Hills to Bath. They had provided their coveted north-south link but had little left with which to equip the new line. Consequently it lacked suitable locomotives and the required additional rolling stock to maintain the greatly increased services now required – it was indeed a very familiar story. By 1875 the company was in deep financial trouble once again and would inevitably have gone back into receivership had the directors not resolved to sell or lease the line. In the end the company leased their line to the Midland and London & South Western Railways jointly. The two companies could do little at first to improve the situation until an Act confirming the lease had been obtained, this being contested strongly and acrimoniously by the opposing Great Western Railway.[5] Shortly after the two railways agreed to take over the line a hideous head-on collision occurred between two trains just north of Radstock which blew the whole operating fiasco of the railway out into the open. This had a profound effect and as soon as they could the two leasing companies began to take control of the situation, their priority being to establish a well-maintained and properly equipped north-south link. Whilst the original S&DR company remained in a notional capacity, the line was henceforth run by a new Joint Committee on behalf of the lessees, the LSWR taking over responsibility for civil engineering whilst the MR concentrated on locomotives, rolling stock and provision of services. Henceforth the Evercreech Junction-Highbridge-Burnham section became very much a branch line.

The new Joint Committee were content to leave the Highbridge shipping interest intact (see Chapter 5) but they did not appear to worry overmuch when the *Flora* was withdrawn from Burnham and it would seem that they made no attempt to replace the vessel.

There is no record of any regular service to Cardiff between 1879 and 1882. Indeed there seems to have been some local feeling about this with agitation to reopen the ferry gaining momentum through 1881. In June of that year Mr. G. Wade, a Burnham solicitor, called on the Midland and LSWR to restart the service but they were unwilling to comply.

Eventually in 1882, John Boyle of Cardiff, for the Bute Docks Trustees (Bute Docks Authority) agreed to send a daily steamer to Burnham. The ship used was *The Lady Mary*, a handsome two-funnelled iron paddler built in 1868 and of 179 tons gross.[6] As a relief ship Boyle used the smaller iron paddler *Wye* (108grt) built in Bristol during 1861. Normally the *Wye* ran the Cardiff-Bristol route when not required at Burnham. Occasionally *The Lady Mary* was used on seasonal excursion work when it could be fitted in whilst it is known that the *Wye* had charge of the ferry service in July 1882 because *The Lady Mary* was undergoing an overhaul. With a steamer service leaving Cardiff at 7.30am and returning from Burnham at 4.30pm (subject to tides) through tickets were issued to places such as Glastonbury and Bournemouth whilst the occasional excursions typically embraced a Cardiff-Burnham-Ilfracombe schedule.

The Lady Mary was kept on the station until the end of April 1883 then returned to the Cardiff-Bristol run. Likewise the *Wye* also found other employment but from May the ferry service was covered by the 1875-built *Nelson*, a two-funnelled iron paddler of 166 tons gross. The relief vessel became the *Water Lily*, a small twin-screw vessel of just 52 tons gross, also completed in 1875. Both ships belonged to Samuel Little of Newport, who was by trade a tailor and outfitter!

CARDIFF & BRISTOL CHANNEL STEAMSHIPS.

The Shortest and Cheapest Route to and from South Wales, the South-east, South and West of England, Southampton, Portsmouth, Isle of Wight, the Channel Islands, and France, via Southampton.

STEAM COMMUNICATION BETWEEN

BURNHAM AND CARDIFF.

☞ Passengers, Parcels and Goods are conveyed at Through Rates between Cardiff and all Stations on the Somerset and Dorset Joint Railway, London, Portsmouth, Gosport, Southampton, Guernsey, Jersey, Lymington, Weymouth, and all the principal Stations on the London and South Western Railway.

THIRD CLASS Tickets for Cardiff are issued from any Station between Bournemouth, Poole, and Highbridge inclusive, and from London and South Western Railway Stations; and from Cardiff, available by any Train leaving Burnham, after the arrival of the Packet.

THE FAST STEAMER

LADY MARY OR WYE,

Or other Steamer, is intended (Wind and Weather permitting, with or without a pilot, and with liberty to tow), during the month of

JULY, 1882,

To ply with Passengers and Merchandise, as follows:—

From CARDIFF to BURNHAM.		From BURNHAM to CARDIFF.	
1 Saturday ... ... 3.45 p.m.		1 Saturday ... ... 7.30 p.m.	
3 Monday ... ... 8.0 a.m.		3 Monday ... ... 6.0 "	
4 Tuesday ... ... 7.30 "		4 Tuesday ... ... 7.30 "	
5 Wednesday ... ... 7.0 "		5 Wednesday ... ... 10.30 a.m.	
6 Thursday ... ... 7.30 "		6 Thursday ... ... 11.0 "	
7 Friday ... ... 8.15 "		7 Friday ... ... 11.45 "	
8 Saturday ... ... 9.15 "		8 Saturday ... ... 12.30 p.m.	
10 Monday ... 10.30 a.m. & 2.45 p.m.		10 Monday ... ... 12.30 "	
11 Tuesday ... ... 4.0 "		11 Tuesday ... ... 12.30 "	
12 Wednesday ... ... 5.0 "		12 Wednesday ... ... 2.0 "	
13 Thursday ... ... 6.0 "		13 Thursday ... ... 2.30 "	
14 Friday ... ... 4.45 "		14 Friday ... ... 2.45 p.m. & 6.45 "	
15 Saturday ... ... 3.45 "		15 Saturday ... ... 7.30 "	
17 Monday ... 6.30 a.m. & 5.15 "		17 Monday ... 8.45 a.m & 7.30 "	
18 Tuesday ... ... 7.0 a.m.		18 Tuesday ... ... 7.0 "	
19 Wednesday ... ... 9.30 "		19 Wednesday ... ... 6.30 "	
20 Thursday ... ... 7.0 "		20 Thursday ... ... 10.30 a.m.	
21 Friday ... ... 7.15 "		21 Friday ... ... 10.45 "	
22 Saturday ... ... 8.0 "		22 Saturday ... ... 11.45 "	
24 Monday ... 8.30 a.m. & 12.30 p.m.		24 Monday ... ... 10.30 "	
25 Tuesday ... ... 1.45 "		25 Tuesday ... ... 10.30 "	
26 Wednesday ... ... 2.30 "		26 Wednesday ... ... 11.45 "	
27 Thursday ... ... 2.30 "		27 Thursday ... 12.30 p.m. & 4.45 p.m.	
28 Friday ... ... 1.45 "		28 Friday ... ... 5.45 "	
29 Saturday ... ... 2.45 "		29 Saturday ... ... 6.30 "	
31 Monday ... ... 7.0 a.m.		31 Monday ... ... 7.0 "	

Single Fare, After-Cabin 3s. 6d. Fore-Cabin 2s. 6d.
Return ditto ... ... 6s. 0d. ditto ... 4s. 0d.
Return Tickets are available for 7 days.

ARRIVING AT

Trains leave BURNHAM at	Highbridge	Bridgwater	Taunton	Exeter	Glastonbury	Wells	T'Combe	Bournemouth	Salisbury	S'hampton	Portsmouth	Waterloo
8.5 a.m.	8.12 a.m.	8.46 a.m.	9.17 a.m.	10.45 a.m.	...	...	...	...	...	...	...	...
8.45 "	8.52 "	...	...	...	9.31 a.m.	9.55 a.m.	10.52 a.m.	12.7 p.m.	12.13 p.m.	1.27 p.m.	2.24 p.m.	2.35 p.m.
11.45 "	11.52 "	12.29 p.m.	12.55 p.m.	2.10 p.m.	12.44 p.m.	1.16 p.m.	1.55 p.m.	3.39 "	3.56 "	5.34 "	6.15 "	5.15 "
1.0 p.m.	1.8 "	2.33 "	3.0 "	4.0 "	...	...	...	...	...	...	...	...
2.45 "	2.53 "	...	...	...	3.50 "	4.5 "	...	...	...	...	...	...
4.20 "	4.27 "	4.54 "	5.33 "	6.35 "	5.38 "	5.33 "	6.45 "	8.55 "	7.44 "	9.30 "	10.25 "	10.7 "

TRAINS LEAVE

Waterloo	Portsmouth	S'hampton	Salisbury	Bournemouth	T'Combe	Wells	Glastonbury	Exeter	Taunton	Bridgwater	Highbridge	Arriving at BURNHAM
...	...	...	8.15 a.m.	7.25 a.m.	9.26 a.m.	7.33 a.m.	10.55 a.m.	6.0 a.m.	7.35 a.m.	8.4 a.m.	8.32 a.m.	8.40 a.m.
...	...	...	...	...	...	10.35 "	10.55	8.25 "	10.2 "	10.39 "	11.27 "	11.35 "
...	...	...	...	...	...	...	...	9.35 "	11.30 "	12.30 p.m.	1.32 "	12.27 p.m.
9.0 a.m.	8.0 a.m.	8.30 a.m.	11.15 "	10.5 "	12.5 p.m.	12.25 p.m.	12.55 p.m.	11.50 "	12.47 p.m.	1.15 p.m.	...	...
10.45 "	10.45 "	11.35 "	1.2 p.m.	11.45 "	2.50 "	3.35 "	3.50 "	...	...	...	4.20 "	4.45 "
11.45 "	12.35 p.m.	1.0 p.m.	2.42 "	3.10 p.m.	4.4 "	4.45 "	5.3 "	2.45 p.m.	4.45 "	5.12 "	5.36 "	5.45 "

All information as to freight, &c., may be obtained on application to Mr. JAMES HADDOW, Goods Manager, London and South Western Railway, Nine Elms, London; or Mr. W. B. MILLS, Waterloo Station; Mr. R. A. DYKES, Traffic Superintendent, Somerset and Dorset Railway, 14, Green Park, Bath; Mr. E. K. CORKE, Steam Packet Superintendent, Southampton; Mr. W. GANNON, 31, Nicholas Lane, Lombard Street, London; Mr A. PEACE, West Quay, Bridgwater; Messrs. E. TAYLOR & Co., 49, Bute Street, Cardiff; and at the Offices of the Cardiff and Bristol Channel Steam Ship Co., Pier Head, Cardiff; also at any London and South Western or Somerset and Dorset Joint Railway Stations.

June, 1882.

BY ORDER.

SOMERSET & DORSET JOINT RAILWAY.

CHEAP EXCURSION TO
BURNHAM
AND
SPECIAL SEA TRIP
BY THE FAST SALOON STEAMER
'SHERBRO

Or other suitable Vessel, (wind and weather permitting,) TO

CARDIFF

On MONDAY, JULY 27th, 1885,
CHEAP EXCURSION TICKETS will be issued as follows :—

STATIONS.	TRAIN.	Fares to CARDIFF and back.				Fares to BURNHAM and back.	
	a.m.	Third Class Rail, Deck, and Fore-Cabin only.		Third Class Rail and Saloon, or Bridges.		Third Class.	
TEMPLECOMBE (Lwr)dep	5 50						
WINCANTON ... ,,	5 57	3s	6d	4s	6d	1s	6d
Cole ... ... ,,	6 7						
SHEPTON MALLET ,,	6 0						
Evercreech New ... ,,	6 7	3s	6d	4s	6d	1s	3d
Evercreech Junction ,,	6 17						
Pylle ... ... ,,	6 22						
West Pennard ... ,,	6 29	3s	0d	4s	0d	1s	0d
GLASTONBURY ,,	6 40						
HIGHBRIDGE ... ,,	7 10	2s	6d	3s	6d	....	
BURNHAM (by Steamer)	7 30						

The Steamer leaves CARDIFF (Pier-Head) in returning at 4.30 p.m., and the Excursion Train leaves Burnham at 7.50 p.m., for all Stations.

REFRESHMENTS ON BOARD.

ROBERT A. DYKES,

Offices, Bath, July, 1885. No. 88 | 300 | 3000.

Traffic Superintendent.

From GOODALL'S Railway Printing Works, 19, Westgate Buildings, Bath and Glastonbury.

41

*(above) The paddle steamer **The Lady Mary** (179grt) lies alongside at Burnham pier in 1883. This ship, belonging to the Bute Docks Authority of Cardiff, was used to keep the daily Burnham-Cardiff ferry open during the 1882-3 period. Note the mooring piles on the extreme left which could be used to help warp ships out of the channel if necessary.*

(Captain James Dew via R. Atthill collection/S&DRT)

*(below) Photographs of ships taken at the pier from the northern side are more unusual. **The Lady Mary** is again seen but this time empty so the captain and crew were probably awaiting a train connection.* *(R. Atthill collection/S&DRT)*

It was at this stage that the Midland and London & South Western Railways had a remarkable change of attitude towards the service. Since the leasing they had religiously pursued a policy of strict economy whilst slowly improving the standard of infrastructure and the services on the Joint line. They were clearly not in the business of squandering money so perhaps it was a little surprising that they should throw caution to the wind and agree to the Joint Committee purchasing a vessel to run the ferry.

The ship in question was the two-funnelled twin-masted paddle steamer *Sherbro* of 239 tons gross. Her purchase was completed by May 1884 when she was registered in the names of the 'Trustees of the London and South Western and Midland Joint Railways'. Built as a government despatch vessel in 1870 she was refitted for the ferry service to carry 400 passengers and 80 head of cattle. Her appearance on the Burnham station, with the background and resources of two major railway companies, heralded a greatly improved service, posters proclaiming her as the 'new fast steamer', offering 'the shortest and cheapest route for goods and passengers to and from South Wales, the South and West of England, Somersetshire, Dorsetshire, Southampton and France via Southampton'. The LSWR had much to do with the French connection and were already operators of a large fleet of steamers to various destinations from the South Coast, their Southampton-Cherbourg service dating from 1869.

Displacing the *Nelson,* the *Sherbro* ran daily services until October. Little's *Water Lily* remained as the regular relief vessel. Indeed there were occasions when the relief vessel was called in to replace her on the regular run which allowed the steamer to run excursions to Ilfracombe. On other occasions the *Sherbro* would run from Cardiff to Burnham on the ferry service then extend her voyage to Ilfracombe and back as an excursion before returning to Cardiff.

Undoubtedly she was a popular ship with the regular users and her capacity to take a large amount of cargo was, at times, well appreciated. Many local people made use of her to take cattle and produce such as apples, potatoes, cider and dairy products across to Cardiff market, returning the same day, although loading and unloading on the open pier was still difficult at times. Mr. & Mrs. Stone of Rosewood Farm were one such farming family who made regular use of the *Sherbro* although Mr. Stone later related to his son an occasion whilst returning to Burnham in a storm when the weather was so bad that water penetrated into the ship's saloons and put the fires out that were used to heat the areas. He recorded that he thought they would never make land.

Coaching stock and locomotives were not allowed onto the 1 in 23 gradient so all passengers had to walk to the station if they were continuing their journey by rail. Once at the station they were at least afforded some protection from the elements because it was

43

Ships Engaged on Somerset & Dorset Railway Passenger Services

Burnham Ferry

Date	Ship	Owner	Operator
1858-60	*Taliesin*	Cardiff Steam Navigation Co.	Cardiff Steam Navigation Co.
1860-63	*Ruby*	Reed, Seymour & Baker (later BTH Co.)	Reed, Seymour & Baker (later BTH Co.)
1863	*Pilot*	Bute Dock Towing Co.	Chartered to BTH Co.
1863-71	*Defiance*	BTH Co.	BTH Co.
1864-67	*Heather Bell*	BTH Co.	BTH Co.
1866-68	*George Reed*	G. Reed (for BTH Co.) (P.L. Henderson from 1867)	BTH Co. (Chartered to BTH Co)
1871	*Diana*	P.L. Henderson, Liverpool	Chartered to BTH Co.
1871	*Avalon*	Great Eastern Railway Co.	Chartered to BTH Co.
1871-78	*Flora*	P.L. Henderson, Liverpool F.C. Winby, Cardiff H. Cousins, Cardiff	Chartered to BTH Co. (later S&DR/S&DJR)
1879-82	No recorded ferry service		
1882-83	*The Lady Mary*	Bute Trustees, Cardiff	Bute Docks Authority
1883	*Nelson*	Samuel Little, Newport	Chartered to S&DJR
1884-88	*Sherbro*	S&D Joint Committee	S&DJR

Reserves on Burnham Ferry

Date	Ship	Owner	Operator
1882-83	*Wye*	Bute Trustees, Cardiff	Bute Docks Authority
1883-87	*Water Lily*	Samuel Little, Newport	Samuel Little

Poole-Cherbourg Ferry

Date	Ship	Owner	Operator
1865-66	*Albion*	P.L. Henderson, Liverpool	Chartered to S&DR.

BTH Co. = Burnham Tidal Harbour Company. Ships operated on behalf of the Somerset Central Railway.

*Photographs of S&D cargo vessels at Burnham pier are rare but in this view the **SS Alpha** is tied up alongside some of the huge mooring piles. Cargoes are known to have been discharged over the pier rather than being landed at High-bridge, road building materials being amongst them.*

(R. Atthill collection/S&DRT)

provided with an all-over roof and, of course had the usual waiting rooms. Passengers waiting for a ship to arrive had no protection whatsoever if they elected to walk down to the pier.

Railway wagons could be lowered down the slip and these invariably carried agricultural produce such as apples, vegetables, dairy produce or cattle. The wagons were shunted to the pierhead and then lowered using a wire rope which passed through a ring set in the stonework at the top of the pier. In 1884 rollers were laid between the rails to protect the rope. According to Captain James Dew trucks were sometimes pushed down the gradient by the engine but with extra trucks added to allow it to stand clear of the wooden section of the pier head. The cattle were usually taken straight from the wagons across the boards and onto the ship but it was not unknown for one to escape and make a bid for freedom along the sands! Local baker and confectioner, Glyn Luxon, recalled an occasion whilst trying to load cattle when considerable trouble was experienced driving them down the pier. In the end

his grandfather jumped up on one of the cows and rode it down, then all the rest followed!

Other cargoes landed at the pier included spartina grass from France or Spain whilst road building materials were also known to have come ashore there.

One marvellous story (perhaps embellished in the telling), recalled by Glyn Luxon, which unfortunately cannot be corroborated, relates to an incident when a locomotive ran away down the pier following brake failure whilst running around its train in the station. Fortunately it did not go off the end because it occurred at half-tide and the water stopped it! Perhaps the incident was never officially reported; certainly it does not seem to feature in any surviving reports.[7]

Unfortunately by 1886 the true amount of ferry traffic that could be attracted was found to be too small in spite of all the efforts and the **Sherbro** spent more and more time on excursion work from Cardiff and less and less on the ferry. This was really not surprising because when the Severn railway tunnel opened during that same year it had a dramatic effect on trade

Burnham station was completed in 1857 and was one of only two on the line to be provided with an overall roof, the other being its contemporary at Wells. Built on land belonging to George Reed the station was a little closer to the pier than originally planned which was probably just as well for intending passengers waiting for ships because there was no other protection during inclement weather. Taken around 1905 from the later 'excursion' platform, the train shed is painted in the attractive LSWR dark brown and buff colour scheme which adorned most of the S&D stations during this period although it was comparatively short-lived. On the right is the goods shed. Looking seaward The Queen's Hotel (sometime The Reed Arms) can just be seen on the esplanade whilst the back of the lifeboat house, built in 1874, is on the left. (S&DRT)

through Burnham. With its construction in mind it is difficult to understand just why the LSWR and MR decided to invest in a ship in 1884 to keep the service going when hitherto it had used chartered tonnage. As a result the *Sherbro* was likely to turn up at Weston, Watchet, Lynmouth and Ilfracombe. During the winter months the Joint Committee decided to lay the ship up. Samuel Little continued to supply his *Water Lily* as relief to the ship and on Whit-Monday in 1887 she was noted running an excursion from Cardiff to Burnham followed by 'trips round the bay'. As it turned out, 1887 was to be the last season for the *Water Lily* as relief ship, leaving the *Sherbro* to run the service on her own for the 1888 season. In the event the ship got no further through the summer than July when the Joint Committee decided to sell her. No time was wasted in disposal and the Cardiff-Burnham ferry was suspended. It was never restarted and the S&D's interest in operating out of Burnham finally came to a disappointing end.

Notes:

1. Bridgwater Customs House Letter Books – No.57/16 dated November 1858 refers. The *Marley Hill* (508tg/399tn) was registered at London to the General Iron Screw Collier Company in February 1854. It was built as a collier primarily to service the needs of the London gas companies. By the mid-1860s she had passed into the ownership of F.H. Powell & Co. Ltd. and was used on the Liverpool-London service. Her registered dimensions were 164.3ft x 26.4ft x 15.0ft.

2. Coincidentally Parliament repealed that part of the Railways Act that forbade railway companies owning and operating ships during 1862. Thereafter once a company obtained ship-operating powers it was free to purchase and operate them.

3. S&DR Company minutes dated 30/8/66, PRO Kew.

4. The Poole & Cherbourg Steam Packet Company was formed to take over the service and it seems that the 230grt iron paddle steamer *Spicy* came south from Liverpool to run the short-lived service which ran only until 1868. This company was no more successful than the S&DR.

5. The period leading up to the lease of the S&DR was fraught with difficulties in which the Great Western Railway played a leading part. A complete account of the events can be found in Vol.2 of the *History of the Great Western Railway* by E.T. MacDermot, revised by C.R. Clinker, 1964.

6. *The Lady Mary* was specifically built by the Duke of Hamilton's trustees to open the Ardrossan-Arran service, entering service in 1868. She developed the trade so successfully that a larger steamer was required so was sold in 1871 but was chartered back to her old owners for a period before finally being sold again in 1876 when the ship came south to the Bristol Channel.

7. S&DRT File X507. Correspondence between G. Luxon, Captain J. Dew, G. Farr and R. Atthill, 1966.

(above, left) A delightful early view taken at Burnham in 1895 as some of the station staff pose with the crew of S&DJR 0-6-0 No.28, Driver Henry (Hennie) Hill and Fireman Braund (in the light coat), both of Highbridge shed. In the background can be seen the water tank beneath which was the small workshop in which up to four men worked producing and repairing the sails of the company's ships and the many wagon sheets. (R. Atthill collection/S&DRT)

(below, left) Johnson 0-4-4 tank locomotives served the S&D well over a lengthy period of time. Supplied in two batches, the first series were constructed by Avonside but No.53 belonged to the second Vulcan Foundry-built series. All were originally used on main-line services but as larger locomotives became available during the 1890s they were progressively relegated to Burnham-Templecombe services as well as being used on the Bridgwater and Wells branches. No.53, seen here at Highbridge with a local train from Burnham, dated from January 1885 but this photo was taken after March 1905 following the fitting of a Johnson boiler. (S&DRT)

5 Highbridge Harbour – The Hub of Services

If the full expectations of the New Wharf area at Highbridge were to be realised and as much coastal trade as possible captured then a fair amount of development needed to be carried out. Both berths and extra sidings were needed which would also make the site more attractive to prospective lessees. Applications for some sites had been received before any serious development had started and with these in mind the positioning of the yards was arranged in 1854. Messrs. J. & C. Rigby, the railway contractors responsible for the building of the Somerset Central, were given the contract for the construction of extra berths at a cost of £550. Further land to the north of the harbour area was purchased and this allowed for the extension of the existing sidings and the addition of others at a cost of £1,000.

Among the tenants at the wharf were Rigby's themselves. The contract for the extensions of the SCR to Burnham and Wells were in the offing at the time, and were, indeed, subsequently won by them, whilst with the contract for the extension from Glastonbury to Bruton following, they were to be associated with the railway until early 1862. At a rental of £50 per year the yard was no doubt convenient for importing rails and other construction materials. They were also able to rent a gantry frame for an additional £50 per year provided that they undertook to load and unload for the public at no more than 1/- (5p) per ton.

One or two other companies rented wharves with river frontage varying from 40 to 150 feet (12.3m to 46.2m) in length. Rents varied from £10-£20 per annum over a period of 14 to 21 years. The SCR did come across some difficulties as instanced by Messrs. Wall & Smith. They were allowed to rent the orchard which then existed next to the eastern end of the harbour on the north bank and with it they gained the sole rights to land goods to the east of Arford's timber yard. This involved the SCR in providing specially constructed berths for two vessels together with additional sidings. For this the SCR required a rental of £50 per annum rather than the £15-£20 expected by Wall & Smith. Following apparent completion the lessees complained that the wall of the quay was not long enough whilst the sidings were neither long nor substantial enough. Finally they complained that the mud had not been removed from the berths.

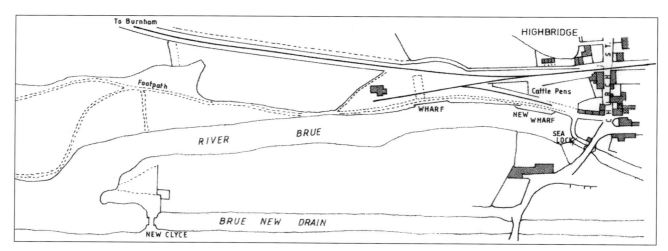

Highbridge Wharf, c1858. This early Somerset Central Railway map of the wharf area post-dates the building of the Burnham branch but shows the modest provision of sidings as built and serving the two original wharves just west of the old canal sea lock, the remainder of the area being, as yet, totally undeveloped. The adjacent road bridge was originally a three-arch structure (the 'High Bridge') and the site of the mediaeval clyce. It is of interest to note that only one set of rails originally crossed Church Street on the level but this was to change radically following the development of the wharf in the 1860s when the Burnham and Wharf lines were separated to improve operational efficiency resulting in a second track being laid over the road. Although the wharf area was the original course of the Brue the main river outflow was via the New Cut (or New Drain) and the Commissioners' 'New Clyce'.

This delightful late 19th-century view of Highbridge well illustrates the wharf when sail still held reign over steam. The two vessels nearest the camera have probably brought timber in from Scandinavia. Outboard of the barquentine is a local trading smack but at least four ketch-rigged trows and cargo vessels are in the harbour. Timber-carrying railway wagons can just be seen to the right together with some of the steam cranes but there is no development at the western end of the wharf yet. (Author's collection)

The respective company solicitors decided that the complaints were justified and that the work should be satisfactorily completed. On the other hand it was also revealed that Wall & Smith had been over-zealous in the protection of their exclusive rights having insisted that railway employees wandered no further than 4ft.(1.2m) from the rails for maintenance work. The negotiations removed this restriction.

To protect Wall & Smith's rights to prevent inconsiderate use of the harbour a number of rules and regulations were formulated and it was laid down that Berth No.1 was to be available to all vessels except that Wall & Smith could not use it if other vessels required it. Berth No.2 was for use by Wall & Smith exclusively. Berth No.3 and the rest of the harbour berths were open to anyone.[1] Two days were allowed for loading and unloading a vessel in Berths Nos.1 & 3. Ships larger than 50 tons were allowed an extra day.

Imports continuing their journey by rail were to be landed to the west of Berth No.2 unless they were handled by Wall & Smith. A further rule imposed by the Act stated: 'All persons throwing any ballast, gravel, stones, rubbish or dirt into the Harbour, are liable to a penalty of 20/-'.[2]

It has already been mentioned that to stimulate traffic through the harbour the SCR reduced tolls on certain items in 1854. When Rigby's had completed the planned developments further reductions were made and a new list of tolls published. This gives some indication of the regular cargoes then using the port facility. Although minerals and some manufactured goods passed through there was a large agricultural content.

As with the canal, repairs were necessary from time-to-time. The lock gates between the harbour and the canal needed attention in 1856 and the wharf wall and gantry frame in 1858. The lock gates were again in need of repair in 1861 by which time the increase in traffic and the demands of the new Burnham and Wells extensions led to further plans for enlarging wharfage and siding accommodation. Extra plant, including cranes, was also ordered.

A further enterprise to develop trade at the wharf was the leasing of a portion of the wharves to 'responsible parties' who would operate steamship services between Highbridge and South Wales thus, according to *Herapath's Journal,* 'connecting the fruit and vegetable districts of Somerset with the consuming population of the mining districts of Wales'.

*Coastal trade formed a vitally important part of the commercial activity at Highbridge and in this interesting scene the 54-ton ketch **Ann** can be seen moored outboard of the ketch-rigged trow **William**. Behind the two classic railway steam cranes stand a rake of four S&DJR cattle wagons, all from a batch of 50 c1885-built vehicles in the 407-456 number range, including Nos.422, 435 and 436. As was usual for such wagons they are covered in lime, used as a disinfectant.*

(Randell Collection/S&DRT)

*Viewed on the same occasion, two more coastal vessels are seen at the Wharf; the smack-rigged Bristol-registered open moulded trow **Flora** is moored outboard of the French-built ketch **Marie Eugénie**. The latter came into the ownership of Clifford Symons of Bridgwater in 1885 and was no doubt in port to load a cargo from the nearby rail-connected brick and tile works of Colthurst Symons & Co. on the Burnham line, one of a number of such firms belonging to the two families following their amalgamation in 1857. After 42 years of faithful service she was finally sold for breaking in 1927. The wooden S&D marine store would shortly be rebuilt into a neat, brick-built structure.*

(Randell collection/S&DRT)

*The elderly 1809-built Severn trow **William** from Gloucester (35 tons net) was a frequent visitor, often bringing coal in from the Forest of Dean although she was later owned in Highbridge. She is seen alongside the rather larger 100-ton topsail schooner **Morning Star**, a ship dating from 1878.*   *(Randell Collection/S&DRT)*

*A tranquil scene at the Wharf in the early 1920s with an Oslo-registered barquentine taking pride of place whilst the two S&D cargo steamers **Alpha** and **Julia** occupy the western berths.*   *(N. Chipchase)*

There is every indication that the development of the harbour was quickly rewarded. At the special general meeting of the SCR held on 30 October 1855 reference was made to

> the great natural advantages possessed by Highbridge as a port for communication with Cardiff and the ports of South Wales, and the comparatively small outlay which would have to be incurred to render it available for an almost unlimited amount of traffic.

The fact that it was so directly served by the railway must have had much to do with its success and post-1857 toll revenue figures reveal a profit of £67-8-10 for the second half of 1858 rising to £132-16-3 in the first half of 1862.

With the formation of the BTH Co. in August 1860 the future development of Highbridge as a deep-water harbour was expected to change the geography of the area considerably as the northern bank of the Brue was cut back and the existing channel leading up as far as Berth No.3 (the wooden wharf) widened. The development was expected to create a new dock in this area with the ability to take considerably larger ships. In the event, and with a pressing need for additional wharfage only piecemeal improvements were made during the early 1860s with the provision of a lengthy, part stone, part wooden wharf which did not seem to conform to the intentions of the new development; it retained the original rail connection and not that planned under the new Act and also the difficult turn into the harbour area. As things turned out the BTH Co. was destined not to play any significant part in events at Highbridge whilst the pending formation of the Somerset & Dorset Railway Company in 1862 would contribute to the ultimate winding up of the company around 1875.

It was not until 1873 that the Somerset & Dorset Railway, having been in severe financial difficulties following its expansion northwards to Bath, finally engaged in its own cargo operation; in that year it acquired three wooden ketches, the *Railway*, *Julia* and *Richard and Emily*, followed in 1874 by its first small steamship, the *Leopard*. They were provided primarily to bring rail over to Highbridge from the steel mills of South Wales. When not so engaged they were employed on general cargo duties. Their use expanded rapidly and this caused the company to consider chartering extra tonnage so in 1875 a fifth ship, the *SS Lincolnshire* (88 tons gross/54 net) joined the railway-owned fleet. Built by C. Mitchell & Co., at Low Walker, Newcastle in 1867 for J. Hawdon & Co.,

also of Newcastle, she may have come south especially for this charter in advance of her sale to the well-known Newport shipowner, Henry Burton & Sons since she was not registered to them until 16 February 1877. Even this did not, apparently, give enough capacity and in 1876 another small steamship, the *Terrier*, was chartered. This vessel of 91 tons gross, 79 net, was built at Whiteinch in 1865 for R. Hannan of Glasgow.

There is no doubt that making the connection with the Midland Railway was a good move but unfortunately the extension strained the existing resources of the railway to their absolute limit and faced with almost certain bankruptcy the directors sought to sell or lease the company to other interested parties. The train of events that happened next is well documented elsewhere but, as mentioned in Chapter 4, in the end the railway was leased by the S&DR to the Midland and London & South Western Railways jointly, the new arrangement being confirmed by an Act of 13 July 1876. Although the lease covered the railway and rolling stock it omitted to cover the ships so these remained in S&DR ownership, a somewhat untidy arrangement which would eventually have to be put right. The new Joint Committee formed by the LSWR and MR to run and administer the Somerset & Dorset was almost immediately confronted with an urgent need to make reforms in order to upgrade the existing civil engineering, stock it properly with locomotives and rolling stock and place the line into profitability. Clearly economies would have to be made alongside the new investment and amongst the earliest casualties was the termination of the charter of the *Lincolnshire* in October 1876.[3] Then on 10 November 1877 *The Bristol Times and Mirror* reported that the 'steamship *Terrier* (Smith) of Glasgow left Swansea for Highbridge with coals, sugar of lead and copper plates on 14 October, and anchored off Port Talbot the same day', but thereafter went missing with all hands. Sad though this was, it was very convenient for the Joint Committee who made no attempt to replace her.

The matter of ownership of the four S&DR ships was quickly tidied up when they were purchased outright from the company by the Joint Committee in late 1875, all being allowed to continue to ply without hindrance. Perhaps the loss of the *Terrier* did have some lasting effect because in 1879 a fifth ship, the small iron screw vessel *Alpha*, was purchased.

For the next six years the five ships all traded together, the *Alpha* being lengthened during 1884 to cope with the longer rails then being produced, but in 1886 the Severn Tunnel opened and like that at Burnham the port's trade was badly hit. By a cruel twist of fate two of the ketches were lost in that same year. The **Railway** was the first to go, wrecked off Cardiff, followed by the **Richard and Emily** which sank during a storm off Nash Light. Neither were replaced. The depleted little fleet was further reduced in 1890 when the **Leopard** was declared 'unfit for further use' and laid up for a couple of years. She remained in the fleet for a further six years until finally sold in 1896 for further trading. This left just the ketch **Julia** and the steamer **Alpha**, both still being employed largely in bringing in rails, iron and coal from Newport. By 1903 the **Julia** was showing her age and the Joint Committee described her as being 'worn beyond repair' – clearly her days were numbered.

Keeping the wharf and the River Brue free of mud was a constant problem to the S&D as it was at all the harbours and tidal rivers in Somerset. As has been noted there had been a long and contorted flooding problem on the adjacent Somerset Levels and many attempts had been made to control the situation, mostly with only limited success. Unfortunately for the S&D its inheritance of the canal and wharf facilities from the SCR and Glastonbury Canal Company before it

brought with it far more problems than they could have possibly anticipated.

The Glastonbury Canal's sea lock was, of course, designed for navigation, the original path of the Brue having been re-excavated, although with the opening of the railway it had become defunct as a navigation. It was retained because it acted very much as a sluice and water from the river was frequently used to give a scouring action for the harbour area. However the water was not always available because the main river outfall had, it will be recalled, been diverted through the much wider New Cut to a large tidal sluice. This lack of water and inability to keep the old channel free of mud would cause the S&D ongoing grief at the sea lock.

The responsibility for drainage and controlling the water on the levels had passed to the Commissioners of Sewers who were to prove to be difficult neighbours to the S&D as did their replacement body, the Somerset Drainage Commissioners who were formed with fresh powers and finances following the passing of the Somersetshire Drainage Act in 1877. A specific re-

The 'Cut' between the sea lock and the River Brue New Drain of 1801 was part of the 13th-century river channel and was later utilised for the Glastonbury Canal. Apart from the sea lock behind the camera it was not, however, railway owned, being the responsibility of the Commissioners of Sewers. It is seen in a drained-down state, to facilitate maintenance on the sea lock, with the New Drain channel just visible in the distance. (Randell collection/S&DRT)

Highbridge. Renewal of outer Sea Doors. Coffer-dam. Sinking commenced 29.6.09.

When the S&DJR renewed the outer sea doors of their old sea lock at the head of the harbour in 1909 they at first had to construct a cofferdam. Sinking of this commenced on 29 June and work on this is still in progress when viewed shortly after. This photo is of interest as the rail-mounted crane is one of the two Thomas Smith-built examples provided originally for Bridgwater Wharf, one of which was known to have been transported to Highbridge following the abandonment of much of that structure in the same year – see also Chapter 7. (Randell collection/S&DRT)

quirement in this Act stated that water must be made available through the old cut to scour the harbour area, thus protecting the railway's interests. The new body set about attempting to improve the flooding situation which still occurred regularly. A number of major improvements were made including rebuilding of the Highbridge Clyce at the seaward end of the New Cut which had suffered from a severe lack of maintenance. Part of the rebuilding included lowering the door cills and deepening by three feet. This action alone was to cause an incredible amount of further trouble to the railway.

In January 1889 Mr. George Lovibond, the clerk to the Somersetshire Drainage Commissioners, wrote to Mr. A. Colson, the S&DJR's resident engineer at Glastonbury drawing his attention to 'the extraordinary condition of the River Brue between the New Cut and the Harbour Gates'. This was blamed on 'the accumulation of mud which has been allowed to go on

and block the flow of water for some considerable time past'. The railway was told in no uncertain terms to put its sea lock gates into proper working order and cautioned against allowing mud and silt to flow back along the old river course into the New Cut. Unfortunately the problem had only really become severe since the Commission had rebuilt and deepened its clyce around 1886 resulting in less water feeding through the S&D property. This in turn was causing added expense to the railway in trying to keep its wharves clear of silt. Ironically the Commissioners were blaming the S&D for a problem that was not of their making. The trouble was that they held considerable legal powers and were really very little interested in the railway's problems in comparison with their own.

Colson decided to refer the problem to the S&D Joint Committee who were reluctant to rebuild their sea lock to the same level as the Commissioners' clyce.

The estimate for this was up to £3,000 and the reasoning was not hard to find. Between 1876 and 1892 the company's ships had incurred a trading loss of £4,000, most of which could be blamed on the opening of the Severn Tunnel and the deepening of the Commissioners' clyce, both in and around 1886. In addition, extra expense had occurred when the S&D were forced to hire small steamers to dredge the harbour whilst on occasions the company's own vessels were used for the same purpose thus denying their use for commercial purposes. The reluctance of Waterloo to authorise any major expenditure becomes obvious but in March 1889 the LSWR engineer, Mr. E. Andrews, compromised and allowed Colson permission to spend up to £300 on deepening the freshwater cut immediately upstream from the lock.

In connection with this work the *Alpha* and *Leopard* were used extensively on mud and silt clearance work in the harbour, their use continuing well into the summer of 1889, no doubt to the chagrin of the Traffic Department. Amazingly by the summer of 1890 the mud had largely reasserted itself, such was the speed at which silting occurred. Some of the local traders using the wharf were also disenchanted, including John Bland & Co. who, in the middle of August 1890, had contacted Mr. Colson requesting that their berth be cleared of mud to enable several large timber cargoes to be landed.

The problem was to dog the S&D for evermore but was exacerbated at times by the irresponsible behaviour of Mr. Long, the Commissioners' clyce gatekeeper who was felt to be extremely unreliable and who failed to co-operate with the S&D staff. Typically he would unexpectedly open his clyce thus denying the S&D sufficient water to pass through its cut to scour the harbour.

The troubles continued year on year, causing Colson to hire a small steamer again in 1899 for a six-month period during the summer to dislodge the accumulations of mud which were rapidly building up in the harbour due to a lack of water on the levels – a particularly difficult time in the year if the summer turned out to be excessively dry.

Many other ships of all types were using the railway facilities at Highbridge through these years. Timber importation provided much of the basic business coming in from the Baltic ports often in sizeable Russian vessels but it was the S&D's own operation concerning the importation of rails from South Wales which gives us a measure of just how important it was. In the year ending 31 May 1903 the *Julia* and *Alpha* together brought over 7,960 tons of rail to the port but chartered vessels brought in a further 10,457 tons. Clearly there was sufficient business in rail alone for another coastal steamer of 150 tons besides the *Alpha*. In consequence a new ship was ordered to replace the *Julia* which was disposed of towards the end of 1904, the year in which the replacement steamship was delivered. This ship was also given the name *Julia* and was the first cargo vessel expressly built for the S&D Railway. At the same time the opportunity was taken to lengthen the *Alpha* for the second time to enable her to take the even longer rails now being used by the LSWR.

Although he was not averse to using the ships on 'mudding' duties, one of Colson's successors, Edward Roche, decided eventually on a different approach to the incessant silting problem and in November 1910 he approached Mr. W. Lunn of the Somerset Drainage Commissioners to see if the S&D could hire their little steam eroding vessel *Pioneer* which they used on the Parrett and which was fitted with a high pressure water jet to dislodge the mud, but the reply was both helpful and discouraging:

Some time ago the Parrett & Tone Committee, who represent The Drainage Districts under whose jurisdiction our Eroder works, decided that in future the Eroder should not be hired out to anybody except our own District's Boards requiring the use of it. They came to this conclusion because it invariably happens, and must of necessity be so, that the time people want to hire the Eroder is always a time when it can do most useful work for themselves.

Have you tried to obtain the use of the Bridgwater Corporation's Eroder? It is more powerful than ours and they are not using it to the extent they contemplated to use it when they have obtained the necessary permission of The Board of Trade.

I am afraid it would not be possible to use an Eroder very long in your Harbour as it is necessary to have flotation and a stream of water for its proper working. If however circumstances permitted of these desiderata an Eroder would soon move all the soft material, but great care would have to be exercised in working it to prevent damage being caused to the banks by washing the foot of them away.

Following this reply, Roche wasted no time in removing 30 truck-loads of mud in one week but where it was transported to is not recorded! Inspector Cox, the man who actually took responsibility at Highbridge for the silt clearing works, wrote to Roche on 25 November:

*Taken in the late 1920s both the Somerset & Dorset's ships, **Radstock** and **Julia**, are seen together at Highbridge. Lying alongside the former is the 34-ton tug **Edward Batters** (ON124623) which was purchased in 1922 by L.W. Nurse who reformed The Bridgwater Steam Towing Co. Ltd. with the vessel in July of that year. The Nurse family were well-known Bridgwater shipowners who otherwise operated only sailing vessels. The little tug had been built in 1908 for The Point of Ayr Collieries Ltd., on the south bank of the River Dee near Prestatyn, North Wales. By all accounts there was not much work at Bridgwater for a tug by the time Nurse purchased her and it seems that she was laid up at Bridgwater dock in the early 1930s before finally going to Newport for demolition in 1934.* (Author's collection)

I beg to inform you that 'Long' has turned the water through our cut twice this week and also had a good flush last Sunday, and we have worked the men in the small boats stirring up the mud so long as there was any water running.

This was followed by a similar communication on 5 December when Cox stated that the water had been diverted through the cut and harbour twice during the previous week for about two hours on each occasion and he estimated that there was between five and six feet of fresh water coming through. This gave him the opportunity to get his gang of men back out in the boats and they successfully reduced the mud by another 6 inches but the unpredictable nature of the clyce operation made it extremely difficult to forecast when any work could be achieved.

All this extra activity did not go unnoticed and on 2 February 1911 the Traffic Superintendent, G.H. Eyre, wrote to congratulate Roche. *Julia* was able to leave the wharf before high water whilst *Alpha* was able to dock fully laden again, before high water. 'Anything of this kind has not been possible for the last twenty years', he wrote. Even so later that year Roche was being plagued by lack of co-operation from the Commissioners' gatekeeper once again. Nothing much had really changed.

As alluded to in the letter from Mr. Lunn, The Bridgwater Port & Navigation Committee had also tried an eroding system using a small boat and water jet with some success but at the turn of the century they were without this facility and relied on a dredger for the dock area in Bridgwater. In March 1910 they completed the 62ft-long steel-hulled *Eroder* which mounted a high-powered water jet system. The S&D were able to hire the vessel for use at Highbridge but by the time the war came in 1914 the Bridgwater Committee soon found it hard to crew the vessel and it only saw intermittent service thereafter. It was finally sold in 1927.[4] The S&D eventually overcame the problem to some extent by using the locally owned tug *Rexford* as a mud dragger in later years when required.

*(above) The S&D's coaster **Alpha** is the only vessel in port in this otherwise forlornly empty 1924-view of the Wharf and the scene makes a stark comparison with earlier turn-of-the-century views.* *(Author's collection)*

*(below) The broad-gauge tracks of the crane road were an odd survivor from earlier days. The **Julia** discharges her cargo of rails from South Wales in this late 1920s view. The building to the left of the ship is Feaver's flour store whilst those to the right form part of the old Eclipse Fuel Company's works.* *(Author's collection)*

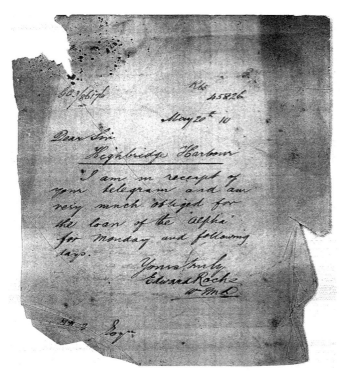

On Friday 20 May 1910, Edward Roche, the line's civil engineer, was forced yet again to borrow the **Alpha** from the traffic superintendent, G.H. Eyre, for 'mudding' duties at Highbridge during the following week. It is noteworthy that the various managers involved were always extremely courteous in their correspondence although the constant misuse of the vessels in this manner must have provided the traffic superintendents with a number of problems. (S&DRT)

(below) Highbridge Wharf, c1900. Once the harbour had been developed by the S&D in the 1860s the siding system was extended accordingly. Nearly 40 years later the picture looked like this with the private premises of the saw mill now well established in the apex formed between the S&D sidings and the Burnham extension. On the far left the original siding layout has been modified and the rail-served flour store built. Also extant at this time was the private siding into the Britannia Brick Works, inspected in February 1883 and worked by a simple two-lever ground frame but removed by 1919 after the works had closed. One of three such yards on the Burnham extension, the other two were a little to the west where sidings served Colthurst, Symons & Co. and the Apex Brick & Tile Works (otherwise Somerset Construction Co.). All provided trade to the harbour. (OS 38.3, 2nd Edition 1903, by permission of the British Library)

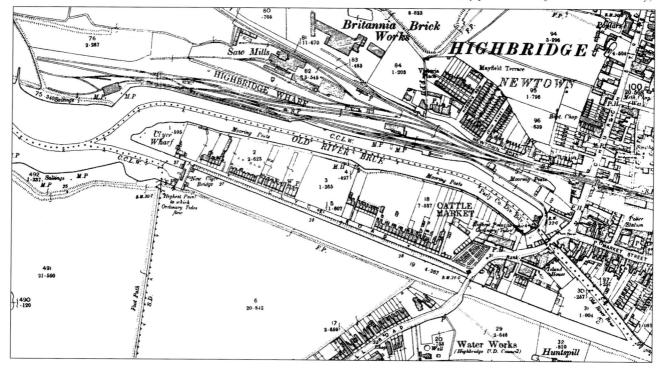

Tranquillity and reflection at Highbridge. Taken on a still summer's day this picture first appeared in the Southern Railway Magazine *in June 1929. The central feature is the S&DJR's steamship* **Radstock**, *then still a very new ship, which sits in the main River Brue channel with Kimber's Clyce Wharf and boatyard behind. Two large cargo vessels are tied up alongside the wharf but to the left of these and just at the entrance into the harbour is the other S&D cargo vessel,* **Julia**. *Several ketches or trows complete this busy scene although by this time many coastal sailing craft such as these were being laid up or disposed of as they failed to find cargoes in the face of steamship competition. (Colin G. Maggs collection)*

Highbridge Wharf, c1930. This map represents the final development at Highbridge with the extension of the siding network into the patent fuel works at the western end and the development of the Saw Mills where two lengthy new timber storage sheds were constructed during the early 1920s. On the debit side all trace of the Britannia Brick Works and its associated siding have disappeared.   *(OS 38.3, Revised 2nd Edition 1915-46, by permission of the British Library)*

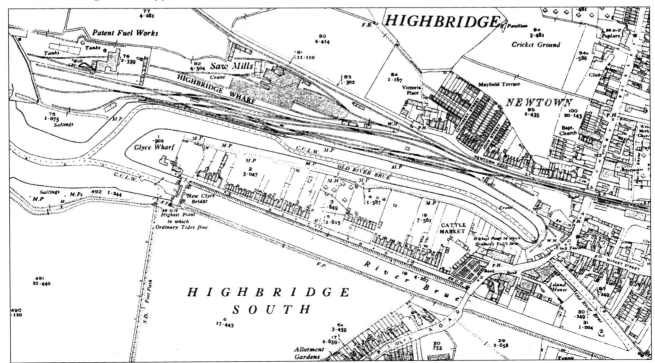

South Western & Midland Railway Companies
Somerset & Dorset Joint Line.
Locomotive Superintendents Office.

REFER TO

IN YOUR REPLY.

Highbridge 29th May 1889

Dear Sir,

The Alpha is going to Mud for you tonight and tomorrow morning instead of working her trial trip – I advise you of this in case you should come in the morning and wonder what she is doing –

Yours truly
W H French

A. Colson Esq.

REFERENCE

(45b)

South Western and Midland Railway Companies'
SOMERSET AND DORSET JOINT LINE.

TOUR

MEMORANDUM.—FROM GOODS DEPARTMENT,
Please Address
Mr. H. BASTARD.
HIGHBRIDGE.

To Glastonbury
12 Oct 1889

Dear Sir,
In consequence of a dense fog in the Channel last night 'Leopard' did not get into Swansea this morning, Consequently, it is very doubtful if she can load there until Monday, in which case you cannot have her for dredging until Wednesday. If, however, you see me Monday morning, I shall be able tell you definitely.

Yours truly

Insp. Hansford

H. Bastard.

Plenty of evidence of the silting problems at Highbridge is shown in these letters. On the left, a letter from Locomotive Superintendent W.H. French to the S&D's Civil Engineer at Glastonbury, Mr. A. Colson explaining why the **Alpha**, which had been under repair, was not on a trial trip.

The second letter (below) was a memo from Harry Bastard, who for many years was Highbridge goods manager and superintendent of the Wharf, to Inspector Hansford in the Engineer's Department at Glastonbury explaining why the latter gentleman would be unable to 'borrow' the **Leopard** from revenue-earning service in order to clean the harbour.

Both letters are dated 1889 and highlight the way in which the ships were often misused.

(Reproduced by courtesy of Duncan Harper)

60

During the First World War the wharf became exceptionally busy indeed and apart from iron, large quantities of extra coal passed through together with additional flour and huge amounts of stone chippings for road making. Timber from the Baltic continued throughout this period and was to remain a staple traffic. Indeed, at its busiest, trade built up to such an extent that it was quite common to see two or three white-painted Scandinavian timber brigs and barques, as well as half-a-dozen local colliers, sail and steam, at the wharf together. Although the wharf had been exceptionally busy during this period the harbour suffered badly from lack of maintenance, so typically a problem during such busy periods: no provision for maintenance was made at all during 1915 and 1916 and there was little progress until 1920 when the Joint Committee then spent over £830.

Matters relating to mud and silt clearance in the harbour came to a head once again in 1920 when the continued non-cooperation of the Drainage Commissioners' staff was noted. In June the S&D convened a conference at the *Railway Hotel* in Highbridge at which all the main bodies involved in drainage on the levels were invited and which was chaired by Colonel S. Preston of the Canal Control Committee, a representative of the Ministry of Transport. It was hoped that the Somersetshire Drainage Commissioners could be persuaded to lower the cills of the S&D sea lock in line with those of the clyce. District Engineer Mr. O.A.G. Edwards (who between 1900 and 1904 had been the Resident Engineer at Glastonbury before moving to Exeter) and Walter Fox, the then S&D engineer, probably knew before it had started that little progress would be made and the only practical suggestion came from the chairman who suggested that a 4ft.-wide trench should be dug into the bed of the freshwater cut to increase the effectiveness of the water flow.

Following the meeting, Edwards prepared a report which he sent to the LSWR's Chief Engineer, Mr. A.W. Szlumper who subsequently discussed the problems at Highbridge with another Ministry of Transport representative, Colonel Pringle. In the course of time this was transmitted back via Edwards who wrote to Fox on 12 August stating that the Colonel

> expresses the view that it was the S&D's duty to form the channel between the Inner Sea Doors and the junction of the old River Brue with the new Cut, such channel to be kept to the level of the Cill of the Inner Sea Doors. Your Plan No. G 6569 shows the recent level of the Mud between the points named and I must now

ask you please to proceed as quickly as possible, with the forming of the channel getting the same down to the level specified, namely, the Cill of the Inner Sea Doors.

> Directly you have got this done, please report to me, when the Chief Engineer proposes to communicate with the Board of Agriculture and Fisheries.

Clearly the issue had now been raised to the highest level within the LSWR and Mr. Szlumper was taking a direct interest in it.

A site meeting was then called at Highbridge at the beginning of August by Edwards which was attended by Fox and other interested parties to discuss the way ahead. Following this, Fox was authorised to engage six casual labourers to help dig out the mud in the harbour which at this time was more than 3ft.(1m) above the cill of the sea lock gates but clearly more drastic action was needed and during the same month the unusual decision was taken to recall the *Julia*. At the time the ship was in the middle of a refit and was actually in drydock at Bristol. Back at Highbridge Fox borrowed the vessel for a couple of weeks on 'mudding' duties before she returned to No.1 berth to complete her refit and for a boiler replacement to be carried out.

Fox also arranged for a temporary dam to be built across the freshwater cut to enable the gang to start to dig out the channel that had been advocated. No sooner had this been completed than the Commissioners closed their clyce gates. The immediate effect was to pen in the fresh water which rose in level until it flowed over the top of the dam and into the old cut with a consequent flooding of the works. The water continued to rise to such an extent that the dam had to be partially demolished and the sea lock gates opened to release it. Any pretence that the S&D engineers could ever reliably work with the unpredictable Commissioners was at an end. Clearly the latter had demonstrated time and again their complete contempt for the railway and its harbour despite the legal obligations placed upon them.

The LSWR Chief Engineer had required of District Engineer Edwards regular updates of the situation and a series of letters now followed giving daily details of the readings on the Commissioners' clyce gauge board at Highbridge and also on a similar board at Edington Junction. On the 8th October he was able to tell Mr. Szlumper that on 30 July they had fresh water running through the harbour for over four hours and that they had also had a flush of water between each tide since. Men were still employed on mudding operations, both in the sea lock and the harbour.

A lot of activity and a wealth of detail. Taken in the early 1930s it looks as though a platelaying gang is giving the crane-road some attention although this photo was taken as part of a sequence marking the trials of the new 3-ton crane which had just been installed and which required much modification to the crane-road track. Trying to empty the contents of the unfamiliar grab into the awaiting trucks must be taxing the crane driver who has a helping hand from another member of staff on a ladder whilst management look on! The tide is out which is why only the top of the funnel belonging to the local Bristol collier **John** *can be seen above the coal tubs whilst waiting patiently by the mess room is one of Fred Wiltshire's shunting horses.*   (National Railway Museum – DY17315)

Then the problems started all over again. On the 9th October Fox wrote to Edwards:

Will you please note Inspector Cox called at my office this morning, and informed me that on the night before last Clyse Keeper Long had instructions to raise the Commissioners' Clyse, with the result that we have had no water through our Harbour since that evening.

'Long' informed Inspector Cox that this was due to the fact that owing to very heavy rain during the last few days, the water had to be very quickly run off, but we should have water through the Harbour in the course of a few days.

On the 15 October this was duly reported to Szlumper, it having taken until Tuesday 12 October for the Commissioners' clyce gatekeeper to lower the gates but thereafter water ran through the harbour and again men in boats were working in the lock stirring up the mud to allow it to be flushed out.

The reports continued on a regular basis thereafter and in April 1921 Cox was still working his men in the boats in the freshwater cut although periodically the clyce keeper would still raise his gates without any warning. However as a result of the much improved situation and the regular flushing the harbour was now getting and the fact that Edwards had received assurances from the Commissioners' engineer, Mr. Haile, that he intended to give the S&D all the water available in the future, it was decided to terminate the employment of two of the men engaged on this work with a proviso that they would be re-engaged if it proved impossible in the future to keep the mud levels down.

This view of the Wharf looking towards the west reveals much of the siding detail. The five main sidings are all seen here, the tracks behind the camera being used mainly to sort wagons whilst those in the far distance were used for storage. The siding on the right originally gave access to the fuel works which was not in use in this early 1930s photograph. The small building in the centre was the rope shed. (National Railway Museum – DY17314)

All this coincided with an acidic letter received on 19 April from the effervescent Lovibond, still in post with the Commissioners after more than 30 years, and addressed to the Somerset Joint Committee at their general offices at Bath. In it he claimed that the constant working of the clyce gates in favour of the S&D had placed an unreasonable burden on keeper Long who now had to visit the harbour to talk regularly with Inspector Cox and that the Joint Committee should contribute to the increased wages the Commission now felt disposed to pay him. He also felt that the Commission's Engineer and his assistant should be entitled to free railway passes! The letter was duly forwarded by Edwards to Fox at Glastonbury for his comment. The reply paints a different picture:

I do not think there is much in the statement as to the additional work being thrown on clyce Gatekeeper 'Long', by the supplying of constant flushes of water through our Cut.

I have been into the matter with Inspector Cox, and there seems no doubt but that the clycekeeper has, on a few occasions, put down the Commissioners' gates whereby we obtained a flush of water, which we might not have done, had the Commissioners' gates not been put down. I do not think, however, that this can be considered as involving much additional work on 'Long', in so far as he lives adjoining the Clyce and so is right on the spot, and the work of lowering the gates is very little.

With regard to the Clyce Gatekeeper having to keep constant watch of the Water level gauge, this man has been at Highbridge attending to the gates, so I am informed, for about 30 years, and his past experience of the water conditions at Highbridge is such that there is practically no necessity for him to actually keep any special watch on the water level.

Seldom photographed from this angle, the full extent of the harbour together with the pronounced curve at its upper end can be seen in this early 1930s view. In the foreground is the 200ft.(62m) stone quay which was developed from the original New Wharf together with its fixed hand crane. Two ships could be berthed here. Immediately below John Bland's Sawmill the remains of the other 150ft.(46m) upper berth can be seen. This was always made of timber and had long since been out of use when this view was taken. Between them these two quays handled vast quantities of timber in early times. Note the public footpath on what was sometimes referred to as the catchwater bank. (National Railway Museum – DY17313)

I am also of the opinion that there is nothing in the statement that 'Long' visits the Harbour to keep in touch with the 'Railway Foreman'. As a matter of fact, 'Long' is one of the chief men in Highbridge Harbour, engaged in unloading vessels that arrive at our Wharf, and the performance of this duty necessitates his visiting the Harbour two or three times a day, and any conversations that have taken place between him and Inspector Cox have been when 'Long' has either been going to, or from his work.

If there is any additional work thrown on 'Long' in providing flushes of water through our Harbour owing to the manipulation of the Commissioners' gates, it is, in my opinion, of a very trivial nature, and I certainly do not think it would be worth 1/- a day. In very fine weather,

such as we are having at the present time, there would be no necessity for the Gatekeeper to touch the gates at all, as if the gates were kept down, all the water that was required to be run off could come through our Harbour. I remember on one occasion, 'Long' himself informed me that in the very dry summer we experienced a few years ago, he had kept the Commissioners' gates lowered for 13 weeks, and never once had to disturb them, during that period.

I do not think that the Joint Committee should pay anything towards the additional wage of 7/- per week which the Commissioners state they have found it necessary to pay 'Long', seeing, as stated by Col: Redman, they are obliged to give us a flush of water under the Somersetshire Drainage Act of 1877, and I think that our case would only be prejudiced if we were to in any way help to pay the Clyce Gatekeeper's wage.

With regard to the Commissioners' desire that a Pass should be granted to their Engineer and his Assistant, there is no doubt but that their present Engineer – Mr. Haile – does seem disposed to do what he can to give us water, and I consider it would tend to assist matters if he was provided with a Pass between Bridgwater, Burnham, Edington & Wells, but I hardly see the need of an additional Pass being issued to his Assistant.[5]

From this communication it suggests that Long frequently took casual stevedoring work at the wharf albeit that he was employed by the Commission.

Such were the ever-present problems surrounding the arguments between the S&D and the Drainage Commissioners even though the Act of 1877 gave the railway a right to have fresh water diverted through the harbour area to scour and clean it.

There was never going to be a satisfactory conclusion to the problems and the ever-present silting continued. At the end of June 1923 both the *Alpha* and *Julia* were again pressed into service as mud draggers. This came about following notice earlier that month by the timber merchants John Bland & Co. that they were expecting a steamer and urgently needed their berth to be cleared of mud but even after this the *Julia* was commandeered, being used between 4.00 and 7.10pm on 11 July and again between 5.00 and 7.50am on 12 July. On that same day she also managed a quick hour between 5.15 and 6.15pm at which point it is stated that 'the boat has gone to sea'!

Apart from her periodic turns at mudding, the *Alpha* was soon back to her usual trade following the end of hostilities in 1918 and was recorded as making up to a dozen voyages to South Wales each month until finally being withdrawn from service in 1925 and scrapped. She was replaced by another new steamship, the *Radstock*, in the same year, this vessel being an updated version of the *Julia*. Despite a failing economy in the country which would lead to the great depression, trade seemed to remain buoyant at Highbridge during the 1920s under the supervision of harbourmaster Nat Francis. At the top (western) end of the wharf at this time Fred Wiltshire could be found with his three shunting horses but steam locomotives were also used and shunters Bill Foster and Bert Ladd would be kept busy eight hours a day with the regular wharf locomotive, 2-4-0 No.27A.[6] Fred, who was also responsible for weighing the wagons, eventually became the harbourmaster and

because of the Second World War he stayed in employment with the S&DJR well beyond retirement age. Even after hostilities had ceased he remained to see the last few years out and was still there when the harbour was finally closed in 1948, by which time he had completed over 50 years in railway service at the wharf. Albert Buncombe was another who spent most of his working life there, working his way up to become head stevedore. Not by coincidence he was also the owner of the tug *Rexford* which was freely used by the S&D for many years.

The fortunes of the S&DJR were, unfortunately, not so rosy as that of its wharf. The First World War undoubtedly did little to help the fine economic balance that the Joint Committee had endeavoured to work and by the early 1920s expenditure was rapidly rising out of control. The Joint Committee responded by forming the Redhead Commission to look into the railway's affairs and when it reported it recommended large-scale changes in the administration. In consequence the London Midland & Scottish and Southern Railways (as successors to the Midland and LSW Railways in the 1923 grouping) took direct control of the S&D in 1930. A number of changes manifested themselves at the time, not least the loss of the famous Prussian Blue livery carried by many of the locomotives and coaching stock and the renumbering of locomotives into LMS stock. Cost-cutting was pursued vigorously and by 1933 the decision had been taken to withdraw from shipowning altogether although the wharf at Highbridge was to be retained. In consequence the 31-year-old *Julia* was sold for scrap whilst her sister-ship *Radstock*, being much younger, was sold for further commercial service. The crew of the latter had stayed together since she was delivered in 1925 and it was a sad day for them.

Private Sidings at Highbridge Wharf

1929

Bland & Company – Timber Yard
Highbridge Anthracite Fuel Works Ltd.
Norris Siding – Coal Yard
Willett's Cake Mills

From the Railway Clearing House Handbook, *1929. Norris's coal yard was situated at the head of the harbour.*

Highbridge Wharf continued to function normally throughout the 1930s under railway control and the S&D continued to provide storage facilities there, although trade was generally on the decline. All that was, of course, to change dramatically in 1939 as the Second World War brought about a useful revival. There was a tremendous increase in imports, mainly of coal, reaching a peak of 1,500 tons a day, which was brought over from South Wales by sea to relieve the hard-pressed railway system, up to three Southern Railway ships being engaged in this traffic.

Once the war was over there was a serious decline in the use of the harbour again, particularly as road haulage began to bite. On 1 January 1948, nationalisation of the complete railway system saw the S&D become part of British Railways but by this time the trading situation had become hopeless. BR wasted little time in losing this unwanted asset. The last timber cargo was imported in the Dutch motor vessel *Jola* (1935/267grt) during June 1948, following which there was little or no activity although the wharf was not officially closed to shipping until the following year. The last locally-owned vessel, other than a few yachts, was Albert Buncombe's tug *Rexford*, which, after so much useful service around the area, was finally towed away to be scrapped in January 1950.

Highbridge Wharf

Train Arrivals and Departures
from 4 October 1920

Down

Burnham	dep:			12.40pm			3.30pm	
Highbridge	arr:			12.45pm			3.35pm	
Wharf	dep:	7.15am	11.45am			12.56pm		1.55pm
		to	to			to		to
		T'combe	E'creech Jcn.			H'bridge Loco (Shunting Engine)		E'creech Jcn.

Up

		10.40pm	12.45pm		1.25pm	3.15pm
		Ex-E'creech Jcn.	Ex-H'bridge Loco (Shunting Engine)		Ex-E'creech Jcn.	Ex-E'creech Jcn.
Highbridge	arr:	2.05am	12.51pm		3.50pm	5.45pm
Wharf	dep:			12.55pm*		
Burnham	arr:			1.00pm		

* Train runs 20 minutes later on Saturdays

From the Working Timebook, 4/10/20.

(left) The small railway town and harbour of Highbridge is viewed from the south-east in August 1930. In the right foreground the River Brue flows past the Somerset & Dorset Joint Railway's works (which closed during this year) and station before entering the straight 1803-built 'New Drain' which by-passed the original cut to the sea lock and head of the wharf area. Meanwhile the railway has crossed the GWR Bristol-Exeter line on the level before passing through the little town, following which it splits to serve the extensive wharf sidings whilst the 'main' line curves away towards its terminus at Burnham, seen towards the top right. Just two small vessels can be identified in the port, both at the western end of the lengthy quay, above which is the old briquette works and the extensive timber sheds belonging to Bland's. The Brue winds its tortuous way into the Parrett estuary with the low relief of Stert Island opposite. (Image supplied by aerofilms.com)

Originally constructed by George England & Co. as a 2-4-0 tender locomotive and acquired by the Somerset Central Railway late in 1861 as No.7, this little engine became No.27 in 1876 and placed on the duplicate list as No.27A in 1881. Rather than being discarded it was retained in stock, reboilered and converted into a neat, side tank engine during 1888. Over the years it found regular employment on the Wells, Bridgwater and Burnham lines but during the First World War it became a regular Highbridge Wharf locomotive and stayed there subsequently until it was finally condemned during 1925 having recorded no less than 1,204,647 miles in its long career. (National Railway Museum, Real Photographs collection)

Unlike most parts of the S&D Railway there are virtually no surviving photographs of engines shunting Highbridge Wharf, presumably as most photographers of the day went there to look for ships. In this rare but somewhat distressed photo, regular shunting locomotive, 2-4-0T No.27A, is viewed with a private owner wagon at the Wharf in the early 1920s towards the end of the old engine's long career.
(R. Perkins/S&DRT)

The Harbour and Wharf Described

Ships proceeding up the River Brue entered the harbour area by turning sharply to port to follow the original course of the river. Straight ahead the latter-day route of the Brue through the New Cut drainage canal ceased to be navigable because of the Highbridge Lower Flood Gates or clyce. The original course of the river then followed the cut occupied by the wharf area to its head at the Glastonbury Canal sea lock and thence via a short canal cut leading back into the Brue.

The eventual development of the wharf area, much of which took place during the 1860s, entailed the construction of a quay some 770ft (237m) in length, partly in wood and partly in stone and concrete, with mooring rings set into the side, covering about a third of the northern bank of the harbour area. Vertical ladders were also provided. Forming an elevated platform, the top of this quay was the 'crane road' upon which a number of steam-operated cranes were located, running on an isolated length of broad-gauge track. Behind this platform a number of sidings were added to enable railway wagons to be drawn up alongside ships being unloaded. Further sidings were eventually built to store wagons and allow shunting operations to proceed.

Immediately to the left as ships entered was another much shorter wooden quay, set at an angle to the above. The original intentions are debatable since this may have been provided as wooden shuttering to prevent bank erosion, yet reference to the First Edition of the Ordnance Survey, dated c1885, gives clear evidence that a short elevated siding was laid along its length with wagon turntables at each end to connect with the rest of the siding system. The map also suggests that there was another siding at a lower level immediately behind. There is little evidence that it was much used although turn of the century photographs show the bank area hereabouts still to be in good condition. However no attempt was made to maintain the timbers and they were allowed to decay completely as the years went by; the original sidings were removed and Feaver's flour store was eventually constructed on the site.

The cranes form an interesting sub-topic in their own right. The provision of self-propelled machines would seem to date back to the earliest times when the new quay was built. There is some confusion as to how many were provided but in most of the earlier views at least five can be seen on the long wharf. All were self-propelled steam machines of 30cwt capacity but there were at least three different types. Three were equipped with covered wooden cabs and afforded some protection to the crane driver. Two of these came from Worsdell & Co. of Birmingham and can be identified by their narrow solid jibs and the small-wheeled bogies upon which they were mounted. The third, and possibly the oldest to survive, was similar but had an open lattice jib; it was mounted on a bogie with much larger wheels and was generally to be seen at the western end of the crane road. Two almost identical steam hydraulic cranes dating from around 1891 complete the line up and can be quickly identified as they had no cabs, leaving their vertical boilers, workings and the poor driver open to the elements.

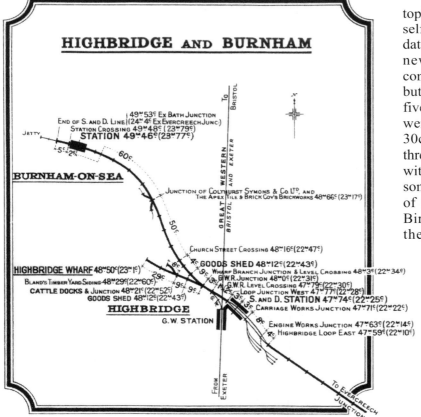

The Midland Railway Distance Diagram of Highbridge and Burnham, Book No.76, Sheet No.62 (fifth edition), 1919. The continuous distances shown are those from Bath Junction. The mileages shown in brackets are those measured from Evercreech Junction which was 25 miles 49 chains from Bath Junction.

At the western end of the Wharf was a crane which seemed to feature in this location for very many years. It differed from the other two fitted with cabs in a number of details but it is easily identified by a completely different jib and its bogie which had much larger diameter wheels. It is unloading new rails which have been brought across the channel from South Wales by the *Julia*, seen on the right in this late-1920s view. The small brick building on the left replaced a wooden structure and housed the S&D's marine store at the near end and the Wharf mess room at the far end. *(Author's collection)*

Crane No.2 was one of a pair of 1891-built 30cwt steam hydraulic machines provided to the S&DJR. Crane driver Bill Spratt is unloading coal from a ship during the 1890s using one of several tubs of varying sizes kept for this purpose. Behind are three typical sailing vessels of the period, the outboard one (with a crew member at the masthead) being the Severn trow *Eliza* from Gloucester (ON 51203). Built in 1864 this 57-ton net vessel survived until the 1940s. *(S&DRT)*

*A different driver, bucket and wagons and a few minor differences to the crane suggest that this is the other 30cwt steam hydraulic crane placed into service during 1891. In typical railway lettering style 'Not to exceed 112 tons' is painted on this crane's jib. Sitting on the mud in mid-stream is the **Alpha**. This view, taken well before the timber sheds were constructed gives some idea of the lengths to which they went to ensure that the stored timber was sheeted. (Rod Fitzhugh collection)*

*(below) A single-cylinder 30cwt steam crane built by Worsdell & Co. of Birmingham, probably photographed before 1900. Once again the S&DJR acquired a pair of essentially similar cranes from this manufacturer, the maker's name being visible, stamped on the machinery framework. With some protection afforded to the operator, foreman fitter Sid Hall poses on the crane. Much else can be discerned about life at the Wharf. Alongside is the Severn trow **Providence** (ON 11694) of 45 tons net. She sank in the Bristol Channel early in the 20th century. A long mixed rake of S&DJR paired single-bolster dumb- and spring-buffered wagons carry many lengths of rail and beyond is the weighbridge house and, rather surprisingly for a siding system such as this, a home signal which was later removed. (Nine of the bolsters can be identified – from the left Nos. 597, 661, 369, 403, 362, ?, 361, 81, 124, ?, 376, ?.) (National Railway Museum – DY8575)*

*Crane No.5 was the second of a pair of machines built by Worsdell & Co. of Birmingham. Although very similar to the other one there are detailed differences in the flywheel and the cab timbering. Once again coal is being unloaded from a sailing vessel using a tub, a labour intensive method which prevailed for many years although a grab crane was finally introduced in the 1930s. There were two trows with the name **Eliza** trading in the Bristol Channel at this time and the 54-ton net Bridgwater-registered vessel (ON56581) can just be seen behind the crane. (National Railway Museum – DY8430)*

There were periods when some of the cranes seemed to be missing but as they were no doubt taken to Highbridge Locomotive Works for repair or periodic overhaul (until its closure in 1930) this would probably explain their absence, although being mounted on broad-gauge bogies this must have made life that little bit more difficult when it came to moving them. Inevitably when photographed they would be equipped with a characteristic tub to handle coal imports, this being lowered into the ship's hold and filled up manually, a time consuming and back-breaking job.

The two steam hydraulic cranes were withdrawn from use in the late 1920s and for a period only the three cab-fitted cranes remained. Then in the early 1930s the railway introduced a new and much larger 3-ton self-propelled steam crane with a mechanical grab in an effort to speed up the discharge of coal cargoes. It was no simple task setting this second-hand crane up at the wharf because it ran on a rail gauge of about 8ft.(2.46m) which was considerably wider than

that of the existing crane-road. In fact the crane bogie was so wide that it only just fitted on the width of the elevated platform so it was decided to place it on that part of the wharf which was stone built because the inside edge of this part was of concrete. Fortunately the rails of the adjacent siding were not aligned as closely as they would have been had it been a conventional station platform so the necessary clearance between cab body and wagons was available. In order to strengthen the inside edge and to provide a safety walkway the platform was extended by three sleepers' widths and a new rail fitted outside the existing rails, thus creating, for a short distance, a rather unusual mixed-broad-gauge configuration.

Although few details are available about this new acquisition it is easily recognised in a number of later photographs because of its size and a series of official photographs were taken of it during trials shortly afterwards when the **Radstock** discharged a cargo of coal amid an audience of management! Photographic

evidence also suggests that the crane was later re-boilered causing the cab to be permanently removed.

The cranes, which noticeably rattled and clanked as they moved along the uneven flat-bottom crane-road rails, were driven amongst others by Bill Spratt and Ern Pitcher whilst foreman steam crane fitter Sid Hall looked after their needs. They were subject to periodic testing and it was during one such operation that one of them, being operated by driver Ern Pitcher, tipped on its side. Fortunately this was to landward; had it been towards the harbour he could well have been drowned. As it was he was rather shaken although not injured so went home to recover. When the wharf foreman heard that he had not been injured he immediately went to his home and insisted on pain of dismissal that he return and finish his shift driving one of the other cranes until his had been righted and repaired. Ern Pitcher later admitted that had he not been ordered back to work at once he would probably have been so nervous that he would never have worked

a crane on the wharf again. In the event he continued to do so for very many years thereafter.[7]

A combined wooden marine store and mess room (later rebuilt in brick), shunters' cabins, warehouses, stables, and other buildings were provided, whilst behind the sidings, served by its own private rail connection, were the extensive wood storage and drying sheds of the sawmill which for many years belonged to John Bland & Company who imported timber mainly from Scandinavia. The storage sheds with their familiar elliptically-shaped roofs were erected around 1923-4.

Beyond the eastern end of Bland's premises a pre-stressed concrete building formed part of the Eclipse Fuel Company together with a pitch reservoir, these premises also being rail connected. The works manufactured fuel briquettes during the First World War at a time when it was feared that there would be a national shortage of coal. Known as the 'Winkle' locally, the building became part of Alexander's

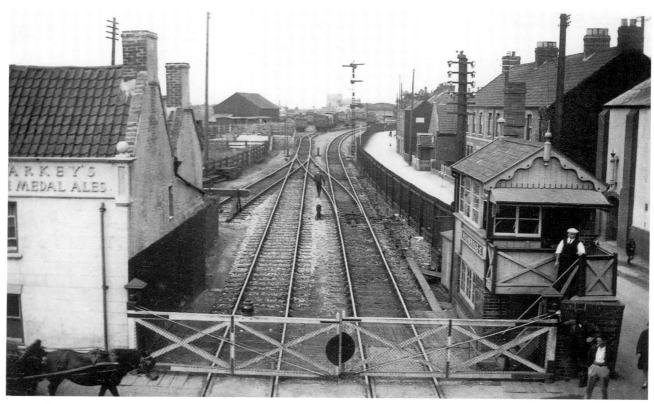

The parting of the Burnham line (right) and the Wharf branch (left) at Highbridge in 1933. The original layout here was very different with just a single track into the Wharf and a junction line to Burnham. It was later substantially remodelled into a separate twin-track configuration, the wharf branch being extended eastwards across Church Street level crossing (the Bridgwater-Bristol turnpike road, later the A38) and under the footbridge (from where this view was taken) for a further 13 chains to a new junction with the parallel Burnham line which was controlled by the S&D's Highbridge 'B' signalbox. The road crossing was controlled by the delightful little Highbridge 'C' box with Newtown Road to its right. The crossover was a later addition and provided a more direct link into the Wharf from the Burnham line, the sidings of which can be seen fanning out in the distance with the cattle pens and headshunt on the left. (National Railway Museum/LGRP collection)

Highbridge Anthracite Fuel Works from 23 December 1924 and survived in use until the 1930s when the disused premises became derelict. During the Second World War it was used as a military depot for the storage of war materials by United States forces. American-built tank locomotives were provided from a larger depot close to the locomotive works for shunting the adjacent sidings at the western end of the wharf during this period.[8] The building, albeit derelict again, was still standing in 1971. Also at this end of the wharf was the flour store operated by Messrs Feaver & Co.

A weighbridge and house were provided and large cattle docks at the eastern end near the junction with the Burnham branch, convenient to Highbridge Cattle Market. This junction was controlled by the diminutive S&D 'C' signalbox which also controlled the level crossing gates over the main road through the town.

As has been noted, various areas of the wharf were originally rented to local businesses and this had caused the original development of the two other short

quays towards the eastern or upper end of the wharf. At the first of these, a 150ft.(46m) single-berth wooden quay, there were originally two small cranes, one of which was a self-propelled steam crane running on its own very short length of isolated rail. This quay fell into disuse and was allowed to decay, becoming unusable by the early 1930s. The other quay, the original New Wharf, some 200ft.(62m) in length and built more substantially of stone, was provided with a fixed crane and could accommodate two ketch-sized vessels. Much of the timber came in over these quays in the earlier years but both were later used to berth S&D ships for periods of lay-up or refit when required. In later years John Feaver & Company, feeding cake manufacturers and millers, established a flour mill in this area although it changed hands sometime before 1920 and was subsequently used by Willett & Son as a corn and cake feed store and mill with stables attached. By the early 1970s it was once again standing empty. A siding, which ran eastwards along this part of the

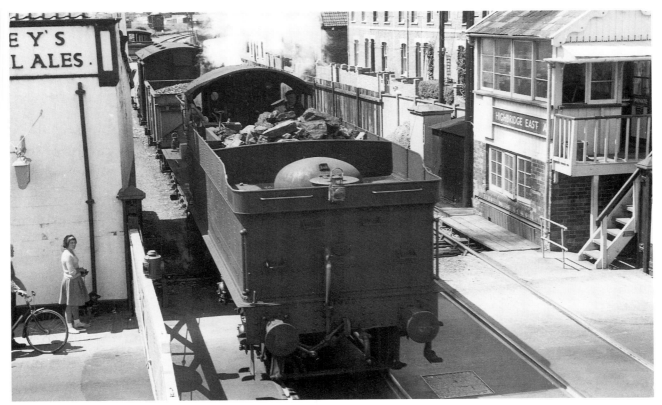

Driver Ron Andrews at the regulator of Collett Class 3MT 0-6-0 No.3210 as he hauls a short freight train along the Highbridge Wharf branch and across Church Street crossing during the closing years of this branch in the early 1960s. (R.E. Toop)

wharf (otherwise known as the 'catchwater bank'), served both the upper quay and the mill premises before later being extended to curve sharply southwards through gates and dividing into two short sidings in the Co-operative Society coal yard (formerly Norris's), close to the main road. One of these sidings crossed Bridge No.283A, built over the original canal sea lock.

Although much of the siding layout remained basically unaltered over the years there were developments and alterations to match the changing needs and trading patterns. The original rail-served facilities were very basic but they were soon extended to serve the newer longer quay at the western end. The building of the patent fuel works to the west of the sawmill saw a further extension into these premises with railway-owned storage sidings being constructed alongside. There were minor alterations as the years passed but most remained.

The sidings continued in use for some years after the closure of the harbour to shipping, those at the west end being largely used to store crippled or condemned wagons, but by the early 1960s they were no longer required. Rail traffic to the wharf was discontinued from 2 November 1964, the official closure date of the wharf branch being 16 May 1965.

Notes

1. The actual positioning and numbering of Berths Nos. 1, 2 & 3 are not shown although in the early days timber imports inevitably came over No.1 which was the original 'New Wharf' at the eastern end of the harbour and which had been rebuilt to accommodate two vessels as Berths Nos. 1 & 2. No.3 was the wooden wharf a little further to the west.
2. 7 & 8 Geo IV c.41.
3. The iron-built **Lincolnshire** could load about 114 tons of coal with registered dimensions of 76.3ft x 20.1ft x 8.5ft. She was sold to a Liverpool company in 1907 and broken up in 1928.
4. 'Steam Eroding Boats of the Somerset Levels' by Mary Miles (SIAS *Bulletin*, Nos.61, 63 and 64). A full and descriptive series of articles covering the vessels designed and placed into service for mud removal and erosion.
5. Letter dated 28 April 1921 Fox/Edwards. This correspondence and the preceding letters and extracts relating to the difficulties of keeping the area free of mud and silt are held in the S&DRT archive collection (A920 series). See also Duncan Harper's article 'Highbridge Harbour', *Pines Express*, issue No.200.
6. From notes by Leonard Grant, S&DRT *Bulletin* No.115.
7. Details from Paul Fry, S&DRT journal *Pines Express*, issue No.198.
8. A number of War Department locomotives are known to have been operated at Highbridge by the US Ordnance during the Second World War until the end of 1944. It is thought that one of these was allocated for use at the wharf whilst others were used at the extensive sidings and depot situated opposite the Highbridge locomotive works. USA 0-6-0T Nos.WD1255, WD1285, WD1394 and WD1557 were recorded amongst others, notably an 0-4-0 Sentinel (WD70232) and a WD Ruston. Further details can be found in *Pines Express*, issue No.192.

6 Cargoes, Commerce and Crews

In order to understand the trade carried on at Highbridge and Burnham it is necessary first to look at the aspirations of the company. The Burnham situation is relatively easy because there the intention was to run a ferry service primarily for passengers although some cattle could be transported, with limited facilities for agricultural produce and other cargoes. Highbridge, on the other hand, was a different proposition. From the earliest days when the SCR inherited the New Wharf and systematically developed it during the 1860s, the intention was not only to provide facilities for local trading vessels mainly within the Bristol Channel but also to attract a foreign trade. The use of the wharf by its own cargo vessels was a later adjunct.

In the early to mid-19th century there were hundreds of small coasting sailing vessels in the Bristol Channel, often with owner/masters who tramped around the coastline taking up any cargo that was offered. In many respects they were the lifeline of the communities on both sides of the channel because this was by far the cheapest and easiest way of shifting relatively large tonnages before the advent of the railways. The ships they used were more often than not built and rigged locally in such places as Bridgwater, Watchet, Bristol or the North Devon and Cornish ports by small ship-builders, or, further upstream by Chepstow, Lydney and Gloucestershire builders. Many seldom ventured out of the Channel although some of the larger vessels were quite capable of doing so and these often traded around Lands End to south coast ports, up the Welsh coast or across to Ireland.

Without doubt the major cargo was coal. Coal was required in large quantities throughout the south-western counties of England and South Wales had the mineral in abundance. There was of course plenty of coal in North Somerset and from 1874 the Somerset & Dorset Railway had tapped into that coalfield but the quantity that came south and west was nothing like that required to service both industry and domestic requirements. The only sensible way was to bring it across by ship. Thus Highbridge was assured one inbound cargo from the beginning.

The industrialisation of South Wales commenced during the latter part of the 18th century when iron-masters from the Midlands moved into the valleys of South Wales where they established iron works because coal was easily mined there and readily available for their furnaces. Initially the iron then had to be shipped across to Bristol from where it was exported, mainly to America. The opening of the Monmouthshire Canal down the Usk valley to Newport in 1794 connected the iron-producing areas with the Severn Estuary and cut out the problem of land transport.

A similar situation also existed at Merthyr Tydfil where yet more ironworks had been established and in 1798 the Glamorganshire Canal was opened connecting with the existing wharves at the mouth of the River Taff a little to the south of Cardiff. Further west still, the Swansea Canal was built to bring iron from the Swansea Valley to the coast.

Both the ironworks and collieries were worked on a relatively small scale to start with but this began to change with the advent of the railways. When they arrived they were able to move both iron and coal in far greater quantities out of the narrow valleys than hitherto which allowed for an expansion of the iron and steel industry whilst at the same time helping to quench the insatiable demand for coal which started to rise considerably as the steam era developed. South Wales was lucky in that its coalfield was noted for the abundance of good quality steam coal and this was very much in demand not only in this country but throughout the world.

Ship loading was at first primitive, with few quays and wharves available, but the Marquis of Bute, a Scottish laird, changed all that. He controlled much of the Rhondda, two valleys which were to provide some of the best coal and supporting up to 140,000 inhabitants in the string of little mining towns that grew up to service the industry, and which was connected by the Taff Vale Railway to the embryonic port of Cardiff. Realising the severe limitations of the riverside wharves the Marquis invested heavily in building new facilities, culminating in the opening of the Bute West Dock in 1839 followed by an East Dock, as trade increased, between 1855 and 1859. Thus provisioned, Cardiff was quickly established as the major coal exporting port in the area and over the next 80 years such a great market was established that this port along with the others had difficulty in keeping up with demand for much of this time.

One of the major problems identified at Cardiff was the constant delay caused by the inefficient ship loading system and congestion brought about by the

Although the volume of trade through Highbridge peaked in 1905 this view taken around 1910 shows just how busy the wharf could be. Nearest the camera is the Newport-owned brigantine **Livonia** *(1874/268nrt) with the Somerset & Dorset Railway's ship* **Alpha** *beyond. (Rod FitzHugh collection)*

Two Baltic traders, the brig **Gerda** *and the Swedish-flagged barquentine* **Lily of Oskarshamn**, *make a fine sight at Highbridge Wharf where they had come to discharge timber cargoes.*
(Craig/Farr collection)

*Judging by the timber on the wharfside these two ships were in port to discharge such cargoes to Bland's, the timber merchants. Nearest is the Scandinavian ship **Codø** whilst alongside her is an unidentified ketch-rigged Severn trow in ballast with her very descriptive 'D' shaped transom showing up well. This postcard view was one of several taken by local photographer Charlie Pearson at Highbridge and admirably shows the size of vessel which could be accommodated, a figure quoted as 750 tons burthen in* Kelly's Directory *for 1914. Further details of the* **Codø** *have proved difficult to find.* (S&DRT)

railway system but the Marquis of Bute, who by now monopolised the industry in the area, felt no great need to invest further despite the continuing complaints of shipowners and collieries. In 1880 over 4 million tons of the mineral were shipped through the port, rising to more than 6 million by 1887. Despite all this the collieries could have produced more and the shipowners would have taken more. Neither were happy at the situation.

The mining interests in the valleys of Gwent and East Glamorgan were largely controlled by Lord Plymouth and, fed up with the constant delays in the Taff Valley, he decided to bypass Cardiff and build a new port at Penarth. The Marquis of Bute invoked delaying tactics where the new railway had to cross the Taff Vale line but in the end the port was successfully established, the coal hoists and quays on the River Ely becoming a favoured pick-up point for coal destined for the coastal trade and one used frequently by the Somerset & Dorset ships.

As it turned out, the real threat to the Bute empire was not to be Penarth and Lord Plymouth but a Montgomery man by the name of David Davies. He sought permission to close the channel between Barry Island and the mainland, some nine miles west of Cardiff, and in the sheltered deep-waters he created two new docks which were opened in 1889 covering 73 acres and lined with the most advanced coal hoists then available. In 1890 Barry Docks were shipping out over 3 million tons of coal but by 1900 they were exporting a massive 7 million tons a year. At the same time Cardiff Docks were running into financial trouble. At this point the Marquis of Bute decided to sell his docks interests but because they were now too small for the larger generation of tramp steamers then in service he had no success and he was eventually forced to build the new 52-acre Queen Alexandra Dock to compete effectively; this opened in 1907.

South Wales reached its peak production in about 1913, with 4½ million tons being shipped from

*High summer at the Wharf. In this busy scene, taken on Tuesday 6 August 1929, there is much to see and a number of ships are being discharged including, in the foreground, the 373grt **Zillah** (ON 111365) of the Zillah Shipping & Carrying Co. Ltd., Liverpool. Completed in July 1901 she had a length of 143ft. (44m) and remained with the company until her sale in June 1943. To her right is the S&D's **Radstock** which is discharging a cargo of coal into some of the many open mineral wagons from the North Eastern and Great Western Railways as well as the parent LMSR. A boatman sculls himself across the harbour whilst two ketch-rigged sailing vessels, the furthest a Severn trow, remind us that the days of sail were not yet a thing of the past although by this time cargoes were getting difficult to obtain in the face of steamship competition. On the opposite shore another sailing vessel is definitely in a state of some distress. This is probably the ketch **Arthur** which arrived with a cargo of coal in 1926 and never sailed again! Our picture is completed by noting two small steam vessels beyond the trow, the inboard one being a tug, possibly the newly acquired **Rexford**, and just three visible cranes.*
(National Maritime Museum – G3677)

Penarth, 10½ million tons from Cardiff and 11 million from Barry. Added to all this, vast tonnages were also shipped out of Newport, Port Talbot and Swansea whilst there were numerous smaller ports such as Llanelli, Saundersfoot, and the Forest ports of Lydney and Bullo which added yet more, the latter providing an outlet for Forest of Dean coal which was of good quality and relatively cheap to produce. It is known that large quantities of coal were dispatched from this area to Highbridge and in 1864 it is on record that the 1809-built trow *William* from Gloucester frequently brought cargoes in from Bullo with 13 trips recorded between June and December alone.[1] Culm (anthracite or coal dust used for firing limekilns) was also imported in quantity and much of this was produced from Saundersfoot.

For all that, Cardiff, because of its early development by Bute and its links with the Rhondda, became recognised as the centre of the coal trade and as a measure of its importance there were still some 120 shipowners in the port in 1920, owning 1.5 million tons of shipping. To cater for the needs of the marine

WHARF HIGHBRIDGE

*When steam met sail – an atmospheric view of the Wharf taken during the early years of the 20th century. As several employees pose for the camera the S&D's cargo vessel **Alpha** is seen in her post-1905 rebuilt form with hatch covers open, derrick-topped and steam up. Alongside, a crew member stands in the ship's tender. Further along the quay a crane driver takes time off whilst unloading an open-moulded trow (note the high side sheeting on the little vessel) whilst a group of people are seen in the distance deep in conversation alongside a visiting barque. All five of the S&D's cranes at this end of the harbour are clearly visible behind which is an enormous amount of stacked timber lying unprotected in the open – if only the 1920s-built timber storage sheds had been there!*   (Author's collection)

*Moving to the early 1930s the lack of water emphasises just how the harbour dried out at low tide. By now the new large 3-ton crane had been installed alongside the three remaining older cranes. Nearest the camera the S&D's own **Radstock** has just completed discharging a cargo of coal. Further along the quay are two steam colliers belonging to A.J. Smith Ltd. of Bristol, the nearest being the **John** (141grt), built by J.T. Price at Neath Abbey as long ago as 1849, and an unidentified vessel which is probably the **Tanny** (1890/164grt) beyond. Further up the pill is a ketch, probably laid up awaiting a cargo, whilst in the foreground is an unrigged sailing vessel which on closer inspection looks to be in a very poor state, and a small unidentified tug. On the right-hand shore the breaking of the sailing vessel seen in the August 1929 view on page 79 is almost complete.*
(National Railway Museum – DY17316)

*This view of the wharf, taken around 1933, shows the 61-ton Bridgwater-registered ketch **Fanny Jane** (ON 10941), an excellent example of a Bridgwater-built Bristol Channel trading vessel. She was turned out of J. Gough's yard in 1858 and originally employed in the local brick and tile trade. Settling down to a long career trading out of Bridgwater under various owners she survived for an amazing 100 years under sail before being stripped of her rig to become a lighter in 1958.* *(Somerset Archaeological and Natural History Society)*

and dockland community the whole area south of the city had developed into Butetown and it was here where the Coal Exchange and shipowners' offices could be found. The core of the town was Bute Street which was probably better known as the infamous 'Tiger Bay', a degrading area of pubs, dance halls, lodging accommodation and, of course, brothels, all of which contrived to give Cardiff a terrible reputation in its time.

Coal from Cardiff was shipped, not only across to Somerset, Devon and Cornwall, but much further afield on ocean-going tramp steamers. The real importance of this to the local trade was that the ships returned to Cardiff and the other ports not only with iron ore for the local industry but also animal foodstuffs and grain from South American countries. These cargoes then had to be distributed throughout South Wales and the South West of England. Highbridge, like Bridgwater, played an important if relatively small part in this.

The decline in coal exports from South Wales started during the First World War when colliery companies quickly lost their world markets which were never won back. In the pits there had been much bitterness between the miners and coal owners over the conditions they were forced to work under. This animosity developed into long and very bitter strikes during the 1920s, culminating in the General Strike of 1926. Just when the shortage of coal was beginning to be felt most it chanced that the Bridgwater ketch *Arthur* (1876/62grt), inbound to her home port with a cargo of this scarce mineral, happened to go ashore on the Lark Spit between Stert Island and Burnham. The subsequent pounding badly damaged the vessel at which point a local opportunist bought the wreck from its owner, patched it up and managed to get it into Highbridge; the coal was off-loaded and sold at great profit. Unfit for sea and beyond economic repair the *Arthur* was subsequently scrapped.[2]

*With cargo discharge well under way the steamship **Bertha** (1906/1216grt) typifies the way in which the timber was stacked high above the main deck and held in place by numerous uprights. The ship was built in Newcastle as the **Ragnar** and became the **Ostanvik** before taking the name **Bertha** in 1932 by which time she was owned in Sweden by Rederi A/B Magnus Stenbock of Halsingborg.* *(Rod Fitzhugh collection)*

Whilst the strikes showed the determination of the miners to improve their conditions, ultimately their sacrifices were paid for dearly by the loss of the export coal market. By the late 1920s the effects were having visual consequences and in 1928 the original docks at Swansea closed, whilst in 1931 the Town Dock at Newport was closed and filled in although the two Alexandra Docks lower down the River Usk were still exporting coal. In 1938 Penarth Dock closed and was subsequently filled in; fuel oil was making a serious impact on the South Wales coal trade whilst foreign demand continued to drop as coal from elsewhere in the world became competitive, and eventually cheaper. By 1939 exports of the mineral from Cardiff had dropped to just 3 million tons annually. Despite the Second World War the decline in this traffic through the ports continued during the late 1940s and into the 1950s and 60s, finally all but terminating during the 1970s.

Not surprisingly coal imports into Highbridge mirrored the fortunes of the South Wales ports and had declined rapidly by the end of the Second World War but because of the quality of the Welsh steam coal a fair amount of that imported was specifically for use as 'Loco Coal' by the railways themselves and the S&D ships were greatly involved in this.[3] Other coal imports went to a variety of destinations in central southern England but overall Highbridge was not as big an importer as neighbouring Bridgwater whilst there were many other harbours and wharves providing for their respective local areas.

Much of the development of the coalfield was, of course, attributed to the iron industry, a product which was itself exported in large quantities and this, in the form of both iron and steel rail, was also brought in to Highbridge in huge quantities providing much of the staple import trade to the little harbour as will be seen.

Also of significance was the import of grain into Highbridge. It will have been noted that this was a common inbound cargo to Cardiff and other South Wales ports, and was also imported through Avonmouth and Bristol City Docks. Probably one of the best known names in the grain trade locally was that of Joel Spiller who founded his corn and flour merchants in 1829 at Bridgwater. When the new company wished to expand in the town their plans were blocked, so in the early 1850s they took an obvious course of action and opened a mill in Cardiff where they could produce 1,200 sacks of flour a week. Eventually they amalgamated with W. Proctor Baker in Bristol in 1894 to form Spiller & Baker Ltd, by which time they were also shipowners. Flour came into Highbridge regularly – as has been noted Messrs Feaver & Co. had a flour store at the wharf – often arriving in the S&D's own ships.

The other staple inbound traffic at Highbridge was timber, huge quantities of which were imported from the earliest days, most from Scandinavia in Baltic traders, including those from Russia, although occasionally from elsewhere, such as Canada. This formed an early example of trade being enticed from foreign ports and was to become important in keeping the local sawmill in business.

Exports from Highbridge where not so prolific and the regular cargoes were mainly confined to bricks, tiles, agricultural products (including cheese) and cattle. Much of the latter two went to South Wales but bricks and tiles could go much further afield. Somerset was, of course, a great producer of cheese but it still seems somewhat surprising to note that a local man, Mr. V. Hardacre, on moving to South Wales, found that the Caerphilly cheese he purchased there was actually made in Highbridge!

Highbridge Wharf

List of Tolls, circa 1856

Coal, Coke, Culm and Cinders:	
if sold at Highbridge	2d per ton
if carried on line	1d per ton
Charcoal	6d per ton
Timber	4d per ton
Iron	4d per ton
Bricks and tiles	4d per 1,000
Stone	1d per ton
Slate	4d per ton
Turf	6d per ton
Manure, bonedust and superphosphates of lime	6d per ton
Cheese	1/- per ton
Hay and Straw	6d per ton
Cider	6d per ton
Creosote	1/- per ton
Iron Ore	1d per ton
Fish	1d per basket
Apples and Pears	1d per basket
Salt	4d per ton
Butter	2d per cwt
Horses	1/- per head
Oxen and Cows	6d per head
Sheep and Pigs	1/- per score
Corn, Wheat, Barley, Oates, Peas and Beans	2d per quarter
Flour	1d per sack
Bark	6d per ton
Hides	1/- per ton
Malt	4d per quarter
Hops	1/- per pocket
Potatoes	$\frac{1}{2}$d per sack

To collect this revenue a tollkeeper was appointed, the first being George Wilton. At a rather later date the collector was a tall, white-haired gentleman called Joseph Lush who was also to become the harbourmaster as well as stationmaster of Burnham and Highbridge.

S&D Ship Services and Crewing

The principal reason for employing the Somerset & Dorset cargo vessels was to bring rail from the South Wales steel mills into Highbridge and they spent much of their year employed in this way. It was at times semi-seasonal in nature, no doubt brought about by the difficulties of sustaining large relaying programmes during the height of each winter.

Rail technology was still relatively new in the 1850s when the Somerset Central Railway was constructed but even by then the need for ever increasing weight and length to match the increasing loads imposed by heavier locomotives and rolling stock meant that 80lb/yd wrought-iron rail, usually between 15 and 20ft. in length, was already in use. By the mid-1870s, 85lb/yd bullhead rails were becoming common, steel, with its increased durability, having largely displaced wrought iron. Steel also allowed the mills to roll longer lengths of rail compared with wrought iron and by 1880 the London & South Western Railway had already standardised on 45ft. lengths. Around 1904 the weights had generally increased mostly to 95lb/yd for main-line work. Bullhead section remained the most common on the S&D.

Rails were brought over from South Wales from the earliest days of the Somerset Central Railway and, as has been noted in Chapter 5, Rigby's, the contractors, even rented wharfage from the company at Highbridge as a depot which they continued to use to service the various contracts they won for the subsequent extensions of the line to Burnham, Wells and Cole. It was probably no coincidence that Sir Ivor Guest of Canford Manor, near Wimborne, who became a director of the Dorset Central Railway, was the son of Dowlais (Merthyr Tydfil) ironmaster, Sir John Guest. Dowlais rails were to become an important traffic through Highbridge in the years to come. In a routine report to the Chairman and Directors of the railway in August 1858, relating to works progress on the Wells extension, the line's engineer, Charles Gregory, had stated that 600 tons of rail and some 30,000 cubic feet of timber had arrived, either actually at the works site or at the wharf at Highbridge. Rigby's did not finish their construction work on the Cole extension until 1862 so it is reasonable to speculate that they continued to import rail throughout this period.

*The **Elemore** (165grt) was another small steam collier which belonged to Bristol-based A.J. Smith Ltd. She is seen completing the discharge of her cargo of coal alongside the wharf. Built by Livingstone & Cooper of Hessle in 1915 the ship came into the ownership of Smith's in 1937 and survived until 1952.* (Rod Fitzhugh collection)

E.R.O. 57387
S. & D. 289

Southern and London Midland and Scottish Railway Companies.
SOMERSET AND DORSET RAILWAY JOINT COMMITTEE.

Highbridge Wharf   **19**

Turn out of the Cargo of Ship

from the Port of

($\frac{1}{20}$)   Signed, _____

WEIGHER.

Truck Numbers.	Weight of Coals—net.	Description.	Station sent.	To whom Consigned.

Mr.

When a ship's cargo was discharged at Highbridge full details were recorded of everything that was forwarded by rail on S&D Form No.289.

It was as late as December 1873 before the S&DR finally decided to enter cargo ship owning, when it finalised the acquisition of the three ketches. All three were purchased with the movement of rail in mind although even then this particular cargo would have been a difficult one to handle given the characteristically small hatches of ships of the period. However there must have been an economic case for using their own tonnage rather than that of other owners and most significantly these vessels were brought into company ownership in time for the final building of the ex-

pensive 26-mile long Bath Extension from Evercreech over the Mendip Hills which opened during the following year. No doubt they contributed to this.

These first ships were adapted for the task and extra tonnage was chartered to cope with the demand during 1875/6, but as the mills produced longer and longer rails the ketches were no longer suitable, whilst the little steamship *Alpha*, purchased in 1879, had to be lengthened twice to cope with them. Although the surviving ketch, *Julia (1)* (the other two were both lost in 1886) traded until 1904 she must have been woefully inadequate for the rail trade by then. Both the *Julia (2)* of 1904 and the *Radstock* of 1925 were built especially with this trade in mind and both had holds of 50ft.(15.4m) in length, with hatches of 36ft.9in.(11.3m) and 39ft.(12m) long respectively.

Rails were brought over both for the S&D and the LSWR and when not imported through Highbridge the S&D ships could be seen going in to the LSW's own railway wharf at Fremington on the River Taw. Those brought into Highbridge were usually off-loaded directly onto S&DJR bolster wagons (originally dumb-buffered single-bolster but later bogie-bolster wagons) which were built primarily for this task. Those not destined for the S&D were taken to Templecombe for onward conveyance by the LSWR (later Southern Railway).[4]

At other times the ships were frequently used to bring iron over from the South Wales ports, again mainly into Highbridge but occasionally they would go further afield to pick up a cargo of stone, typically visiting both Porthgain in West Wales and Porthoustock on the south coast of Cornwall. They were also occasionally used for local coastal tramping so it was not particularly unusual to see a variety of other merchandise in their holds, usually simply described as 'general cargo'.

Crewing of the ships varied considerably depending upon their type. Ketches were generally built to carry four; master, mate and two deckhands although latterly they often dispensed with one of the deckhands to keep running costs to a minimum. The steamships normally carried a crew of six; the master, mate, engineer, fireman and two deckhands. The masters fell into two groups: those who had worked their way up in the employment of the S&D and who had been with the company for a number of years and those who had been engaged from other local trades in the channel. In all cases they were extremely experienced in the difficulties of the area in which they had to operate.

The ships all operated within the 'Home Trade limits' (i.e. between the River Elbe in the east and Brest in the west) and this simplified crewing arrangements. Life on a small coaster was certainly not easy

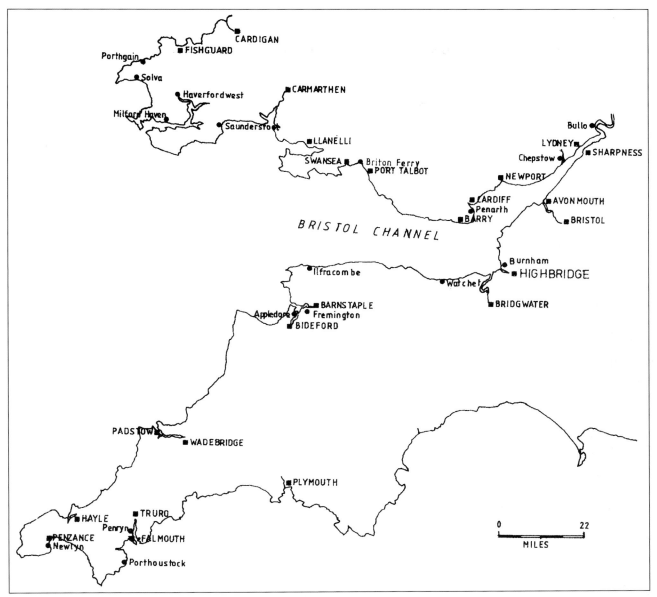

The principal ports of South Wales and South West England, most of which saw visits by S&D ships either on a regular or occasional basis.

and the crews were worked hard if they were to keep their job. Security in the job was minimal although crew members preferred working for a company like the S&D than a tramping company because the ships were operated largely in a permanent trade and did not rely on cargoes being fixed around the coast with the consequent risk of being paid-off at a moment's notice if the ship failed to find a cargo or became inactive for any other reason.

Officers had few real privileges although the master, mate and engineer would often be retained on the company payroll if the ship became inactive such as when docking down had to be carried out for a survey.

All were working hands during the normal day-to-day operation of the vessel along with their crew members. The seamen and firemen were 'signed on' when needed but just as easily 'signed off' if there was no work.

Mates normally held a certificate of competency with masters gaining an additional certificate although in the years before 1854 this was not an essential requirement if the ship was engaged in the home trade. Many of the local masters and mates worked their way up from seamen rather than through deck apprenticeships and were extremely well qualified by experience alone. The engineers were also certificated but again this had not always been a requirement. Likewise

Typical S&D Cargo Ship movements at Highbridge, 1912

1912, a year taken at random, was typical of a normal year in the life of the two S&D cargo vessels, the *Alpha* and *Julia (2)* on station at the time. In addition to their usual runs, during March and April both ships found time to bring rails over to the LSW wharf at Fremington on the river Taw whilst on 24 March the *Alpha* unusually took a cargo of scrap iron out of Highbridge bound for Newport. On 8 April the *Julia* arrived at Highbridge with a cargo of stone from the little harbour of Porthgain out in West Wales. However their daily bread-and-butter work mainly consisted of bringing in cargoes of rails, iron and coal from a variety of South Wales ports, their typical routine for a sample two-month period in that year being listed below:

Su	Aug 25	JULIA to Swansea in ballast
M	Aug 26	ALPHA to Saundersfoot in ballast
Tu	Aug 27	ALPHA from Saundersfoot with coal. JULIA from Swansea with coal.
W	Aug 28	ALPHA to Newport in ballast. JULIA to Newport in ballast.
Th	Aug 29	JULIA from Newport with iron. ALPHA from Newport with coal.
F	Aug 30	ALPHA to Newport in ballast.
S	Aug 31	
Su	Sept 1	ALPHA from Newport with iron. JULIA to Newport in ballast.
M	Sept 2	ALPHA to Newport in ballast
Tu	Sept 3	JULIA from Newport with general cargo.
W	Sept 4	JULIA to Newport in ballast
Th	Sept 5	
F	Sept 6	
S	Sept 7	JULIA from Newport with rails
Su	Sept 8	
M	Sept 9	
Tu	Sept 10	JULIA to Newport in ballast
W	Sept 11	JULIA from Newport with general cargo. JULIA to Newport in ballast.
Th	Sept 12	
F	Sept 13	ALPHA from Swansea with coal. ALPHA to Newport in ballast. JULIA from Newport with rails
S	Sept 14	ALPHA from Newport with rails
Su	Sept 15	
M	Sept 16	JULIA to Newport in ballast
Tu	Sept 17	JULIA from Newport with rails. ALPHA to Newport in ballast.
W	Sept 18	ALPHA from Newport with rails. JULIA to Newport in ballast.
Th	Sept 19	
F	Sept 20	ALPHA to Cardiff in ballast (thence to Briton Ferry)
S	Sept 21	
Su	Sept 22	
M	Sept 23	
Tu	Sept 24	JULIA from Newport with coal and rails.
W	Sept 25	JULIA to Newport in ballast
Th	Sept 26	ALPHA from Briton Ferry with coal. ALPHA to Newport in ballast
F	Sept 27	JULIA from Newport with iron. JULIA to Newport in ballast.
S	Sept 28	ALPHA from Newport with coal and rails.
Su	Sept 29	
M	Sept 30	
Tu	Oct 1	
W	Oct 2	ALPHA to Newport in ballast.
Th	Oct 3	JULIA from Newport with coal.
F	Oct 4	ALPHA from Newport with coal. JULIA to Cardiff in ballast.
S	Oct 5	
Su	Oct 6	
M	Oct 7	ALPHA to Newport in ballast
Tu	Oct 8	
W	Oct 9	
Th	Oct 10	ALPHA from Newport with iron. JULIA from Newport with iron.
F	Oct 11	ALPHA to Porthoustock (Cornwall) in ballast
S	Oct 12	
Su	Oct 13	JULIA to Newport in ballast
M	Oct 14	ALPHA from Porthoustock (Cornwall) with stone. ALPHA to Newport in ballast.
Tu	Oct 15	JULIA from Newport with iron.
W	Oct 16	ALPHA from Newport with coal. JULIA to Newport in ballast.
Th	Oct 17	JULIA from Newport with coal and iron. ALPHA to Newport in ballast.

This busy pattern of operation continued to the year's end with, typically, the *Alpha* arriving from Saundersfoot with coal on 20 November and from Cardiff with coal and rails on 13 December, whilst the *Julia* went to Barry in ballast on 22 November and to Briton Ferry (Neath) for coal on 8 December.

many had worked their way up from fireman and had gained their practical engineering experience 'on the shovel' rather than through a formal apprenticeship.[5]

At sea the crews of the *Julia (2)* and *Radstock* could if necessary be split into two four-hour watches of three but because the ships were not generally tramping and mainly only engaged in local trips across the channel it was more usual to operate them without going into a formal watch system. The local nature of the voyages also meant that crew members could see something of their families whilst at Highbridge between voyages, a distinctly more palatable arrangement for them than most who were engaged in a life at sea. As soon as the ship arrived in port all hands were engaged in opening up the hatch covers and removing the beams in preparation for unloading. At Highbridge the company employed its own cranage and labour, greatly helping the crew who would otherwise have to man the derrick winch. Once the hold was cleaned out, the beams and hatch covers were replaced in readiness for sailing and the crew would go back into watches if required. No overtime was normally paid for work in port.

Sam Evans was typical of one of the long-standing employees of the S&DJR and was a regular crew member of the *Radstock* for many years. He began his working life in the locomotive department at Highbridge shed in May 1917, moving to Wells locomotive depot before transferring to Templecombe shed as a fireman in 1924. There he might have stayed, eventually being promoted to driver, had the *Alpha* not paid off together with its crew during July 1925. A new crew was signed on for the *Radstock* and Sam was one of two who applied for the post of fireman, starting work on the new vessel in September 1925. Then under the command of Captain William D. Sharman, there was also a mate, an engineer (William Winter from the *Alpha*), Able Seaman William Hill and one other.

Sam recounted that the crew would normally report for work one hour before high water time with the exception of the engineer who would have arrived on board before the rest to check the water tank and light up the boiler to raise steam. Although the fresh water carried was adequate for most trips, water could be taken at any of the ports visited.

Sailing from Highbridge the *Radstock* was normally in ballast. Delays were frequent because of the need to wait for tides in order to get into the various ports, docks or up rivers. These waits often allowed the crew to get their heads down for an hour or two.

When loaded, the ships would sail as soon as possible but again they often had to wait for the tide. Bad weather could cause difficulties and gales would almost always ensure that they would run for the nearest port and shelter. When travelling in ballast the discomfort was, of course, worse. Indeed Sam recalled an occasion when they were stuck in Newlyn harbour (near Penzance) on the *Radstock* for four or five days. One or two passengers were also sometimes carried – or more correctly given a lift – particularly between the nearest South Wales ports and Highbridge; a small if probably unofficial residue, perhaps, of the former Cardiff-Burnham ferry service![6]

One of the earliest company masters was Captain Ezekiel Lovering Barron who took over the *Ruby* from Captain David George during 1861. Barron was born in Ilfracombe in 1819 and was an experienced Bristol Channel mariner when he was engaged by the railway. His first command was the *Goddess* (ON23401) from 1855 to 1857, but between then and 1860 he was master of the 1857-built, 303-ton steamship *Clifton* (ON18580) of Bristol. It was, however, to be his unfortunate experience to be involved in the mishap of the *Ruby* in August 1863 (see Chapter 8). No blame was attached to him and he was destined to go on to have a lengthy career with the Somerset & Dorset Railway in its passenger fleet moving firstly to become master of the *Defiance*, then the *George Reed*, followed by a very brief spell in the *Heather Bell* before returning to his old command, the *Defiance*. Barron stayed in that ship until July 1871 when the company withdrew from the ownership of passenger vessels and reluctantly severed his employment. After a gap of nearly 13 years, following the reintroduction of passenger services with the *Sherbro*, Captain Barron was quickly back in the employ of the S&D as master until her eventual sale in 1888.

A contemporary of Barron was Captain William Densham, born in 1815 and a native of Barnstaple. He became mate of the *Robert Bright* in 1856 followed by the *Pioneer* (ON14364) in 1857 before joining Barron as his mate in the *Clifton* in the same year. The two stayed together until Barron relinquished his command in 1860 and Densham took over. Remaining as master until 1864 he then joined the S&D where he teamed up with his former colleague again. Thereafter he commanded the *Defiance*, *Heather Bell* and *George Reed* between 1864 and 1868, in turn with Barron.

Many crew members spent only short periods in the ships but, equally, a number gave many loyal years of service to the company. One such was James Farthing who joined the *Heather Bell* as a seaman in his late twenties and rose through the ranks to become master of both the ketches *Julia* and *Railway*. Edward Fletcher was another who saw service in no less than six of the S&D's ships and who also commanded several vessels including the steamers *Leopard*, *Alpha*, and *Julia*.

The steamship **Royal Firth** (411grt) was typical of the small coasters which used the port. Built in 1921 and owned by the Border Shipping Co. Ltd. (G.T. Gillie & Blair Ltd., managers) of Newcastle, she was designed with one long hatch and frequently found profitable cargoes of machinery, boilers and long lengths of steel which made her particularly useful for carrying rails, one of which can be seen being lifted out of the hold (left and above) at the western end of the Wharf. The sequence of photographs recording the unloading of the **Royal Firth** date from the mid-1930s after the S&D had withdrawn its own ships in this trade. The ship's tender has been slung outboard using one of the two derricks, a common solution when the vessel's own lifting facilities were not needed as the boat normally resided on the hatch cover during passage. A closer view of the unloading operation (below) shows the rails being stacked onto the adjacent bogie bolster wagons.
(above and left: National Railway Museum – DY17219 & DY17220; below: Author's collection)

High tide at the Wharf and Albert Buncombe's tug Rexford is moored alongside the crane road during a slack period. For many years the helmsman had been open to the elements but the little vessel was eventually fitted with a wheelhouse. (S&DRT)

Towage Dues between Burnham and Highbridge 1900-10 period

Towage dues were laid down by the Bridgwater Port & Navigation Committee. Those applicable to Burnham and Highbridge were listed (in old pence) as follows:

To or from Burnham and Highbridge, one tide's work:

Vessels under 10ft. draft water per ton	2d
Vessels under 11ft. draft water per ton	3d
Vessels under 12ft. draft water per ton	4d
Vessels above 12ft. draft water per ton	5d

Steam Tug *Rexford*

Official Number:	145752
Type:	Screw Tug
Construction:	Iron
Tonnage:	60grt/9nrt
Completed:	1895 by Millbay Docks, Plymouth
Engine:	Steam, 40 nhp
Length:	70.2ft. between posts
Beam:	15.8ft.
Depth:	7.5ft.

Although built in 1895 this tug was not registered as the *Rexford* until 1922, the owner being stated in 1929 as H.J. Pulsford of Poole. A reference that she was sold on 3 August 1933 to a Shanghai owner could not possibly have succeeded and it would seem more likely that she came to Highbridge in 1929, by this time under the ownership of Albert E. Buncombe who was also an S&D employee at the Wharf and one-time head stevedore. In 1940 the tug was still in his ownership but remained registered at Poole*.

It is interesting to note that there were no known resident tugs at Highbridge before this vessel during the time when sailing ships, often of quite large tonnages, had to make the difficult passage up the Brue so they had to call for assistance from a Bridgwater operator if required. However with the advent of larger screw steamships and the absence of sails, manoeuvrability would have been difficult. Never owned by the S&DJR the company seemed to enjoy almost exclusive use of the *Rexford* for mud dragging as well as for towage duties although the vessel also towed ships up to Dunball and beyond when required. The little vessel was finally towed away herself for scrapping in January 1950.

* Source: Mercantile Navy Lists.

Born in 1862 Charles Rawlings spent most of his seagoing career in the employment of the S&D, initially in sail before rising to command the steamers *Alpha* and *Julia*, retirement coming in 1928 after more than 33 years with the company. Typical of the close-knit family reputation of the S&D, his son Charlie (Jnr.) was also an employee who by the 1930s was one of the locomotive drivers at Radstock.[7] Albert Guy, Benjamin Huckman, Alfred Hunt and John Hutchings are among a number of others who all had long careers with the company culminating in commands whilst mention must be made of the extraordinary number of Winters who appear in the company books. More than a dozen were involved, almost all employed as firemen of which at least six were promoted to engineers within the fleet of steamships over the years.

Arguably one of the best known S&D employees at Highbridge was Henry Dare Luxon. Born in 1853 he was just 13½ when he joined the S&D as a deckhand in 1866. His long sea-going career started on the day that Captain Barron arrived with the new steamer *George Reed*. This ship did not stay long on the Burnham-Cardiff station but the young Henry

Luxon followed his captain on to the *Heather Bell* before they both transferred to the *Defiance* where surprisingly the young lad had a spell as a steward! Presumably this was the only vacancy at the time but one can only surmise that it did not suit him because by 1870 he had re-engaged on the ship as a seaman in which role he stayed until its sale in 1871 when his employment was terminated.

Seeking further work, Luxon left the S&DR and between 1871 and 1874 he served in a barque, the *Margaret Ann*, sailing from Plymouth to the Cape Verde Islands and Gulf of Mexico, returning to Cardiff. His next trip was in the *Jesse Boyle* from Cardiff to the West Indies. After this he served in steamships trading in the Mediterranean and Black Seas. In 1874 he joined the local schooner *Taunton Packet*, owned by Captain Henry Press of Burnham.

In 1875 and with some valuable deep-sea experience both in sail and steamships, he rejoined the Somerset & Dorset Railway and became a crew member of the *Leopard*. Over the years following he also saw service as a seaman in two of the company's ketches, the *Richard and Emily* and the *Railway*.

The Ramsey-registered 90-gross ton steam coaster *Staffa* was built as the *Nellie* at Irvine by J.H. Gilmour in 1892 and was originally in the ownership of McKinney & Rafferty of Glasgow followed by a long period with David McBrayne before taking her new name in 1925 and passing to Osman J.N. Enyon of Angle, Pemrokeshire to whom she belonged when photographed at Highbridge on Monday 29 March 1937.　　　　(Keen Collection, Bristol Industrial Museum)

*The steamship **Forshult** heads into the River Brue around 1936. Out of sight on her starboard quarter (save for a wisp of smoke above the bows) the tug **Rexford** had her firmly under control. Built in 1918 by Eriksbergs M.V. Aktieb at Gothenburg, the 658-gross ton coaster was owned by Uddeholms Aktieb (F. Olsson, managers) of Uddeholm, Sweden. The **Forshult** was a regular visitor to Highbridge. In the photograph below she has taken the ground whilst unloading proceeds at the Wharf but this is a much earlier view of the 1918-built ship and was taken during the early 1920s. Throughout her long life she remained under her original owners and survived until 1949.* *(above: S&DRT; below: Author's collection)*

In 1876, at the young age of just 23, he achieved his first command as master of the **Railway**, a job which lasted for two years. In 1880 he took over the **Richard and Emily**, then in 1883 he transferred to his first steamship, the **Alpha**, remaining with her until 1904 when he was sent by the company to Southampton to take delivery and command of the new steamship **Julia**, on which vessel he remained until he was badly injured in an unfortunate accident at Highbridge Wharf in July 1915. Then aged 62 he never fully recovered and died in July 1916 leaving a widow and family of nine children, four of whom also worked for the S&D (as did his seaman brother Walter). In his long trouble-free career Henry Luxon had the distinction of serving on eight of the twelve ships in the fleet, more than any other employee.

Captain William David Sharman came from a long line of Bridgwater mariners and was one of several experienced local seafarers who came to the Somerset and Dorset late in life when he took over the command of the steamship **Julia** from Captain Edward Fletcher in 1922. Born in the early 1860s Captain Sharman had served in many local sailing vessels and was well-known in the area. By 1889 he had already taken

command of the smack **Henry** and followed that with the **Cygnet** (1891-2), the schooner **Ermenilda** (1892-4), **Rolla** (1896-7 and 1902-3), the schooner **Octavius** from 1899 to 1901 and the ketch **Florrie** from 1904 until 1912 amongst others. From the **Julia** he transferred to the **Radstock** as master to complete his long career only retiring when he reached the age of 70.

Another well-known local figure was William Henry Morse who hailed from Watchet. Born in 1877 he was on the Watchet schooner **Josephine and Marie** as an ordinary seaman by the time he was 15, moving to the ketch **Lizzie**, before being promoted to mate of the schooner **Aurora** between 1896 and 1898. By 1906 he was master of the schooner **Coronella**, a post he retained until 1913 before making the transition to steam. For many years thereafter he commanded the little steamship **The Karrier** which was owned by a local syndicate, the Watchet Trading Company. Captain Morse's regular work was to carry local farm produce and general cargo mainly to the Welsh ports, returning with cargoes of coal. In 1924 **The Karrier** was sold and he next turns up at Highbridge in the employment of the S&DJR where he succeeded Captain Bill Sharman as the master of the **Radstock** in 1929/30.

*The sale of the **Radstock** by the S&DJR in 1933 was far from the end of the vessel's association with Highbridge. Under her owner/master, Captain W.H. Morse, the little ship was often to be seen at the familiar wharf where she was photographed on 29 March 1937 with the steam coaster **Staffa**.* *(Keen Collection, Bristol Industrial Museum)*

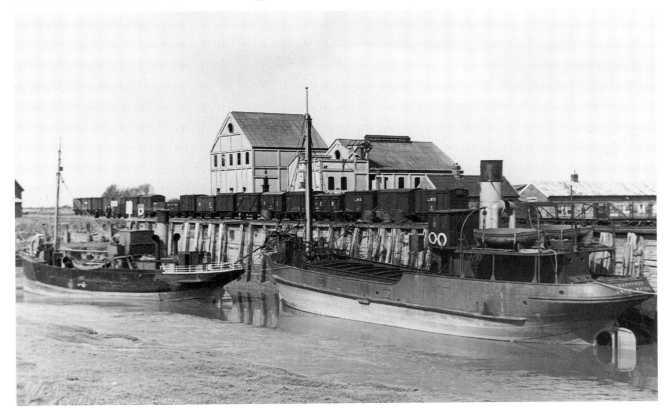

*Deals, battens and boards – loose sawn timber, often pine or fir, was regularly consigned into Highbridge, stacked high on the decks of the Scandinavian ships engaged in this trade. In today's pre-packaged era such sights as this have long since gone but in this view the Norwegian-flagged **Primula** (1918/1,024grt) of Oslo is photographed as she passes up the Brue on 2 July 1939 with one such cargo from the Baltic. Built by de Haan & Oerlemans of Heusden she was owned through the 1930s by Skibs A/S Boss and managed by Wahl & Co.*   *(Craig/Farr collection)*

In 1933, following the decision of the S&DJR to dispose of its small shipping fleet, Captain Morse found himself in the unusual but ideal position to purchase the **Radstock** and become what was then commonly an owner/master. No longer employed by the railway, he returned complete with the ship to his native Watchet where he continued to trade the vessel successfully (often back into Highbridge) for some years until the Second World War intervened. Bill Morse remained the owner until the middle of 1942. For her crew, the sale of the **Radstock** by the S&DRT in early 1933 was a sad day as they had stayed together since the vessel had been delivered new in 1925. Sam Evans, the fireman, was one of the luckier ones. Transferred ashore, he was given a job back on the railway but employment was difficult in this period and the only vacancy for him was as a platelayer, a far cry from his original footplate job at Templecombe.

Notes:

1. For a detailed account of the trow **William** see Colin Green, *Severn Traders*, pp.11-15.
2. Slade, W.J. and Greenhill, B., *Westcountry Coasting Ketches*, p.68.
3. The quality of Welsh steam coal, much of which came from the Rhondda Valley, is well known and was in great demand in the railway industry. Although it can take a long time to ignite and combust it will then glow brightly to radiate intense heat over a long period unlike many house coals which burn rapidly. North Somerset coal was not entirely suitable for locomotive use although it was known to have been used by the S&D, particularly at Radstock and Templecombe sheds.
4. G.H. Wheeler, 'Somerset & Dorset Joint Railway', *Southern Railway Magazine*, 6/29.
5. Examinations of competency for prospective masters and mates were made compulsory by the Mercantile Marine Act of 1850 (effective 1851) and extended to the home trade under the Merchant Shipping Act of 1854. Exemptions were made for those already employed in those capacities before 1 January 1851.
6. Sam Evans originally recalled his memories to the S&DRT orally in 1984. Readers are referred to the tape 'Somerset & Dorset Memories' Vol.2 – Conversations on 'The Branch' and 'Shipping'.
7. Handley, C., *Radstock Coal & Steam*, Vol.2, p.87.

7 Bridgwater Wharf

Somewhat ironically, in view of all the fuss Bridgwater Corporation made when it objected to Burnham pier, a third sea outlet was established by the S&D just below the town docks in Bridgwater itself where a wharf was constructed on the east bank of the tidal River Parrett.

The Bridgwater Railway, a seven-mile branch which connected with the S&D's Highbridge-Evercreech Junction line at Edington Junction, was an independent company somewhat late into the railway business. It was originally intended that the LSWR should operate the line but during the two-year period between signing the contract and opening, the S&DJR took on the dubious task on behalf of the LSWR because it was geographically more convenient. The branch was inspected in early July 1890 and opened with due ceremony on 21st of that month, the Bridgwater Railway Company remaining independent until purchased by the LSWR in 1921 as a preamble to the creation of the 'Big Four' in the grouping of 1923. For all general purposes the line was always considered to be an integral part of the S&DJR's system.

The branch ended in a modest two-platform terminal station on the northern side of Bridgwater, parallel but some distance to the east of the River Parrett from which it was separated by an area known as Castle Field. The terminus was equipped with a small goods yard, engine shed and turntable together with the usual facilities such as cattle pens, goods shed and crane. There was no connection at that time with the GWR Docks branch which ran from the West of England main line (formerly the Bristol & Exeter Railway) at right angles and immediately to the south of station and yard. This line ran across the river via a telescopic drawbridge to Bridgwater Dock.

The wharf branch left Bridgwater (later renamed Bridgwater North) station yard by one of the sidings which was extended to The Leggar, a road crossing, before turning progressively through almost 180 degrees in a broad curve. In the process there was a lengthy loop before a short siding branched off to serve

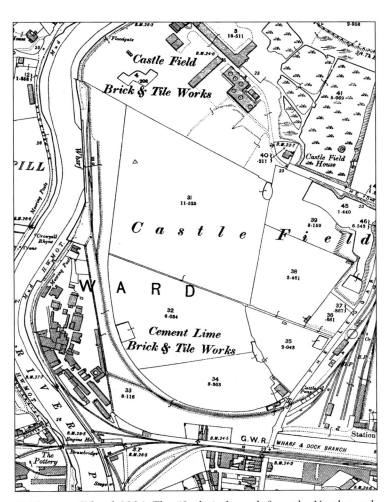

Bridgwater Wharf, 1904. The 48-chain branch from the North goods yard and station, which swung through nearly 180 degrees around Castle Field, can clearly be seen connecting with the railway's wharf on the bank of the River Parrett. There is no evidence to suggest that this wharf, which opened with the Bridgwater branch in 1890, was ever very busy in its relatively short life; by 1912 it had been abandoned by the S&DJR although the track remained in use for the storage of wagons until 1942. The wharf was a little downstream (i.e. north of) and opposite Bridgwater Dock which was served by the GWR Wharf and Dock branch seen at the bottom of the map. There was no physical connection between the two lines despite their close proximity. (OS 50.11, 2nd Edition 1904, by permission of the British Library)

the riverside cement works and brickyard of Barham Brothers Ltd.[1] The line continued for a short distance beyond the works to terminate at the 400ft.-long (123m) wooden wharf which was set into the riverside mud banks. The total length of the wharf branch was 48 chains.

*Almost the total length of the Somerset & Dorset wharf can be seen in this view together with the two cranes and the grounded coach body which was probably used by the railway's wharf staff. Judging by the lack of railway wagons the wharf is not doing much rail trade at this time. Taken from Saltlands on the west bank of the river a number of the distinctive kilns can be seen in the distance to emphasise the one-time importance of the brick and tile industry to the Bridgwater economy. The two vessels at the wharf both belonged to local coal merchant George Bryant & Sons and both were constructed at Brinscombe in Gloucestershire. The 1827-built trow **Palace** (ON 10887, 43 tons net) is on the left and the 1823-built ketch **Stroud Packet** (ON 11658, 45 tons net) is on the right. Both are light and with side covers on the trow and hatch covers on the ketch in place it would suggest that they are just waiting for the next tide to sail.*

(Rod Fitzhugh collection)

As constructed, there were two tracks on the wharf itself, forming a run-round loop, together with a separate siding a little inshore. Finally there was a crane road. The wharf rails appear to have been fastened to a concrete base on longitudinal sleepers.

The branch line, including the wharf extension, had been built by Messrs. Catbull, Son and de Lungo of London who had used local suppliers for bricks, cement and lime whilst the timber for the wharf itself was provided by none other than Messrs. Bland & Co. of Highbridge. In the report on the official inspection of the line which appeared in the 9 July 1890 edition of the *Bridgwater Mercury* it was stated that:

Communication with the riverside is afforded by a siding running down to a substantial timber wharf situated on the foreshore of Castle Field, between Messrs. Barham Bros. cement works and Messrs. Colthurst, Symons & Co's brickyard, the river being thus 'tapped' below the docks and the communication works of the Great Western Railway Company.'

Responsibility for the wharf extension was entrusted to the stationmaster at Bridgwater, Mr. H. Hawkins, who came from the S&D at Shepton Mallet to take over this job. The wharf itself was under the supervision of a company wharfmaster whose red-brick dwelling stood nearby. Apart from the weigh-house there was for many years a grounded coach body at the southern end which may have been used as a rest room for the crane drivers and staff.

The wharf was known to have handled coal, culm and timber amongst other imports and was used by a number of trading vessels which regularly used the River Parrett including the ketch-rigged vessel **Stroud Packet** and the Severn trow **Palace**, both of which were owned by the local Bridgwater coal merchants, George Bryant & Sons. Another ketch recorded at the wharf in 1907 was the **Irene**, the very last vessel of its type to be constructed in Bridgwater in that same year. Evidence of ships of the parent S&D fleet using the wharf are not so readily available and whilst there is a photo of the **Alpha** stuck in ice in mid-stream in this area it was taken before the wharf had been completed.

Despite its relatively young age, a few years later when urgent repairs were required to the wharf, a decision was made to shorten the usable length and abandon the rest. In consequence 255ft.(78.5m) were no longer used from 1909 and the area fenced off. By 1912 the remainder was in such poor condition that the Joint Committee decided, after discussions with the Bridgwater Railway and the Bridgwater Navigation Trustees, to remove the entire structure and replace it with mooring posts on the understanding that if future traffic necessitated, a wharf would be reinstated. Although it was unlikely that it was used after this time there doesn't seem to have been any particular hurry on the part of the S&D to carry out the job, at least not in its entirety, and by 1929 only the northern part had actually been demolished, which was still the case in 1953.[2] As a result the sidings onto it were only shortened. However, the branch as a whole (which according to a former railway guard on the line once saw as many as 45 wagons shunted over it daily) fell into disuse. The wharfmaster's house remained in use by the railway until the 1920s (and continued in habitation for many years thereafter).

Two similar travelling steam cranes were provided. They ran on their own track in much the same way as those at Highbridge. Built by Thomas Smith of Rodley, near Leeds, both were primitive affairs with no cab protection for the operator. When the wharf was cut back in length in 1909, one was transferred to High-bridge where one of its first tasks was to help with the replacement of the outer doors of the sea lock. The fate of the other one is not known although it would not have lasted much longer than 1912. Meanwhile the wharf weighing machine was soon found to be inconveniently placed and it was transferred back into Bridgwater North yard.

Latterly the branch was used to store wagons but in 1942, as part of the drive to recover redundant materials for the war effort, the rails over the last 26 chains were lifted and salvaged. The remaining track survived until as late as 1964. So ended yet another characteristic venture – clearly the wharf did not handle much trade, although it was equipped well enough, and it was always the cinderella of the S&D marine services.

Notes:

1. Barham Brothers brick and tile works had its own rail-served wharf a little upstream from the S&D's but this was connected to the GWR Docks branch.
2. The truncated remains of the wharf are shown on the 1929 Ordnance Survey which is backed up by photographic evidence dating into the 1950s. This still shows about half of the wharf *in situ*. All trace has now been lost.

One of the two identical steam cranes provided at the S&D's wharf at Bridgwater was this Thomas Smith-built example from their crane works in Rodley, near Leeds. The crane ran along its own dedicated track the length of the 400ft.(123m) quay which was situated between Barham's brickyard and Colthurst Symon's premises. Behind the crane is the river, with the houses in Chilton Street, Crowpill, visible through the trees. In 1909 the wharf was cut back to just 145 feet (44.6m) when the remainder was taken out of use as unsafe, but by 1912 even this had been abandoned. One of the two cranes was transferred to Highbridge in 1909 for further use.
(National Railway Museum – DY8515)

The 400ft.(123m)-long S&D wharf at Bridgwater. A number of open mineral wagons sit on the adjacent sidings, some loaded, together with a couple of four-wheeled bolster wagons with timber, whilst one of the two steam cranes rests with protective tarpaulin over it. Moored alongside is the last Bridgwater-built ketch, **Irene**, *completed by F.J. Carver & Son Ltd. and later used in the local brick trade. The 98 gross/78 net ton vessel (ON 111394) has staging below her bowsprit and it is thought that the ship is seen towards the end of her fitting out following her launch on 5 June 1907. The* **Irene** *became the last ketch to trade in UK waters, continuing until 1960, following which she was preserved. (Rod Fitzhugh collection)*

It is hard to imagine that Bridgwater was such a busy and important port for so many years looking at this view of the deserted River Parrett on 27 May 1996. Taken from the entrance to the dock tidal basin towards Castle Field, absolutely no trace of the substantial S&D wharf remains but it was situated on the far bank in front of the modern industrial buildings. By 1965 virtually all seagoing traffic had ceased on this part of the river, the dock formally closing on 31 July 1971. (Chris Handley)

*This aerial view of Bridgwater dates from August 1953 when the port was in serious decline. By this time the S&D's Bridgwater branch had been abandoned but the North station, centre left, remained in use for goods traffic having been connected to the Great Western's branch which runs prominently across the telescopic bridge towards the dock, lower right. Although the S&D's wharf branch had long since been disused, the outline of the 180-degree turn that it made around Castle Field from the station to the wharf on the bank of the Parrett can still be made out. Close scrutiny reveals that the track is still in situ to a point next to the double-gabled factory unit just above the extensive premises of Barham Brothers' brick and tile works. Despite stating that the wharf would be removed after 1912 no serious attempt was made by the S&D to do this and the remains can still clearly be seen on the lower left of the photo. Alfred Peace's little steam coaster **Parret** (sic, 1915/120grt) waits in the tidal basin whilst another ship clears, with the extensive coal yard of Sully & Co. above the vessel, but otherwise there is precious little shipping about in the dock and nothing at all at the town quays, this being the last year in which the telescopic bridge was opened to allow passage.* (Image supplied by aerofilms.com)

8 The Somerset & Dorset Fleet

Although the Burnham-Cardiff ferry service was initially maintained by chartered tonnage, as soon as the Burnham Tidal Harbour Company was formed and it gained permission to operate ships on behalf of the Somerset Central Railway the first purchases were made. The **Ruby** was transferred to the company, the **Heather Bell** and the **Defiance** following on purchase whilst the **George Reed** was registered to George Reed himself on behalf of the company. By the time the latter was ready for delivery the financial situation was critical and its registration suggests that he had to dip into his own pocket to accept the ship into service from the builders. Permission to operate ships was vested in the Somerset & Dorset Railway Company following its formation in 1862.

The initial excursion into passenger ship-owning lasted from January 1860 until October 1871, all four vessels being used on the ferry service. Thereafter, until the acquisition of the **Sherbro** in May 1884, the service was either maintained by chartered tonnage or suspended.

No vessels were owned by the company between October 1871 and December 1873 when the S&DR bought three small ketches for cross-channel trading, mainly in coal and rails. Although separate from the ferry service the ships were owned in the same way as their passenger counterparts had been. The first small steam screw vessel was added to the fleet in October 1874.

Following the lease of the S&DR to the Midland and LSW Railways jointly in 1875 the new Joint Committee resolved on 29 October 1875 to purchase the four cargo vessels from the S&DR Company for a total of £3,050.[1] The value placed on each at that time was:

Leopard	£1,000
Richard and Emily	£650
Railway	£700
Julia	£700

Transfer was effected during the first week of December 1875, and this was confirmed by the minutes of the S&D Directors on 13 December.

Apart from a brief excursion into passenger tonnage again in May 1884 when the **Sherbro** joined the fleet until July 1888 for the ferry service, the S&DJR concentrated entirely on its cargo vessels, adding the steamer **Alpha** and eventually acquiring new tonnage in the form of a second **Julia** and the **Radstock**.

Unlike many larger railway companies the S&DR did not have a marine department. The ships were administered by the railway's traffic superintendent but the day-to-day operation of the cargo vessels was entrusted by the traffic department to the goods manager at Highbridge who for many years was Harry Bastard. (A full list of those involved appears in Appendix 4).

Ship Registration and Ownership

Under the terms of the Merchant Shipping Act every ship was required to have a manager or 'ship's husband', defined as the person or persons responsible for the ship. The ship's husband's name had to appear in all the ship's registration papers. A company itself could not be cited as an owner so individual names had to appear. In practice this was normally an officer of the managing or owning company, often the secretary. S&D ships were so registered.

Ships Dimensions

Dimensions quoted are the those given on the ship's registry papers. These are length, breadth and depth measured in feet and tenths of a foot. Length is measured from the fore-side of the stem to the aft-side of the stern post. Breadth is the widest measurement taken to the outside of the hull planking/plating and depth is the distance measured from the floor of the hold to the underside of the main deck. From this it will be noted that some ships may be considerably longer so 'overall length' (oa) is often quoted together with the length 'between perpendiculars' (bp), as the distance from the bow at the waterline to the aft-side of the stern post.

Tonnages

Measurement of ships' tonnages has changed many times over the years. Until 1835 the tonnage of a vessel was related to the weight of cargo it could carry and this was sometimes referred to as 'Tons Burthen'.

In 1836 the 'New Measurement' system was introduced, based on the internal volume of a vessel below the main deck level. Thus 100 cubic feet would equal one ton, the word 'ton' deriving from the number of casks or 'tuns' of wine a ship could carry in years past. Steamships had their engine-room space deducted to give NET tonnage for the assessment of harbour dues.

With additional superstructure being added above main deck level, the method of calculating tonnage was again altered, this time by the Merchant Shipping Act of 1854 (which came into effect in 1857). All enclosed areas of a vessel were now measured to arrive

The Somerset & Dorset Railway Shipping Fleet

Name	Official Number	Type	Tonnage Gross/Net	Owner	Passenger/ Cargo
Ruby	3185	Iron Paddle Steamer	155/ 98	BTH Co.	Passenger
Defiance	11542	Iron Paddle Steamer	150/ 96	BTH Co.	Passenger
Heather Bell	22090	Iron Paddle Steamer	152/ 95	BTH Co.	Passenger
George Reed	29559	Iron Screw Steamer	170/115	G. Reed (for BTH Co)	Passenger
Railway	25456	Wood Ketch	59	S&DR Co.	Cargo
Julia (1)	47304	Wood Ketch	69	S&DR Co.	Cargo
Richard and Emily	27824	Wood Ketch	82	S&DR Co.	Cargo
Leopard	44106	Iron Screw Steamer	67/ 42	S&DR Co.	Cargo
Alpha	78559	Iron Screw Steamer	82/ 48*	S&DJR	Cargo
Sherbro	73721	Wood Paddle Steamer	239/119	S&DJR	Passenger
Julia (2)	111393	Steel Screw Steamer	197/ 78	S&DJR	Cargo
Radstock	111395	Steel Screw Steamer	195/ 78	S&DJR	Cargo

* The *Alpha* was lengthened twice. In 1884 her tonnage increased to 94/55 and in 1905 it increased to 111/76.

at GROSS tonnage, but the crew's accommodation and navigation areas were added to the engine-room space then deducted from the gross tonnage to arrive at net (or registered) tonnage which was primarily used for due-paying calculations. This was known as the 'Moorsom' method of measurement.[2] Although further changes to the deductions were made in 1884 and again in 1914, the former reducing net tonnage and the latter increasing it, it is this system which is used in this book. It should be noted that the space below deck on the three S&D sailing vessels was minimal and only net tonnages were normally quoted, a situation which pertained for some years after 1854 on all sailing vessels although this began to change from about 1868. Tonnages of ships could be altered for many reasons during their life, normally through modification or change of use but occasionally they were recalculated following survey.

Summary of Tonnage Measurement

Displacement Tons:	The amount of water displaced by a ship's hull measured in cubic tons.
Gross Registered Tons: (GRT)	Measurement of cubic capacity of the ship's closed spaces, including all the holds and deck houses.
Net Registered Tons: (NRT)	The cubic space of the ship's earning space such as the cargo holds, not including engines, bunkers or crew's accommodation. 1 ton = 100 cubic feet.

Livery and Houseflag

HULL:	Black with red boot-topping.
UPPERWORKS:	White. *Alpha* and *Julia (2)* were changed to brown. The *Radstock* was painted brown from new.
FUNNEL:	Light buff. The *Alpha* and *Julia (2)* were changed to light buff with black top. *Radstock* was completed as buff with black top from new.
HOUSEFLAG:	The Joint Committee's house flag was blue, defaced with the white letters 'S&DJR'. It is not known if a houseflag was extant during SCR and S&DR days.

The Paddle Steamers

The singular most successful early marine development and application of the steam engine was in the ubiquitous paddle steamer which made its debut during the 1820s. By the time of the 1860s paddle steamers were a well-established form of transport and whilst the early screw steamers had by now appeared there were many advantages in running paddlers, particularly on short ferry and excursion work. It is not surprising that the company chose to operate no less than four on their ferry services, three of which were built between 1854 and 1858.

Invariably driven by large, slow-turning, reciprocating engines they seldom turned the paddles at speeds much in excess of 25rpm yet the vessels had the advantage of a good turn of speed, ease of manoeuvrability combined with quick acceleration and an equally impressive ability to stop, all ingredients that were required of ships that frequently had to come alongside piers and slipways often in adverse tidal conditions. They were also relatively shallow draughted and usually stable in service. One disadvantage was their susceptibility to paddle damage and disablement.

The public had had plenty of time to get used to such vessels and they generally proved popular in service although one could argue that their comfort was rather less than desired since these early ships were not provided with very much covered accommodation whilst deck houses and other superstructures were kept to a minimum leaving many passengers exposed to the weather, often for lengthy periods. Excursionists might have been prepared to put up with the sometimes appalling weather conditions on their occasional trips in the Bristol Channel but regular ferry users probably found the ships less appealing. With open bridges it was no picnic for the master and crew either – just an accepted part of their life.

Although registered at Bridgwater, because of tidal limitations all the paddle steamers were based at Cardiff from where they were supported (bunkering, catering, etc.). The only exception was the *Sherbro* which ran seasonally and was laid up at Highbridge during winter.

The Ketches

Technically a 'ketch' is a type of sailing rig but the term has generally been corrupted over the years to mean a small two-masted coastal sailing cargo vessel. In many cases the mainmast (or foremast) was constructed in two parts, the lower mast and a top mast which overlapped or 'doubled' it. The mizzen mast was stepped forward of the rudder. Sails were originally square rigged but later a fore-and-aft rig became much more common and all three of the S&D's ketches were so rigged. The main and mizzen sails were set on gaffs (top) and booms (bottom) whilst above the main there was usually a square-headed gaff topsail. Between the mainmast and bowsprit up to four further sails could be set although this was sometimes reduced to three. From the forward end of the bowsprit these were the flying jib, boom jib, standing jib and staysails.

Although the actual dimensions varied from vessel to vessel, typically the mainmast of a ketch would be in the region of 60ft.(18.5m) in height from keelson to head and about 15in.(380mm) in diameter at deck level. Additionally the topmast would be upwards of 30ft.(9.2m) long tapering from about 8in.(200mm) to just 4in.(100mm) at the truck (top). Mizzen masts also averaged 60ft.(18.5m) being some 10in.(250mm) in diameter at deck level and 5in.(125mm) at truck. Bowsprits could vary in length depending on how the ship was rigged but typically were up to 30ft.(9.23m) in length. Such vessels would have a capacity of up to about 120 tons when carrying a heavy cargo such as coal although this would be considerably reduced when lighter loads such as grain were carried.

This rig was particularly easy to handle with a small crew and as such they were a cost-effective form of transport which explains why the S&D were content to place a lengthy reliance on ships of this type.

Accommodation was often situated in the foc'sle, simple in style and somewhat cramped. All cooking was carried out in the same area for which a small coal-fired stove was supplied, that duty invariably falling to one of the deckhands.

The Steam Coasters

The vessels operated by the S&D were amongst the smallest of their type trading in the Bristol Channel. Two of them, the *Julia* and *Radstock* were purpose-built for the rail trade and are described as short, raised quarterdeck vessels. All had a similar net tonnage, a single hold and a derrick although they normally traded between ports with shoreside handling facilities so probably didn't use this latter feature much.

Facilities were basic and crew comfort fairly primitive as befits all ships of the type during this period. Apart from the hold, the engine and boiler together with bunker space took up by far the largest amount of room. There was little room for accommodation but each was provided with a small galley, a WC and lamp store. Berths for up to seven were provided. Officers were accommodated below the main deck right aft with a separate cabin for the captain, another for the

Somerset & Dorset Ships – Chart of In-Service Dates, 1860-1934

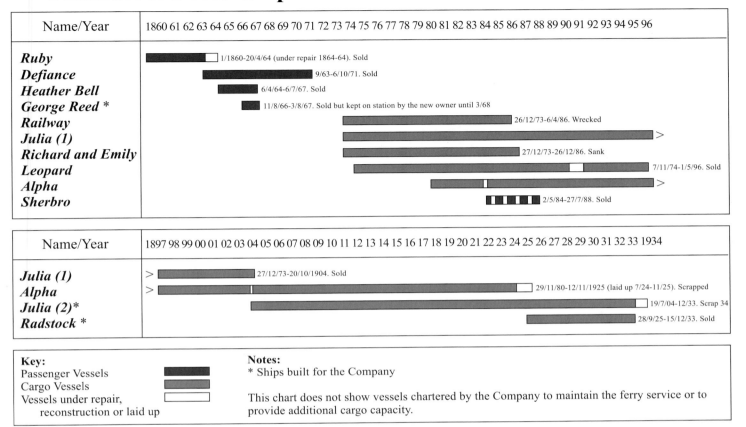

Name/Year	1860 61 62 63 64 65 66 67 68 69 70 71 72 73 74 75 76 77 78 79 80 81 82 83 84 85 86 87 88 89 90 91 92 93 94 95 96
Ruby	1/1860-20/4/64 (under repair 1864-64). Sold
Defiance	9/63-6/10/71. Sold
Heather Bell	6/4/64-6/7/67. Sold
George Reed *	11/8/66-3/8/67. Sold but kept on station by the new owner until 3/68
Railway	26/12/73-6/4/86. Wrecked
Julia (1)	>
Richard and Emily	27/12/73-26/12/86. Sank
Leopard	7/11/74-1/5/96. Sold
Alpha	>
Sherbro	2/5/84-27/7/88. Sold

Name/Year	1897 98 99 00 01 02 03 04 05 06 07 08 09 10 11 12 13 14 15 16 17 18 19 20 21 22 23 24 25 26 27 28 29 30 31 32 33 1934
Julia (1)	> 27/12/73-20/10/1904. Sold
Alpha	> 29/11/80-12/11/1925 (laid up 7/24-11/25). Scrapped
Julia (2)*	19/7/04-12/33. Scrap 34
Radstock *	28/9/25-15/12/33. Sold

Key:
Passenger Vessels
Cargo Vessels
Vessels under repair, reconstruction or laid up

Notes:
* Ships built for the Company

This chart does not show vessels chartered by the Company to maintain the ferry service or to provide additional cargo capacity.

---

mate and engineer and a small saloon with a stove for heating. The seamen and fireman were accommodated beneath the foc'sle head where four berths were provided together with a table and stove for heating.

Crew Lists

Crew lists for the S&D ships still exist for the period from 1863 to 1913 and give a fascinating insight into the engagement, transfers and promotion of more than 200 seamen who were engaged by the railway to operate their vessels over the years. They are not, however, comprehensive and the reader should be aware that some accuracy has been lost in their original transcription.[3]

When considering the names it should be remembered that many of the seamen, firemen and stewards often signed on only for a particular voyage and would not necessarily have an allegiance to the S&D. In many cases it was a question of taking work wherever it could be found; on the other hand some show a remarkable loyalty to the company. A number of the seamen took temporary promotion to mate but were just as often reverted; a few occasionally signed on as both firemen and seaman at different times. There are many cases of large family involvements with sons following fathers,

often with the same Christian names to complicate matters, but it was a male preserve; only two females appear on the crew lists, both stewardesses.

Ship Repairs and Maintenance

With all the resources of Highbridge Locomotive Works barely a mile down the line from Highbridge Wharf it is not surprising to learn that the S&D should turn to the skills within the company when ships needed repairs that were within their capabilities, and this would seem to include almost everything. Indeed, the maintenance of the ships was totally entrusted to the Locomotive Superintendent and his staff who would also arrange dry docking and surveys when required. Both the *Alpha* and the second *Julia* were re-plated by the locomotive works staff, whilst the ships' boilers were always removed to the works to be repaired by the boilermakers and fitters in the locomotive boiler shop. Indeed one former works tradesman, Sam Lane, recalled how in his earlier days he formed part of a team which regularly worked at the Wharf when repairs or maintenance was required on the ships. He started his apprenticeship in 1924 and worked in all the workshops, and on a great many of the S&DJR

locomotives until 1930 when the works closed. In that time he was involved in the repairs of the boiler in *Julia* whilst he also recalled repairing the steam dynamo on the *Radstock*.

To carry out the work the ships would be berthed at the original New Wharf near the old timber crane. Here the boilers could be lifted onto the quayside and then onto wagons to be transported the short distance to the works. On one such occasion in 1884, when the *Alpha* had her boiler removed for repairs, extra labour was engaged in March of that year for this job and not discharged until completion on 17 May.

Dry-docking of the ships obviously caused them to be sent away; for instance the *Alpha* was in Bristol in late December 1902 and early January 1903 and on one occasion the *Julia* was called back from docking at Bristol in August 1920 to help clear mud at Highbridge before completing her refit in the top berth at the Wharf.

Ships' engineers were usually extremely resourceful, able to cope with a wide variety of first-aid measures when the ship was away from home although they had only very limited repair facilities on board.

The ketches were not neglected either and, resourceful to the last, the S&D converted the base under the Burnham water tower into a small sail loft known as the 'Sheet Repairing Depot'. A foreman and three sheet-makers were engaged here in making and repairing the ships' sails, a task which was carried out by hand. They also made the numerous wagon and other sheets required by the railway. Sails were also carried on the steamships for many years, this being a Board of Trade requirement dating from the early days of steam when it was considered that if an engine failed the ship could be sailed – no doubt a difficult proposition as normally only a main trisail and a small jib were carried. A number of the S&D ships can be seen with their emergency sails furled. It took until 1938 for this requirement to be abolished although it seems highly unlikely that latterly the sails ever saw the light of day.

The Redhead Commission report of 1922 criticised the manual nature of the sheetmakers task and argued that it could be better done by one of the parent companies. This recommendation was not acted upon immediately but eventually this small department was closed in 1930 along with Highbridge Works.

Most wooden vessels required frequent maintenance and they were prone to leaking as the wood 'worked', particularly in heavy weather. Masters and their crews were usually competent at first-aid repairs but the Locomotive Department employed shipwrights to cope with maintenance. Charles Clatworthy was one such who was employed by the company for 43 years from June 1866 until July 1909 whilst Charles Willis was engaged as a shipwright (having previously been listed as a carpenter) from June 1888.

Ruby

Official Number:	3185
Signal Letter:	HSQJ
Type:	Single-deck Paddle Steamer
Construction:	Iron, square stern, single mast
Builders:	James Henderson & Sons, Renfrew, Glasgow
Completed:	1854
Tonnage:	155.02grt, 97.66nrt*
Engines:	2-cylinder simple by Barr & McNab, Greenock
Horsepower:	90 (est.)
Speed:	20mph
Length:	177.4ft.* (54.58m)
Beam:	17.1ft.* (5.26m)
Depth:	8.3ft.* (2.55m)
Forward Dining Saloon length:	40 to 50ft.(12.3 to 14.4m)
Aft Saloon length:	75ft.(23.1m)

*Figures relate to the ship as she entered Burnham service after lengthening.

The *Ruby* was built by James Henderson & Sons of Renfrew in 1854 for packet and excursion services in the Firth of Clyde. The search for this, the first vessel for the Somerset Central Railway, led George Reed, along with two of the line's other promoters, Henry Danby Seymour and Sir Edward Baker Baker, Bt. to the Clyde. The *Ruby* cannot have been exactly what the promoters had in mind but with their desire to take over the running of the Burnham-Cardiff ferry service quickly from other less reliable operators they were prepared to buy the vessel on behalf of the railway following which she was sent back to her builders to be lengthened and had her beam increased with consequent increase in tonnage to suit her for her new job.

When completed she was prepared for her wintertime passage south. For this trip she was placed under the command of Captain Peter L. Henderson who was to become very well-known to the railway as a shipbroker working out of both the Clyde and the Mersey. Taking a small paddle steamer down the west coast of Britain during winter was never a pleasant prospect but Captain Henderson left the Clyde on 28 January 1860 and completed the journey successfully during which time he also succeeded in rescuing the 25 crew members of the *Ann Mitchell* of Glasgow.

Until then her registered ownership was still with the three above named gentlemen but on 14 April 1860 she was formally re-registered in Bridgwater in the name of Robert Arthur Read, secretary of the SCR. The promoters, anxious to dispel the poor publicity that the service had initially gained, were determined to provide a reliable and regular service, the scheduled crossing time being set at 1¼ hours. It was, therefore, rather unfortunate that during the following month they instructed Captain George to put to sea with 60 passengers on board during a severe gale against his better judgement. Placed in a rather unenviable position he was forced to return to Burnham for shelter in the lee of Stert Island resulting in the inevitable unpleasant publicity.

Also in March the Bremen ship *Albert* ran aground on nearby Gore Sands at Burnham. Captain George managed to tow her off, subsequently taking the ship to Cardiff for which help the German master offered just £30. With considerable indignation Captain George had the ship arrested to secure £500 which he felt was nearer the sum deserved for such help but even this was compromised and the final figure agreed was just £200.

From March 1860 the *Ruby* settled down on the service, even running her first excursions in July to Newport and Ilfracombe. The only incident of note occurred the following November when she collided with the 1841-built Bridgwater schooner *Lass of Courtown*.

Captain Ezekiel Barron took over from Captain George during 1861. Apart from disabling a paddle in May 1862 when she struck some wreckage, the directors must have been well pleased that they had at last created the sort of service that had been their ambition.

Then, on 18 August 1863 her career at Burnham came to an abrupt end. The entry in the *Shipping Protest Register* is curt and to the point:

RUBY, 97 Tons. Cardiff 18 Aug. 63. Cargo of goods and passengers. Bound for Burnham pier on entering which a gale from the North West drove her on the mud and the vessel has sustained considerable damage in consequence thereof.

In fact as Captain Barron was bringing the ship alongside the pier the crew failed to secure her at their first attempt because of the difficult conditions and the wind quickly slewed her stern around so that instead of coming to rest in the cut, she settled substantially across it with her stern high on the mud bank beyond. Although unable to move, passengers were brought ashore over the bows after which the cargo and stores were removed in a frantic attempt to lighten her, all to no avail. As the ebbing tide fell the ship broke her back just in front of the heavy boiler. Clearly the limitations of the narrow cut and the open nature of the pier which had been forced upon the SCR were all too obvious to see.

This accident brought further criticism from the press and the *Western Mercury* had this to say:

The crowning disaster to that unfortunate vessel ... She broke her back and now lies in the gutway with her deck planking torn up, her sides bulging and her copper sheathing rent and gaping. No blame whatsoever can be attached to Captain Barron, but some misunderstanding between the Secretary and the Harbour Master has let the shareholders in to the tune of £700, at the lowest estimate given for repairs ... Should the *Ruby* again be put on the station in good repair, we shall anticipate in course of time another accident, while the infatuation of the shareholders attempts to sail her in a ditch. *Ruby* accidents are among the ordinary topics of our seaside existence – they come as regularly as the tide.

The comments seem particularly harsh since it had never been the SCR's intention to build anything other than a proper pier and the problems associated with the objections by the Corporation of Bridgwater a few years before seemed to have been conveniently forgotten.

William Patterson, a well-known Bristol shipbuilder,[4] was swiftly brought in to refloat her since she was now blocking access to the pier. He built a large cradle using baulks of timber strained tightly together with a number of chains but suffered several setbacks before succeeding in refloating her. Just six days after the accident, a most creditable time given the circumstances, he managed to tow her out of the cut following which she was taken to Bristol for permanent repairs.

Although the Burnham Tidal Harbour Company had been formed by the SCR some three years before the accident the *Ruby* had never been officially transferred; a few weeks after she arrived at Bristol, a Bill of Sale dated 15 October 1863 confirms this and she was formally re-registered. The repairs must have taken a considerable time because that friend of the company, Captain Peter Henderson, bought the *Ruby*

back on 20 April 1864. At the same time he provided them with a replacement ship, the *Heather Bell*.

The subsequent career of the *Ruby* is still shrouded in mystery partly because there were a number of other ships with the same name. She was removed from the Bridgwater register and on the 11 July 1864 re-registered at Liverpool. In 1867 she was recorded as being owned by a George Edmiston and was still in Liverpool ownership during 1868.[5] This was the time of the American Civil War and a number of ships had crossed the Atlantic to be used as blockade runners. At least three other *Rubys* have been identified as being engaged in this trade but none quite fit the description of the Bridgwater *Ruby* so it becomes difficult to establish the final demise of this little ship.

Masters and representative crew members of the *Ruby*, 1860-1863		
MASTERS:	Captain David GEORGE	Feb 1860-1861
	Captain Ezekiel L. BARRON	1861-August 1863 (thence to *Defiance*)
MATE:	Edward HALFORD	1863
ENGINEER:	Robert H. STRONG	1863
SEAMEN:	David George	1863
	John Hutchings	1863
	John King	1863
	Frank Puddy	1863
	William Smith	1863
	William Kidgell	1863
FIREMEN:	William Hires	1863
	John Martin	1863
	John Marley	1863
	George Read	1863
STEWARD/STEWARDESS:	George Kingston	1863
	Mary Ann George	1863

*This remarkable early image of the **Ruby**, taken by an unknown photographer, shows the vessel lying in the gut alongside Burnham pier shortly after she broke her back immediately in front of the boiler on 18 August 1863. It looks as though her single mast has been struck whilst her funnel remains intact and complete with a balance weight which was used to allow it to be lowered. Sitting end-on behind and to her right is a paddle tug which may have been the **Pilot**, the vessel chartered as a replacement.*

(Robin Atthill collection/S&DRT)

Defiance

Official Number:	11542
Signal Letters:	KTCL
Type:	Single-deck Paddle Steamer
Construction:	Iron, Square stern, 2 masts.
Builders:	Thomas Wingate, Whiteinch, Glasgow
Completed:	1856
Withdrawn:	1879
Tonnage:	150.29grt, 95.62nrt
Engines:	2-cylinder diagonal, by Thomas Wingate
Horsepower:	86 (est.)
Length:	152.3ft.(46.86m)
Beam:	18ft.(5.54m)
Depth:	8.3ft.(2.55m)

Thomas Wingate built the **Defiance** at Glasgow speculatively in 1856. In the following year she found a foreign buyer but returned to his ownership and to Glasgow registration in 1863. It is not known where she had been in the interim. In September that year she was resold to the BTH Co. (deed of transfer dated 15 October) and re-registered in Bridgwater to the secretary Robert Arthur Read on 14 October. The company had originally planned to run the ship alongside the **Ruby** but the untimely demise of the latter vessel in August 1863 caused the charter of the paddle tug **Pilot** until the completion of the purchase of the **Defiance**.

Displaced from the **Ruby**, Captain E.L. Barron took command of the ship in September 1863 and once in service on the Burnham-Cardiff ferry she gave very good value, becoming the longest-serving passenger vessel in the fleet. She was also used for excursion work. Throughout 1864 Barron shared command with his junior colleague Captain Densham until the latter moved to the **Heather Bell**. It seems that the original intention was that Densham should have become master of the **Defiance** alongside Barron in the **Ruby**. When the new screw steamer **George Reed** was delivered in 1866 Captain Barron moved to her but in 1867 he was back again and stayed with the **Defiance**.

Behind the scenes there followed an extraordinary period of turbulence regarding ownership and on 31 July 1866 the BTH Co. mortgaged the ship, all 64 shares being formally transferred to Mr. Edward Tuckett of Stuckey's Banking Company, Langport. However this was eclipsed on 1 January 1867 when the mortgage (and all 64 shares) was transferred in its entirety from the bank to none other than George Reed personally. A little over four years later, on 25 May 1871 the same process was repeated when Reed transferred the mortgage to Sir Edward Baker Baker, Bt. It is no coincidence that this was also the period when the parent S&DR was in receivership.

The *Shipping Gazette* for 26 January 1870 gives a notice of sale by auction to take place at Bristol on 23 February 1870 but other events would suggest that this did not happen for more than a year. At that time it was stated that the ship had received a thorough overhaul of her hull and engines at a cost of £1,200 in 1866. Coal consumption was stated as 11cwt per hour at an average speed of 8 knots. There were cabins and good accommodation for cargo and/ or cattle.

In July 1871, after nearly eight years on the run, she was withdrawn by the Burnham Company and put up for auction by the mortgagee but found no sale until 6 October when the vessel was purchased by James Habgood, Jnr., a Bristol metal dealer. Habgood had intended to resell her as going concern but the ship may not have been in good condition by this time because she attracted no buyers. She languished unused until eventually, in 1879, he decided to scrap her.

Masters and representative crew members of the *Defiance*, 9/1863-10/1871

MASTERS:	Captain Ezekiel L. BARRON	cSeptember 1863-August 1866 (to *George Reed* as master)
	Captain William DENSHAM	Relief to Capt. Barron 1864 (then to *Heather Bell*)
	Captain Ezekiel L. BARRON	1867-July 1871(from *Heather Bell*)
		(Capt. Barron transferred from *Heather Bell* back to
		Defiance together with other members of his crew)
MATES:	John KING	1866 (to *Heather Bell* as mate 1867)
	Benjamin HUCKMAN	1867 (from *Heather Bell* as mate; to *Heather Bell*
		as master)
	George MANSFIELD	1867
ENGINEERS:	Joseph WILLIAMS	1866-1867
	Alfred T. SMITH	1867-1870
SEAMEN:	Joseph Lendon	1866
	William Kidgell	1867-1870
	Albert Guy	1866
	James Farthing	1866-1870
	Alfred Hunt	1869-1870
	William Wood	1868
	John Profut	1870
	Robert Kidwell	1866-1867
	S. Pound	1866
	William Smith	1866
	William Trood	1867
	William Hedgel	1868
	Henry D. Luxon	1870-1871*
FIREMEN:	George Lewis	1866
	John Winter	1866
	James Winter	1866-1870
	John Martin	1867-1870
STEWARDS/STEWARDESSES:	John Harris	1866
	William Hood	1866
	Henry D. Luxon	1867-1869*
	John Probeart	1866-1869
	Mary Ann George	1866-1867
	James Mansfield	1870

* Henry Luxon was signed on this ship as a 17-year old steward but transferred to seaman.
In addition Hugh Winter was in the crew list and probably employed as a fireman.

Heather Bell

Official Number:	22090
Signal Letters:	NKBQ
Type:	Single-deck Paddle Steamer
Construction:	Iron. Scroll on head, round stern, two masts
Builders:	James & George Thompson, Glasgow
Completed:	1858
Withdrawn:	1879
Tonnage:	151.55grt, 95.48nrt
Engines:	2-cylinder simple expansion, oscillating by builders 31in.(794mm) diameter x 36in.(923mm)
Horsepower:	60 nominal
Length:	135.5ft.(41.54m)
Beam:	18.1ft.(5.57m)
Depth:	8.3ft.(2.55m)
Engine Room Length:	26.6ft.(8.0m)

The *Heather Bell* was built and engined by James & George Thompson of Glasgow in 1858 and had been ordered and built to the specification of Christall, Gray and Bateson of Wick. Initial service probably found the ship on the Wick-Orkney run but in 1864 she was sold to Captain Peter Henderson. His acquisition was extremely timely indeed although he may well have been looking for a suitable second ship for the SCR because it would seem that they had already intimated that they wanted a two-ship operation on the ferry service. Because of the accident to the *Ruby* Henderson agreed to purchase that ship from the BTH Co. whilst still under repair but at the same time he sold the Company the *Heather Bell* in what now looks to have been a part-exchange deal of some sort.[6]

*(left) The **Heather Bell** (1858/152grt) lies in the cut at Burnham Pier sometime between 1864 and 1867, the period in which she was used by the S&DR on the Burnham-Cardiff ferry. For the majority of this time she was under the command of Captain William Densham.*
(G. Luxon collection via R. Atthill /S&DRT)

The *Heather Bell* joined the *Defiance* on the Burnham-Cardiff ferry shortly after her purchase on 6 April 1864 when she was registered to the BTH Co. at Bridgwater in the name of the secretary, Robert Arthur Read, and ran successfully for the next few years, mainly under the command of Captain W. Densham. The economic plight of the S&D led to a similar train of events as with the *Defiance* and the ship was mortgaged by the BTH Co., all 64 shares being transferred to Edward Tuckett of Stuckey's Bank, Langport on 1 August 1866. The ship continued in use during the first half of 1867 but clearly the situation was such that one of the two ships would have to go. As a result the *Heather Bell* was placed on the sales list. On 6 July 1867 she was sold and re-registered to the Jersey & Continental Steam Packet Company (John Allen, owner) of St. Helier, the BTH mortgage being discharged by the bank on 13 July. She was sold again in 1869 to James Stark of London. Early in 1871, following yet another sale, she appeared on the South Coast under the ownership of George Burt of Swanage.

Based at Poole, Burt ran the ship on its inaugural trip on 1 May 1871 habitually using her on the Lulworth, Swanage, Bournemouth and Isle of Wight trips.[7] She was withdrawn from that service and replaced by another ship in 1876 but Burt kept her in his fleet probably until 1879 when she was sold for scrap.

Masters and representative crew members of the *Heather Bell*, 4/1864-7/1867

MASTERS:	Captain William DENSHAM	1865-1866 (then to *George Reed* as master)
	Captain Ezekiel L. BARRON	c4/1867-1867 (then to *Defiance* as master)
	Captain Benjamin HUCKMAN	1867-6/1867
MATES:	Benjamin HUCKMAN	1866-1867 (to *Defiance* as mate, then back to *Heather Bell* as master)
	John KING	1867 (from *Defiance*)
ENGINEERS:	John GRIFFITHS	1866
	John WILLIAMS	1867
SEAMEN:	Alfred Hunt	1866
	William Smith	1866
	Robert McCrete	1866
	John Hutchings	1866
	Uriah Winter	1866
	William Kidgell	1867
	James Thatcher	1866
	George Mansfield	1866
	Frank Type	1866
	Eli Hunt	1866-1867
	James Farthing	1867
	John Witten	1867
FIREMEN	John Martin	1866-1867
	James Winter	1867
	Daniel Hilfall	1866
STEWARDS/STEWARDESSES:	Martha Huckman	1866
	Mary Ann George	1867
	Harry Kingston	1866
	William Wood	1867
BOY:	Thomas Davies	1866

George Reed

Official Number:	29559
Type:	Single-deck Screw Steamship
Construction:	Iron. Male bust at stem, round stern, 2 masts
Builders:	J. & W. Dudgeon, Cubitt Town, London
Completed:	August 1866
Withdrawn:	17 December 1872. Wrecked
Tonnage:	169.55grt, 115.29nrt
Engines:	2-cylinder simple by builders
Horsepower:	60 nominal
Length:	169.3ft.(52.1m)
Beam:	18.0ft.(5.54m)
Depth:	7.7ft.(2.37m)
Engine Room Length:	24.3ft.(7.5m)

The *George Reed* was the only ship specifically designed for the requirements of the Burnham-Cardiff ferry service and was ordered by the Burnham Tidal Harbour Company for delivery in 1866. Considering the reliance on paddle steamers at the time, it was, perhaps, a little unusual if not a bold step for the company to specify an iron screw ship. Named after the foremost citizen of Burnham and Somerset & Dorset Railway Company director, George Reed, her builders delivered the ship in August of that year. It was registered formally to him on 11 August and like other members of the fleet carried a Bridgwater port of registry. Captain E.L. Barron took command.

The *George Reed* was described as being a good sea-boat, very fast and having excellent passenger accommodation. Nevertheless the severe financial difficulties that were by then besetting the Somerset & Dorset reflected on the fortunes of the BTH Co. and George Reed, therefore, was obliged to operate the ship on behalf of the company largely on his own account.

In the event the vessel had a very short and undistinguished life with the company. It is not clear now whether this was because of the perilous financial state of the company or the fact that the ship was a screw packet and was found unsuitable for the berthing conditions at Burnham. Whatever the reason Captain Peter Henderson was called upon to purchase the vessel which he duly did with the help of a mortgage from S.M. Loutit of London on 3 August 1867. However he did not remove the ship from the station and she remained on the run but on charter to the Burnham company. During 1866 and 1867 Captain Barron shared command with Captain Densham, the latter staying with the ship for the beginning of the 1868 season. In the following March the mortgagee became restive with the arrangement and ordered her sale. The charter was terminated and on 19 May 1868 she was sold to George F. Pitman of London before passing to another London merchant on 11 April 1872. On 17 December of that year she was wrecked off the Maldive Islands, a long way from her home and a strange resting place for this S&D ship.

Masters and representative crew members of the *George Reed*, 8/1866-5/1868

MASTERS:	Captain Ezekiel L. BARRON	1866-1867 (thence to *Heather Bell*)
	Captain William DENSHAM	1866-May 1868 (shared command with Capt. Barron)
MATE:	John PASSMORE	1866
ENGINEER:	John GRIFFITHS	1866-1868 (from *Heather Bell*)
SEAMEN:	Eli Hunt	1866
	William Wall	1866
	Henry D. Luxon	1866*
	John Bull	1866
	Charles Bussey	1866
FIREMEN:	Henry Gregory	1866
	John Winter	1866
	Harry Hunt	1866
STEWARD:	Thomas Hansford	1868
BOYS:	Samuel Russell	1866
	Albert Luscombe	1868

* Amongst the crew was the 13½-year old H.D. Luxon who had joined this, his first ship, on its arrival at Burnham as a deckhand and who would rise to become master of later S&D ships.

Railway

Official Number:	25456
Type:	Single-deck sailing cargo vessel
Rig:	Gaff-rigged Ketch
Construction:	Wood, carvel, square stern
Builders:	John Higham, Strood, Kent
Completed:	1855
Withdrawn:	1886. Stranded. Constructive total loss
Tonnage:	59grt/nrt. (Quoted as 68grt after 19/2/1877)
Engines:	Nil
Length:	72.4ft.(22.28m)
Beam:	18.4ft.(5.66m)
Depth:	6.05ft.(1.86m)

The smallest and oldest of the Somerset & Dorset Railway's three sailing vessels was the **Railway** which was completed in 1855 as a very typical Medway coasting sailing barge by John Higham of Strood, close to Rochester. The ship was owned by Henry Everist but following his death she was re-rigged as a ketch and sold by auction at the bargain price of £240.

Her new owner carried out further unspecified repairs and as a result the deck layout arrangements are uncertain. Following this she was again placed on the market in 1873 and found a buyer, the S&DR, who required the vessel to help carry rails, iron and coal from South Wales to Highbridge. She was formally registered at Bridgwater (from Rochester) to R.T. Rees for the S&D Company officers on 26 December 1873.

On 8 December 1875, when 20 years old and in common with all other ships in the fleet at that time, her registered owners became Ralph Heneage Dutton of Romsey and Edward Shipley Ellis of Leicester, on behalf of the S&DR Company. The **Railway** was, in turn, resold to the Midland and London & South Western Railways jointly at a book cost of £700, the sale being confirmed on 13 December.

Some unspecified alterations to the ship were made over the winter of 1876-7 which altered both her dimensions and tonnage the latter being increased to 68 gross. In consequence she was re-registered at Bridgwater on 19 February 1877.

Ellis died on 3 December 1879 so on 26 May 1880 the registered owners became Dutton and Matthew William Thompson of Guiseley. The **Railway** thereafter remained in regular S&D use until 6 April 1886 when she stranded at the entrance to Cardiff docks. Although fortunately there was no loss of life she became a constructive total loss and her registration was formally cancelled on 12 July.

Masters and representative crew members of the *Railway*, 1873-1886

MASTERS:	Captain James FARTHING	1874	
	Captain Henry D. LUXON	1876-1877	
	Captain Alfred HUNT	1879	
	Captain Charles BRICE	1880	
	Captain Alfred HUNT	1880	(to *Julia (1)* as master)
	Captain Charles BRICE	1881-1882	
	Captain James FARTHING	1884	
MATES:	George WOODS	1874, 1876	
	Albert BOUND	1877	
	Albert BEARD	1877	
	George CLAPP	1879	
	William BLAKE	1879	
	John KING	1880-1881	
	Edward FLETCHER	1882	(to *Julia (1)* as master)
	George COPP	1882	
	Henry WOODWARD	1884	
SEAMEN:	John Reed	1874	
	James Hopkins	1874	
	George Clapp	1876, 1880-1881*	
	William Manley	1877	
	John Manley	1877	
	William Gamblin	1879-1882	
	John Gamblin	1882	
	Walter Luxon	1884	
	Abraham Dunn	1884	
	Francis Hopkins	1874	
	Henry Cosway	1876	
	Joseph Templer	1876	
	Uriah Winter	1877, 1882	
	John Working	1877	
	John King	1879**	
	Eli Hunt	1884	
	William Blake	1877	

*   George Clapp promoted to temporary position of mate in 1879 but reverted to seaman.
** John King was formerly the mate of the **Heather Bell** and had reverted to seaman before promotion to mate in 1880.

Julia (1)

Official Number:	47304
Type:	Single-deck sailing cargo vessel
Rig:	Gaff-rigged Ketch
Construction:	Wood, carvel, square stern
Builders:	Joshua Wright, Milton, Nr. Sittingbourne, Kent
Completed:	1863
Withdrawn:	April 1922. Scrapped Pill, near Bristol
Tonnage:	68.85grt/nrt
Engines:	Nil
Length:	80.3ft.(24.7m)
Beam:	18.6ft.(5.72m)
Depth:	6.2ft.(1.91m)

The wood ketch *Julia* was built by Joshua Wright at Milton in Kent and, like the Company's ketch *Railway* was probably rigged in typical West Country style although as she was built on the East Coast the original layout of the hull, decks and rigging is not so certain.

The vessel probably came to the Bristol Channel soon after construction where she is recorded as being registered in Bristol to an unknown owner[8] but in 1873 she was re-registered in London. Following her sale to the Somerset & Dorset Railway Company she was transferred to the Bridgwater register on 27 December 1873, the day after the *Railway*.

Purchased by the Joint Committee for £700[9] in late 1875 her registration was transferred on 8 December, on behalf of the S&DJR, to R.H. Dutton and E.S. Ellis. When Ellis died on 3 December 1879 it was transferred to Dutton and then to Dutton and Matthew Wm. Thompson of Leeds on 26 May 1880. However, Thompson died on 1 December 1891 followed by Dutton on 8 October 1892, the registered owner then becoming John William Mansfield, a Barrister of London. On 29 June 1896 the ship was further transferred to George Ernest Paget, esq., of Loughborough and Wyndham Spencer Portal, esq., of Basingstoke. A final change saw Robert Armstrong Dykes (the S&D's traffic superintendent) replace Portal by 1899. All these were, of course, the ships managers or husbands!

The *Julia* spent most of her working life transporting iron, rails and coal from Newport to Highbridge, with occasional trading elsewhere in the Bristol Channel but in 1903, forty years after she was built, the S&DJR described her as worn beyond repair. They then ordered a new screw vessel of the same name in replacement before her final withdrawal in October 1904 when she was sold for £50.

She might have had her time with the S&D but her career was far from over because the *Julia* was sold to Alfred R. Wilkins, a Bridgwater shipwright, on 20 October 1904. It would seem that his motive was speculative since he set about refitting the ship for further trading and she was resold on 5 November following to master mariner Thomas R. Brown of 8 Lily Mead Avenue, Bristol although she still retained her Bridgwater registration.[10]

Remaining in Brown's ownership until final disposal she was fully crewed until at least 1913 so it appears that the ship remained rigged but there is a possibility that when her sailing days were over she may have been employed for a few years as a barge in Bristol City Docks. Oddly, in the twilight of her life Brown mortgaged the vessel with Lloyds Bank Ltd. on 12 March 1920. The vessel survived at Bristol only for another couple of years when the Bridgwater registry was closed with the entry 'Broken up at Pill, 1922 (April)'.[11]

Masters and representative crew members of the *Julia (1)*, 1873-1904

MASTERS:	Captain John HUTCHINGS	1874-1877	
	Captain James FARTHING	1877-1880	(to *Alpha* as mate)
	Captain Alfred HUNT	1880-1882	(to *Richard and Emily* as master)
	Captain Edward FLETCHER	1883-1889	
	Captain Albert GUY	1890	
	Captain Edward FLETCHER	1890-1891	
	Captain Albert GUY	1891	
	Captain Edward FLETCHER	1892-1894	(to *Leopard* as master)
	Captain William CREEMER	1894-1895	
	Captain Edward FLETCHER	1896-1904	(to *Alpha* as master)
MATES:	Uriah WINTER	1874-1876	
	Robert WOODWARD	1877-1878	
	John McKAY	1879-1880	
	William BLAKE	1880-1881	
	Robert WOODWARD	1882	
	John KING	1883	
	Albert NEATH	1883-1884	
	Samuel BROWNING	1889	
	John KING	1890	
	Albert NEATH	1890-1900	
	James CASWELL	1901-1903	
	Albert NEATH	1903-1904	
SEAMEN:	Edward D. Rawles	1874, 1877	
	Charles Pople	1877	
	Richard Bound	1877	
	Richard Court	1879	
	Sydney Court	1879-1881	
	John King	1882, 1889	
	George Thomas	1883, 1891	
	William Manley	1883-1884, 1890-1891	
	George Coombs	1884	
	John Caswell	1890-1892, 1896-1897	
	Isaac Caswell	1894	
	Charles Rawlings	1903	
	Charles Brice	1874	
	Uriah Winter	1877	
	George Brown	1879	
	William Blake	1879, 1882	
	Robert Woodward	1880-1882	
	James King	1882	
	J.H. Coombe	1883	
	George Clapp	1883-1884	
	Samuel Browning	1890-1904	
	James Caswell	1890-1899	
	Albert Neath	1901-1902	

*(left) Two fine views of the wooden ketch **Julia** viewed off Stert Point at the mouth of the River Parrett. This vessel was already ten years old when it entered Somerset & Dorset Railway service in 1873 but was not finally disposed of by the company until 1904. The **Julia** displays a traditional ketch sail plan including a square-headed gaff topsail but is carrying only three headsails. Although she appears to be under tow she was in fact very close to the shore and has dropped anchor. The lower view reveals a crew of four on board.* (National Railway Museum – DY8521 & DY8522)

Richard and Emily

Official Number:	27824
Type:	Single-deck sailing cargo vessel
Rig:	Gaff-rigged Ketch
Construction:	Wood, carvel. Round stern
Builders:	Chatfield Shipbuilding Yard, Lewes, Sussex (formerly Rickman & Godlee)
Completed:	1862
Withdrawn:	1886. Sank

Tonnage:	As purchased	81.62grt/81.62nrt
	1875	85.94grt/85.94nrt
	1879	84.47grt/73.63nrt

Engines:	Nil
Length:	84.3ft.(25.66m)
Beam:	21.1ft.(6.42m)
Depth:	6.7ft.(2.0m)

Masters and representative crew members of the *Richard and Emily*, 1873-1886

MASTERS:	Captain Albert GUY	1873-1879	
	Captain Henry D. LUXON	1880-1882	(to *Alpha* as master)
	Captain Alfred HUNT	1883-1886	
MATES:	John WOODWARD	1874	
	Alfred HUNT	1874	
	Eli HUNT	1874	
	John LYNIVER	1876	
	George CLAPP	1876-1877	
	Charles HARRIS	1877	
	Alfred HUNT	1878	
	John BOUND	1880-1882	
	William PEAK	1883	
	Albert NEATH	1886	
	William BLAKE	1886	
	John KING	1886	
SEAMEN	Charles Lane	1874	
	H. Creed	1874	
	Thomas Ware	1874	
	David Jarman	1874	
	George Coggins	1874, 1876	
	George Templar	1876	
	Francis Counsell	1876-1877	
	Francis Hopkins	1876-1877	
	Joseph Creemer	1878, 1882	
	Frank Withers	1878-1882	
	Albert Neath	1880-1883	
	Henry Woodward	1882-1886	
	Walter Luxon	1886	
	Richard Chapman	1886	
	Samuel Hunt	1886	
	Amos Hall	1886	

Like the *Railway* and *Julia* before, the *Richard and Emily* was another East Coast vessel but which was ketch-rigged to suit West Country conditions. Originally registered in Newhaven her early ownership is not known although she must have been trading in the Bristol Channel already because on 15 September 1873 she was in difficulties causing Burnham lifeboat to be called out to her.[12] Shortly after this incident she was purchased by the Somerset & Dorset Railway Company and registered to them on 27 December 1873, the same day as the *Julia*.

Like her two sister ships she was also purchased by the Joint Committee but at a book cost of £650, (the sale being confirmed on 13 December 1875) and registered to R.H. Dutton and E.S. Ellis on 8 December 1875 when a change in tonnage was also noted, then later to Dutton and M.W. Thompson on 26 May 1880. In the interim she was again re-registered when another change in tonnage was recorded in 1879.

She also found employment in the traditional rail, iron and coal traffic bringing the products of the South Wales steel mills and collieries over to Highbridge for the use of the S&DJR and the LSWR whilst also handling general cargoes when not so employed.

Nothing much is heard of the *Richard and Emily* until tragedy struck during a particularly severe gale on the night of 26 December 1886, when she floundered off Nash Light whilst on the Burnham-Swansea run. Fortunately there were no casualties. Her Bridgwater registration was cancelled on 27 January 1887.

Leopard

Official Number:	44106
Type:	Screw steam coaster
Construction:	Iron. Round stern, two masts
Builders:	Hyde & Row, Bristol
Completed:	1861
Withdrawn:	1911. Scrapped
Tonnage:	66.99grt, 41.76nrt
Engines:	1-cylinder vertical developing 25hp and driving a single screw by Muir & Co., Greenock Cylinders 22in. x 18in.(564mm x 462mm)
Horsepower:	25 nominal
Steam Pressure:	40 psi
Bunker Capacity:	18 tons coal
Length:	91.5ft.(28.15m)
Beam:	14.8ft.(4.55m)
Depth:	8.2ft.(2.52m)
Engine Room Length:	24.0ft.(7.4m)

The *Leopard* was originally built as a small passenger-cargo vessel for the Llanelli Navigation Company which was formed in January 1863 with this ship specifically for their Llanelli-Bristol service. She proved rather too small for the trade so in October 1867 she was sold to Swansea shipbroker, James Hazel, for £1,000. She then had several owners before the Swansea register records her sale on 7 November 1874 to Robert Arthur Read, the renowned SCR/S&DR company secretary at Glastonbury on behalf of the Somerset & Dorset Railway Company. Unlike the recent additions of the ketches, the plan was to use this ship chiefly as a collier trading between the South Wales ports and Highbridge with bunker coal.

Following the resolve of the Joint Committee to purchase the vessel for £1,000 from the S&DR Co. her registered ownership was transferred to R.H. Dutton and E.S. Ellis in early December 1875. On 29 November 1880 (following the death of Ellis) she was re-registered at Bridgwater and like the other vessels her managing agents became R.H. Dutton and M.W. Thompson for the company. After Thompson's death on 1 Dec 1891 Dutton became the managing agent until his death on 8 Oct 1892 when London barrister John William Mansfield took over.

Her cargoes ensured that she was seen in a variety of South Wales ports, normally with coal for Highbridge but she was known to trade elsewhere. In 1888, for instance, she operated a shuttle run between Swansea and Llanelli with loads of up to 75 tons of copper ore.

She continued to trade until 1890 when she was declared unfit for further service and not to be replaced,[13] and laid up at Highbridge. This was, perhaps, rather premature. A memorandum dated 24 October 1891, sent from Highbridge to Mr. A. Colson, the resident engineer at Glastonbury, suggests that the latter wanted to use the ship for mudding but evidently work was being carried out because George Dyer, an employee in the goods department replied:

I have seen Mr. Bastard and Mr. Chatworth and the (sic) cannot tell any thing about the 'Leopard'. For a few days they have to drill out the stern bush.[14]

The ship was clearly not serviceable at the time and would appear to have had propeller shaft troubles which were being worked on.

The crew lists do not record any crew on the ship in 1891 but by 1892 Fred Dyer was listed as the master with Gabriel Pope as mate and James Pugsley as engineer which suggests that any repairs required had been completed by this time and that she was once again back in service. From then on she continued to be crewed until the S&DJR sold her in 1896. Since 1879 she had worked alongside the similar *Alpha* and it is thought that her size, although limiting the amount of cargo she could carry, made her ideally suited to Highbridge.

Following the sale on 1 May 1896 her ownership passed to James Ford of Cardiff, a steam tug owner, but almost immediately she was transferred to William M. Tucker, also a tug operator, who took the vessel on mortgage from Ford on 8 May. The ship continued to trade at least until 1909, keeping her Bridgwater registration until she was finally broken up as late as 1911.[15]

Masters and representative crew members of the *Leopard*, 1874-1896

MASTERS:	Captain Albert GUY	1881-1890	(to *Julia (1)* as master)
	Captain Fred DYER	1892	
	Captain William CREEMER	1893	(from/to *Alpha* as mate)
	Captain Edward FLETCHER	1894-1896	(to *Julia (1)* as master)
MATES:	John CASWELL	1881	
	James CASWELL	1882	
	John BOUND	1882-1883, 1889	
	J. CASWELL	1890	
	Gabriel POPE	1892	
	Joseph PUGSLEY	1892	
	Francis DYER	1893	
	Frederick DYER	1894	
ENGINEERS:	William WINTER	1881-1883	
	John BOUND	1884	
	William WINTER	1886-1890	
	James PUGSLEY	1892	
	Gabriel POPE	1893	
	Frederick GUY	1894	
SEAMEN:	Edward Fletcher	1881-1882	
	Albert Fletcher	1881	
	John Caswell	1882-1883, 1889	
	James Pugsley	1883-1884	
	John Bound	1886-1887, 1890	
	Thomas Hale	1889-1890	
	John King	1890	
FIREMEN:	George Baker	1881	
	Uriah Winter	1881	
	James Baker	1882-1883	
	William Winter	1884	
	James Pugsley	1886-1889, 1894	
	Amos Hale	1889-1890	
	Frederick Guy	1894	

A glance at this list will show the same names cropping up in various different positions and it is difficult to imagine how Gabriel Pope could be mate one year and engineer the next! Given that the names refer to the same person it is, perhaps, more creditable that James Pugsley started on the ship as a seaman before becoming a fireman and, much later, the ship's engineer.

*(left) The **Leopard** is viewed at the 150ft.(46m) wooden upper berth at Highbridge Wharf. The little steamship was a neat and businesslike vessel which served the Somerset & Dorset Railway well, mainly as a collier. With the bridge and wheel situated abaft the funnel and the boiler clearly visible, the ship was typical of the period. This photo is believed to have been taken shortly before the ship's prolonged lay-up in 1890. A wealth of detail completes the picture with a small hydraulic steam crane running on its own short length of track and similar to the ones seen on the main wharf crane road. A number of tree trunks are probably sitting on an unseen bolster wagon next to a series of S&DJR sheeted wagons. The railway buildings on the far left date from the earliest days but were demolished in the 1920s whilst sitting in front of H.F. Isaac's Highbridge Ironworks (as the sign proclaims), and just visible, is, rather unusually, a North Staffordshire Railway open wagon well off course and far from home. (National Railway Museum – DY8523)*

Sherbro

Official Number:	73721
Signal Letter:	QVCF
Type:	Passenger/cargo Paddle Steamer
Construction:	Wood, carvel. Round stern, 2 masts
Builders:	John White, West Cowes, Isle of Wight
Completed:	1870
Withdrawn:	1892. Reduced to a lighter
Tonnage:	238.77grt. 112.05nrt
Engines:	2-cylinder single expansion oscillating developing 120nhp, by Humphreys, Tennant & Co., London Cylinders: 45in. x 40in.(1,145mm x 1,018mm)
Horsepower:	120 nominal
Steam Pressure:	22psi
Length:	152.5ft.(46.92m)
Beam:	21.9ft.(6.74m)
Depth:	11.6ft.(3.57m)
Engine Room Length:	41.4ft.(12.74m)

In 1869 an iron screw barque was laid down by Thomas Royden as the *Sherbro* for the African Steamship Co. Ltd.[16] but significantly the name was changed to the *Soudan* at the request of the Colonial Office who had just ordered a new steam yacht from White's of Cowes for use as a government despatch vessel. This two-funnelled paddle steamer completed in 1870 was to be named *Sherbro*, a corruption of Cerberos which is both an island off the coast of Sierra Leone and a river in West Africa: she was built specifically for duties in that area which accounts for the government's choice of name, her handsome appearance and the roominess of her accommodation.[17]

She had been sold out of government service in 1876 after only a short career, and returned to London where she was given an immediate survey. Purchased by the Salvage Steamship Co. it is unclear what they did with her but in 1878 she was resold to A. Leutner, also of London, when it was stated that she would be converted into a salvage steamer. He formed The Wreck Recovery and Salvage Company during the following year and the *Sherbro* was placed under the command of Captain Jackson who would stay with her despite a succession of changes in registered ownership, invariably involving Mr. Leutner together with others. There is no evidence that the conversion ever took place and it is unclear as to what use the vessel was put to before she came on the market yet again in 1884.

In what proved to be the final attempt to run a successful Burnham-Cardiff ferry service the Midland and London & South Western Railway Companies, through their Joint Committee at a meeting on 5 March 1884, took the unusual decision to acquire a vessel rather than continuing the charter arrangements then in force.

On that day it was resolved that Mr. S.W. Johnson (the well-known Midland Railway Locomotive Superintendent) and Mr. Corke (of the LSWR) should inspect the *Sherbro* which was then lying for sale in the West India Docks, London. Subject to their approval they had the Joint Committee's permission to offer £4,500 for its purchase.[18]

Clearly the inspection of the vessel was favourable but the price tag was a little more than authorised because on 2 April the Joint Committee announced the purchase of the *Sherbro* for £4795-10-0.[19] The ship was re-registered at Bridgwater in the names of the Trustees of the London & South Western and Midland Railways jointly (R.H. Dutton and M.W. Thompson managing agents), for the S&DJR on 2 May 1884. Arrangements were made to provide coaling facilities at Cardiff and the ship was initially insured for £5,000 for the period 1 June to 31 October 1884.[20]

Before being placed into service she received an overhaul during which time the vessel was altered to accommodate 400 passengers and some 80 head of cattle. The Joint Committee also made strenuous attempts

*(right) At 239 gross tons, the paddle steamer **Sherbro** was the largest S&D-owned ship to be used on the Burnham-Cardiff ferry service. In this view the fine lines of the former government despatch vessel are clearly seen as Captain Ezekiel Barron takes her astern to clear Burnham pier with a good crowd during the late 1880s.* (S&DRT)

Masters and representative crew members of the *Sherbro*, 5/1884-7/1888

MASTER:	Captain Ezekiel L. BARRON	June 1884-July 1888
MATES:	J. COX	1884-1885
	Henry WHILE	1886-1888
ENGINEERS:	W.F. BLACKMORE	1884
	Charles GILBODY	1886
	Andrew WHITE	1886
SEAMEN;	John King	1884-1886
	Walter Luxon	1884-1886
	S. King	1884
	Charles West	1884
	G. Thomas	1884
	Samuel Browning	1886
	Samuel Hart	1886
	William Manley	1886
FIREMEN	Henry Newick	1884
	W. Winter	1884
	A. Norman	1884-1886
	L. Baker	1884
	James Blackmore	1884
	George Befeledge	1886
	George Deplige	1886-1887
	Joseph Baranes	1886
	Henry Martin	1886
COAL TRIMMERS:	Henry Martin	1884
	Henry Farthing	1886
STEWARD:	Walter Vickery	1886
BOY:	William King	1884

to promote their new acquisition and an initial 500 copies of an illustrated advertisement were obtained by July 1884.[21] Captain Jackson seems to have come with the ship but he was not to remain for very long, quickly being displaced by a well-known former employee, none other than 65-year old Captain Ezekiel Barron, last seen when in command of the *Defiance* in 1871.

From details of the vessel's insurance it is clear that the ferry service would be a summer-only operation as the S&D did not intend to use her during winter and it is recorded that she was laid up on 1 November 1884 at Highbridge Wharf, an event that was repeated on the same date in 1885.[22] These must have been amongst the extremely rare occasions when S&D passenger vessels were to be seen at Highbridge.

In the event the ship was to sail under the S&D flag for only four years during which time it became increasingly obvious that the ferry service could never be made to pay, a situation compounded by the opening of the Severn Railway Tunnel in 1886.

In October 1886 it was reported that improved condensing arrangements were being installed[23] but the ship did not sail again during that winter although she returned to service as planned during the summer of 1887. Following the usual winter lay-up the *Sherbro* again returned to service during the early summer of 1888 but in July of that year the Joint Committee decided that there was no future in the operation and decided to sell her. No time was wasted in disposal; the latter part of the season's sailings were abandoned forthwith and she was sold to the Cantabrica Navigation Company of Bilbao for £2,250,[24] her Bridgwater registration being cancelled on 27 July. Interestingly the Joint Committee were not officially advised of this until a meeting on the 8 August.

Renamed *Express* by her new owners, she sailed on coastwise Spanish services for several more years but in September 1892 was withdrawn and reduced to a lighter after which nothing further is known.

Alpha

Official Number:		78559
Type:		Single-deck screw steam coaster
Construction:		Iron. Round stern
Builders:		Messrs. W. Swan & Son, Maryhill, Glasgow
Completed:		1877
Withdrawn:		1925. Scrapped
Tonnage:	1877-84	82.39grt, 47.79nrt
	1884-05	93.52grt, 55.35nrt
	1905-25	111grt, 76nrt
Engines:		2-cylinder compound developing 22nhp and driving a single screw, by Muir & Houston, Glasgow
		LP cylinder : 1012in. x 15in.(277mm x 382mm)
		HP cylinder: 20in. x 15 in.(513mm x 382mm)
Horsepower:		22 nominal
Steam Pressure:		80 psi
Length:	1877-84	65.2ft.(20.1m)
	1884-05	74.2ft.(22.8m)
	1905-25	86.2ft.(26.5m)
Beam:	1877-84	17.8ft.(5.48m)
	1884-05	17.8ft.(5.48m)
	1905-25	18.0ft.(5.54m)
Depth:	1877-84	8.2ft.(2.5m)
	1884-05	8.2ft.(2.5m)
	1905-25	8.0ft.(2.46m)

The small iron screw steamer *Alpha* was completed at Maryhill, Glasgow during 1877 for local owners and was registered in Glasgow. The Joint Committee minutes of 7 March 1879 refer to the purchase of the vessel at a reduced price of £1,550. The ship was registered at Bridgwater to Edward Ellis of Leicester on behalf of the Somerset & Dorset Joint Railway but not until 29 November 1880.[25] Following the death of Ellis the vessel was re-registered on 19 November 1890 in the names of R.H. Dutton and M.W. Thompson. She was employed, like her sister ships principally in the rail trade, but often carried more general cargoes.

At the end of 1883 the *Alpha* grounded on a mud-bank at Highbridge, the repair of the resulting damage being estimated at £300. However by this time much longer rails were being produced by the steel mills for use by the various companies and as the length of the *Alpha* was no longer adequate to accommodate them the opportunity was taken to lengthen the vessel by 9ft.(2.77m) at the same time. This, it was estimated, would cost an additional £250.[26] The work commenced in March 1884 when extra men were taken on by Highbridge Locomotive Works to cope with the repairs and lengthening. This suggests that the ship was not drydocked but simply moved to the upper New Wharf in the harbour. The total job took two months and on completion the extra men were discharged. It increased the ship's gross tonnage to 93.52 and required her re-registration, which event occurred to the same two gentlemen as ship's managers on 23 May 1884.

When Thompson died on 1 December 1891 Dutton became sole managing agent but when he died on 8 October 1892 there was a re-registration to John William Mansfield until the ship was transferred to George Ernest Paget of Loughborough and Wyndham Spencer Portal of Basingstoke on 29 June 1896. Following the latter's death he was replaced by Robert A. Dykes, the S&D's traffic superintendent (on behalf of the LSWR and MR) who in turn was replaced by his successor G.H. Eyre.

When the old ketch *Julia* was being replaced in 1904 by a purpose-built steamship of the same name, the opportunity was again taken to lengthen the *Alpha* to carry yet longer rails. This time an extra 12ft.(3.7m) was added and this increased her gross tonnage to 111. She was then re-registered at Bridgwater directly to the LSWR Company on 10 April 1905 although this was a mistake because on 20 April it was altered to the LSW and Midland Railway Companies jointly. Shortly before this, Captain E. Fletcher had taken over command from Captain Luxon, remaining with the vessel until relieved by Captain C. Rawlings in July 1915.

The ship suffered another accident in 1920 whilst at Highbridge Wharf's No.2 berth when she was sucked into the mud and failed to rise again with the tide. A similar incident had recently happened with another ship at nearby Watchet. She was totally submerged to the detriment of her cargo of 130 tons of flour, possibly one of the worst cargoes that she could have been carrying! A successful salvage operation then followed and the ship was soon back in service.[27]

*An early 1880s view of the **Alpha** shows the little ship in her original form before the first lengthening in 1884. Complete with furled main and jib sails in compliance with contemporary regulations the ship is seen leaving her berth at Highbridge in ballast against a backdrop of an interesting assortment of S&DJR open mineral wagons (from the left: Nos.647, 676, 42A, 739 ,173 and one un-identified wagon behind the crane). (National Railway Museum – DY8460)*

Transferred under the powers of the Railways Act of 1921 the *Alpha* was again re-registered, this time to the Southern Railway Company and London Midland & Scottish Railway Company jointly and continued to trade for another three years or so. Then in July 1924 she was finally laid up leaving the steamship *Julia* to continue on her own for a few months pending the completion of a replacement ship which was then being built.[28] In April, shortly before the new vessel *Radstock* was delivered, offers were invited for the purchase of the ship.[29] Presumably this was for disposal because that is what next happened to this veteran vessel following cancellation of her registration on 12 November 1925.

Masters and representative crew members of the *Alpha*, 1879-1925

MASTERS:	Captain William BROOKS	1881-1882	
	Captain Henry D. LUXON	1883-1904	(to *Julia (2)* as master)[30]
	Captain Edward FLETCHER	1904-July 1915	
	Captain Charles RAWLINGS	July 1915-1924[31] (to *Julia (2)*, 1925, as master)	
MATES:	James FARTHING	1881-1883	
	Frank WITHERS	1884-1886	
	Albert NEATH	1889	
	Edward FLETCHER	1890	
	William CREEMER	1890-1891	
	Edward FLETCHER	1891	
	Charles RAWLINGS	1892	
	William CREEMER	1892	
	Charles RAWLINGS	1893	
	William CREEMER	1894-1899	
	Charles RAWLINGS	1900-1901	
	William CREEMER	1901-1903	
	William COX	1904	
	William BLAKE	1906-1913	
ENGINEERS:	John WINTER	1881-1892	
	Isaac WINTER	1892	
	James WINTER	1893	
	Isaac WINTER	1894	
	Joseph WINTER	1896	
	John WINTER	1896	
	William CREEMER	1900	
	John WINTER	1901	
	Joseph WINTER	1901-1902	
	John WINTER	1903	
	Joseph WINTER	1903	
	Samuel BROWNING	1904	
	William WINTER	1906-1909	
	Arthur BAKER	1910	
	William WINTER	1911-1913	
	A. WINTER	1916	

SEAMEN:	Joseph Creemer	1881-1884	F. Dyer	1893
	Frank Withers:	1882-1883	W. Bound	1894
	James Parley	1884	Charles Rawlings	1894-1900
	William Creemer	1886-1889	James Winter	1900
	Albert Neath	1890	John Woodward	1903-1904
	Amos Hale	1891	Alfred Bound	1904
	William Hale	1892	Samuel Browning	1906-1908
	Charles West	1892	Arthur Baker	1911
	Matthew Linegar	1893	John Caswell	1912-1913

FIREMEN:	Albert Bound	1881-1891, 1906-1908	John Winter	1898
	Albert Browning	1882	George Winter	1898
	William Winter	1890, 1904, 1910-1911	Robert Payne	1900-1903
	James Pugsley	1891	Alfred Buncombe	1903
	Henry Newick	1892	Fred Lyddon	1910-1911
	William Hale	1893-1896	John Saunders	1912-1913
	Frederick Winter	1896	Fred Tout	1913

Note: Full crew records are not available from 1913.

*(above) The **Alpha**, twice lengthened, is seen in 1924 in her final form. At the end of the following year she was laid up pending disposal and sold for scrap. Note the addition of a black top to her buff funnel, a more sensible colour for a steamship.* *(S&DRT)*

*(below) The **Alpha's** distinctive stern is clearly visible here. Vast quantities of Baltic timber are stacked on the wharf, mainly in London North Western or Midland Railway wagons, awaiting departure.* *(Author's collection)*

When the Glastonbury Canal was first cut, transhipment of goods between river/canal craft and seagoing ships often took place in this area, the original New Wharf. With the arrival of the Somerset Central Railway in 1854 this quay was rail connected and in constant use but following the extensive improvements carried out during the 1860s and provision of a new long quay; it was less busy and was often used as a lay-up berth which is why the S&D's steamer **Julia** has taken the ground here, probably to undergo part of her refit sometime after the First World War. Behind and under the bridge is the old entrance to the canal, the famed sea lock, still in use at this time to control water levels but long since disused as a navigation. The brick arch is a later addition over which ran a short siding into the Co-operative Society's coal yard and closer inspection will reveal two men unloading a coal wagon next to a covered goods wagon, all of which are partly shielded by a fence. On the left is the static timber crane and another rake of open mineral wagons.

(Author's collection)

Julia (2)

Official Number:		111393
Type:		Screw steam coaster
Construction:		Steel
Builders:		Mordey Carney (later Thornycroft), Southampton, Yard 434
Completed:		1904
Withdrawn:		Dec. 1933. Scrapped 1934
Tonnage:	As built	196.86grt, 85.31nrt
	1906	194.04grt, 75.21nrt
	1907	194.04grt, 78.19nrt
Engines:		2-cylinder compound driving a single screw, by builders
		HP cylinder: 14in. x 22in.(359mm x 564mm)
		LP cylinder: 30in. x 22in.(769mm x 564mm)
Horsepower:		300 indicated
Steam Pressure:		150 psi
Length:		105.3ft.(12.6m)
Beam:		21.1ft.(6.5m)
Depth:		9.1ft.(2.8m)
Quarterdeck Length:		41.0ft.(12.6m)
Fo'c'sle Length:		14.0ft.(4.3m)
Hold Length:		50ft.9in.(15.6m)
Hatch Length:		36ft.9in.(11.3m)
Hatch Width:		8ft.0in.(2.46m)

The *Julia* was a steel vessel built at Woolston in 1904 specifically to the design of the Somerset & Dorset Joint Railway to replace the old wooden ketch of the same name. She was the first vessel in the S&D's fleet to be built of steel and when completed was put to work alongside the *Alpha* on the traditional rail trade developed by the company although she also carried a large quantity of iron, coal, stone and other cargoes during her working life.

The vessel was actually registered at Bridgwater on behalf of the London & South Western and Midland Railway Companies jointly to George H. Eyre of Bath (S&DJR traffic superintendent 1902-1920) on 19 July 1904 but under the powers of the 1921 Railways Act her registered ownership was transferred to the Southern and LMS Railways jointly from 1 January 1923.

Captain Henry Luxon, formerly master of the *Alpha*, was instructed to stand by the ship in Southampton and take command on completion, a situation he enjoyed for the next 11 years during which time the ship was re-registered in 1906 and again in 1907, on both occasions recording slightly different tonnages.

One day in July 1915 he left the ship at Highbridge Wharf to walk home. As he crossed the complex pattern of sidings he fell and broke his legs. He shouted to the ship's engineer who was ahead of him but he did not hear so with extreme difficulty and in much pain he managed to climb back on to the elevated crane-road, then down one of the vertical iron ladders set into the quayside to the ship and into his cabin. Here he remained until unloading commenced next morning when he was discovered by Mr. Luke.

Captain Luxon was then carried along the Wharf to an awaiting car and taken to Bridgwater hospital. The Works staff made him a pair of simple wooden crutches to help him get about but sadly although his legs healed the unpadded arm-rests aggravated a cancerous growth under his armpit and just a year later he died without having returned to work.[32]

Following his accident in July 1915 Captain Luxon was replaced by Captain Fletcher from the *Alpha* who stayed with the ship until 1922. Reboilered in 1920, the size of *Julia* was found to be ideal for operations into and out of Highbridge and also the River Ely coal

staithes on the other side of the Bristol Channel as well as the all-important rail trade for which the vessel was primarily built. On this type of work she continued, along with the *Alpha* (until the latter was scrapped in 1925) and, later, the *Radstock*, for the S&DJR until the parent companies decided to wind up the shipping fleet for economic reasons in 1933. By this time the *Julia* was 30 years old and was not considered worth re-selling. Accordingly she was disposed of as scrap to Mr. J. Cashmore, Eagle Works, Great Bridge, Staffs., for £202 delivered as and where lying.[33] Her registration was cancelled on 20 December 1934.

Masters and representative crew members of the *Julia*, 1904-1933

MASTERS:	Captain Henry D. LUXON	June 1904-July 1915 (from *Alpha*)[34]
	Captain Edward FLETCHER	July 1915-1922 (from *Alpha*)[35]
	Captain William SHARMAN	1922-July 1925 (then to *Radstock* in command)[36]
	Captain Charles RAWLINGS	July 1925-6 July 1928 (from *Alpha*)[37]
MATE:	Charles RAWLINGS	1906-July 1915 (then to *Alpha* in command)
ENGINEERS:	John WINTER	1906-1909
	James WINTER	1910
	John WINTER	1910-1911
	John CASWELL	1911
	John WINTER	1912-1913
SEAMEN:	John Caswell	1906-1907, 1910
	John Woodward	1906-1907, 1912-1913
	James Woodward	1908
	James Caswell	1908
	Arthur Baker	1912-1913
	Reginald Baker	1913
	Lionel Hill	1920s
FIREMEN:	John Saunders	1906-1911
	James Woodward	1910-1911
	Frederick Lyddon	1912-1913
	George Young	1913

Note: Full crew records are not available from 1913.

*(left) Having navigated the River Brue the steamship **Julia** sits off the harbour following her maiden voyage in 1904 in what was a typically posed photo of the period. Dressed overall for the occasion, the first flag from the masthead probably being the S&DJR houseflag, the little ship makes a fine sight with her crew and full complement of invited guests, almost certainly more than were ever carried again! But had they come far? At best they would have been embarked at Burnham but interestingly the ship is loaded to her marks whilst both her tender and one of her lifeboats are missing; maybe they had just been embarked and the boats were out of sight. In the background a number of S&D wagons can be seen on the sidings at the western end of the wharf with the characteristic kilns and chimneys of the two brickworks, Colthurst, Symons & Co. and the Apex Tile Company, between Highbridge and Burnham also just visible.*   *(National Maritime Museum – N24352)*

The **Julia**, at Highbridge Wharf, looks in excellent condition so maybe this was taken shortly after her arrival in 1904. Certainly she is in ballast and looks ready to go to sea when the tide allows, with both lifeboats housed, hatch covers in place and tender shipped, canvas dodger fixed to bridge and sails furled. A closer look reveals at least four men on board, with a couple apparently wearing bowler hats; another employee stands in one of the several S&D five-plank open mineral wagons seen behind. Unfortunately the white-painted superstructure eventually gave way to a much more practical if rather less attractive brown whilst her funnel was extended and again for very obvious reasons gained a black top.   *(National Railway Museum - DY8520A)*

The **Julia** in the upper berth or New Wharf at Highbridge which was habitually used for refitting in later days. The boiler, seen on a wagon on the right, has been removed by the rail-mounted crane. Boiler repairs had been undertaken by the S&D's own railway workshops, a mile or so to the east, until they closed although it seems that movements of this nature may have been a little out of gauge. *(Author's collection)*

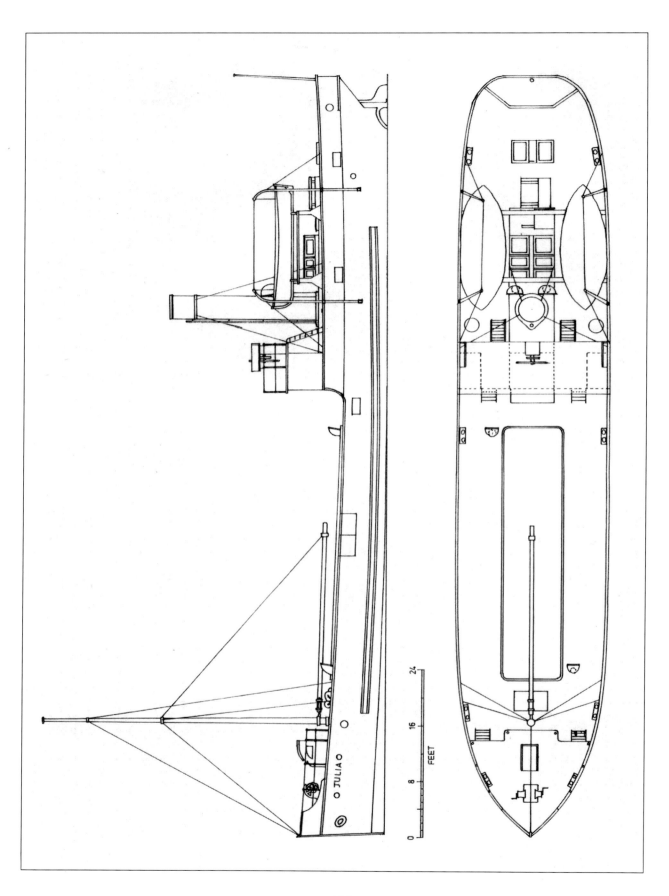

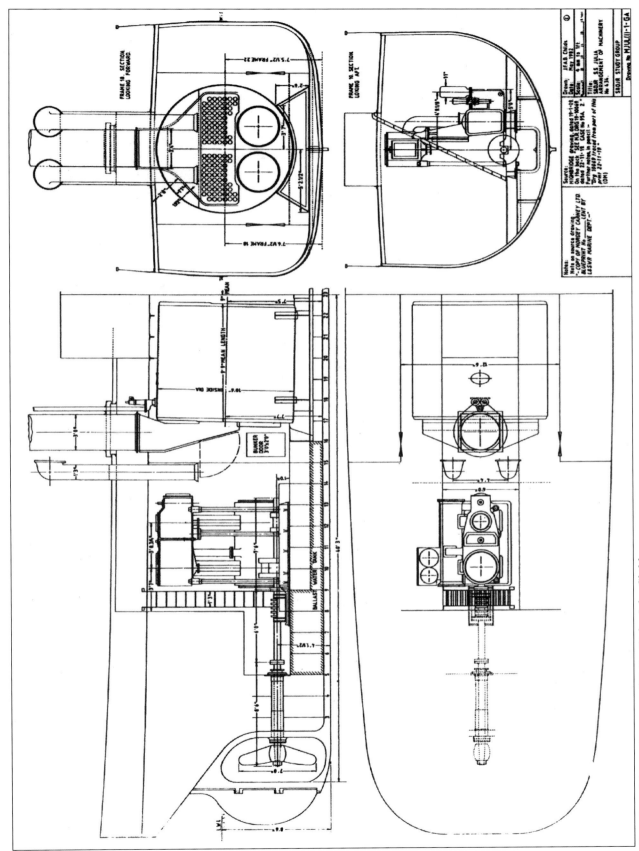

*Drawing of the engine room of **Julia** (2) by John Childs*

Radstock

Official Number:	111395
Signal letters:	MPBC
Type:	Screw steam coaster
Construction:	Steel
Builders:	J. Crichton & Company, Saltney Yard, Chester (Yard 410)
Completed:	September 1925
Withdrawn:	1958. Scrapped
Tonnage:	195.42grt, 77.62nrt
Engines:	2-cylinder compound driving a single 4-bladed screw by Plenty & Sons Ltd., Newbury
	LP Cylinder: 13in. x 18in.(333mm x 462mm)
	HP Cylinder: 26in. x 18in.(667mm x 462mm)
Horsepower:	275 indicated
Boiler:	Single-ended: Grate surface 33 sq. ft., Heating surface 1,000 sq. ft.
Steam Pressure:	150 psi
Steering Gear:	Steam operated
Length:	105.6ft.(bp), 110.1ft (oa),(32.49m/33.9m)
Beam:	21.1ft.(6.49m), 22.1ft.(oa),(6.8m)
Depth (Moulded):	9.7ft.(2.98m)
Draught:	9.6ft.(2.95m)
Freeboard:	7.5in.(192mm)
Fo'c'sle Length:	14ft.6in.(4.46m)
Quarterdeck Length:	44ft.6in.(13.69m)
Forepeak Ballast Tank:	18 tons water capacity

The *Radstock*, a short raised quarterdeck vessel, was the second steel screw ship to be built for the Somerset & Dorset Joint Railway and was completed in 1925 by J. Crichton & Co. at their Saltney yard on the River Dee, near Chester. The ship was delivered on Monday 28 September 1925[38] and formally registered at Bridgwater to the Southern and LMS Railways jointly on 30 September. She was built as a specific replacement for the *Alpha* which was withdrawn and scrapped in that same year. Unlike other members of the fleet she was registered with Lloyds and allocated their '+100A1' survey classification.

Essentially the *Radstock* was built for the rail trade, her steel all-riveted construction being a little heavier than might otherwise have been expected. The steering gear was steam operated and as such the vessel was very much an up-to-date version of the *Julia* with almost identical dimensions and tonnage. Indeed she represented the final development of the small steam-powered coaster; post-war recession had led to a sharp decline in the building of new tonnage whilst those constructed from this period were mainly motor vessels. As events turned out, of course, the parent companies decided to wind up the shipping interests of the S&DJR in 1933 so the vessel had a relatively short career with the railway.

There has been some interesting speculation as to how the name *Radstock* was chosen and it has been suggested that when the time came to decide upon a name the S&D traffic superintendent, Mr. G.H. Wheeler, received a letter from the LMS headquarters at Derby asking him to submit a list of suitable names for consideration. After due thought he made this list, one of which was 'Essendee' which would have perpetuated the railway's title. The list was returned to Derby but, it is said, it definitely did not include the 'Radstock' on it. Consequently there was some surprise when it was learnt that this was to be the name.

*The **Radstock** was launched in August 1925 at the Saltney yard of J. Crichton & Co. Ltd. on the River Dee near Chester and delivered at the end of September. The little ship is seen above as she is prepared for sea trials at the yard in September. Below she steams boldly away from the yard and heads downstream towards the open sea and her trials. As yet the ship has no water ballast in her tank and unusually the whole of the boot-topping can be seen, whilst a ladder gives easy access to the empty hold.*　　　　　　　　　　　　　　　　　*(Flintshire Record Office)*

Who made the final decision and why was not apparently known at the time, and is now very probably lost in history, but certainly it seems that it was no one locally.

During her time with the S&DJR the *Radstock* had a rather uneventful career trading mainly out of her home port of Highbridge. The first master was Captain W.D. Sharman of Bridgwater. At 64 years of age he had been employed by the railway company for about 4 years at the time and transferred from the command of the *Julia* with an increase in salary from £210 per annum to £230pa.[39] Sometime around 1929 or 1930 Captain Sharman retired and Captain William H. Morse of Watchet was appointed by the S&DJR to take over.[40]

Like her sister ships in the fleet the *Radstock* was employed mainly on local coasting and this primarily took the vessel across to the South Wales ports where rolled steel rails were loaded and brought back to Highbridge for use both by the S&D itself and by the Southern Railway. When not so employed the ship was used to carry other bulk cargoes including iron from Newport and coal and culm from a variety of ports including the River Ely coaling wharves at Penarth.

The ship was given a full survey in December 1932 at Newport but following the decision by the Joint Conference of the owners to dispose of its small fleet in 1933, the *Radstock* was put up for sale since she was only eight years old. She found a ready buyer in the incumbent master, Captain Morse, who made an immediate offer to purchase the vessel. He agreed to the asking price of £1,500 and paid the S&D in cash. The ship was handed over on 15 December 1933 and an agreement to operate made on 3 January 1934.[41]

*The **Radstock** unloads coal at Highbridge Wharf in the early 1930s. This view of the ship admirably shows off the final development of the small steam coaster before motor vessels were built in quantity. With the derrick topped and slung outboard the coal can be unloaded. Closer inspection reveals that there are a number of people both on the ship and quayside looking on, some of whom are dressed in heavy coats and bowler hats together with the odd briefcase. That is because the centre of attraction was not the ship but the newly acquired 3-ton steam grab crane which was undergoing its first trials at the time in an effort to speed up discharge. Hiding in the background is Crane No.2, one of the S&D's two rail-mounted breakdown cranes. The coal was being loaded into one of a large number of six-plank open mineral wagons many of which were constructed for the S&D (Nos.1122-1186) as Loco Coal wagons in 1902 and subsequently taken into LMS stock so there is little doubt that the ship is delivering best Welsh steam coal, much of which is for use in the railway's own locomotive depots.*   *(National Railway Museum – DY17223)*

Captain Morse took his new acquisition back to his home port of Watchet where he continued to work the ship for many years mainly in the coal trade but keeping her looking neat and tidy in the process.

At Donniford, close-by, the army established a camp and gunnery range during the mid-1920s. In 1935 a small number of Queen Bee pilotless target aircraft (Tiger Moths with floats) were introduced. The first were catapulted from a cruiser but later a shore-based catapult was built at Donniford. Those aircraft that survived the ravages of the gunners landed on the sea and this enabled Captain Morse to secure charters from the RAF to recover them, the **Radstock** being just about big enough to carry one aircraft on its hold covers.[42]

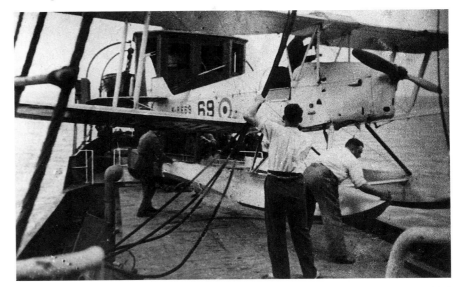

*De Havilland Queen Bee aircraft K8669 sits comfortably on the hatch covers of the **Radstock** having been recovered from the sea off Watchet in 1938 following a live shoot by gunners from nearby Donniford range. Details of the ship's wheelhouse, hatch, deck and lifeboat arrangements can all be seen. The RAF acquired 350 Queen Bee radio-controlled, pilotless aircraft following its first flight on 5 January 1935. The aircraft was used both as a landplane and as a twin-float seaplane to provide live gunnery practice.*

(Colin G. Maggs collection)

*A large crowd welcomes the **Radstock** as local master Captain Bill Morse brings the vessel alongside in Watchet Harbour in July 1938. No doubt the attraction was the Queen Bee aircraft sitting on the hatch covers. The ship's hull has recently been repainted light grey and white. On the right Captain W.J. Norman has just arrived with the Wansborough Paper Company's former Clyde puffer **Rushlight** (1902/118grt). This little ship traded from the harbour for over 40 years from 1910, apart from a brief period in the First World War when she went back to Scotland. She was mainly engaged in bringing culm from Cardiff for the nearby paper mills and was eventually broken up at Llanelli in 1953. (Colin G. Maggs collection)*

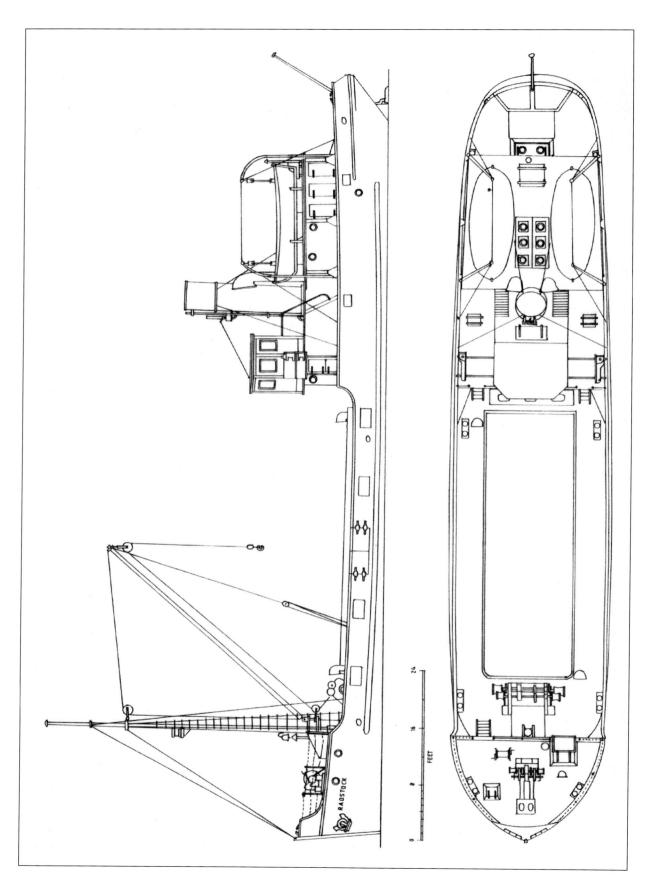

Between such charters the **Radstock** continued to ply locally often bringing coal in from South Wales to various Somerset and North Devon ports whilst the ship regularly visited her old home of Highbridge no doubt for the S&D.

During the summer of 1937 she appeared with a light grey and white hull following a repaint, then in the following December she was again surveyed, in Cardiff. In January 1940 a full boiler survey was carried out prior to being requisitioned by the War Ministry; Captain Morse remained the owner and probably stayed in command. It is said that she initially moved to Portsmouth to tend the navy[43] and was certainly seen at Weymouth at this time but by the end of the year she was preparing to voyage further afield.

In January 1941 'T' Flight of No.1 Anti-Aircraft Co-operation Unit formed at Weybourne on the North Norfolk coast and they received the **Radstock** in February for use as a salvage ship, and a seaplane tender together with a number of Queen Bee aircraft.

Clearly the ship's reputation had gone before her! On 6 June the Prime Minister, Winston Churchill, and a number of distinguished people witnessed firings at these aircraft, one landing on the sea to be salvaged by the **Radstock**. The radio-controlled aircraft were moved away on 29 April 1942.[44]

On completion of this task preparations were made to release the **Radstock** from war service and in May 1942 she was given a full '+100A1' Lloyds survey at Southampton. She was allocated to the Bristol company A.J. Smith Ltd. by the local Ministry of War Transport shipping controller, Alfred Duggan. Duggan was himself the owner of a fleet of coasting vessels and acted as agent for a number of other ships but unlike Smith's he did not work in the coal trade, The actual sale to Smith's is recorded as 29 June 1942 following which the ship returned to the Bristol Channel and settled down to trade very much as before mainly with coal for Bideford, Barnstaple, Watchet and Bridgwater.

*The **Radstock** was not a particularly frequent visitor to Bristol in her earlier years but here she is in the Avon Gorge inbound for the City Docks on Saturday 20 July 1946 when in Alfred Smith's ownership. Although little changed from her S&D days there has been some trouble with the wheelhouse which has gained a couple of hefty bracing wires. The hull has reverted to black whilst the funnel is in Smith's colours.* (Keen collection, Bristol Industrial Museum)

Alfred J. Smith had traded in and around the Bristol Channel since 1887 and also had interests in Fowey, the business largely being that of carrying coal from the South Wales ports to consumers on the Bristol side of the channel and providing coal bunkering services. *Radstock* was only occasionally seen at Bristol unlike the other similar-sized steamers in the fleet, the *Elemore, Tanny* and *Roma*.

Shortly after the war, in 1946 the *Radstock* was a frequent visitor to Bideford where she delivered coal to the gasworks on the eastern side of the River Torridge. The ship then carried Smith's funnel colours. In June 1948 she was again surveyed in Cardiff to Lloyds '+100A1' but her future was becoming increasingly uncertain so she was laid up at Appledore Quay awaiting sale.

Facing a gradual post-war decline in the coal trade A.J. Smith Ltd. was liquidated in 1949 and the *Radstock* continued in lay-up without a buyer. In 1951 a new holding company, Bristowe Shippers Ltd., was formed by Jocelyn Smith together with two large Bristol coal factors, Renwick, Wilton & Dobson and Thomas Silvey & Co. to take over the assets. Renwick's were no strangers to shipowning having operated colliers elsewhere. The three above-mentioned ships were duly transferred to the new company together with the *Radstock* which followed on 22 February 1952. The ship, until now still registered at Bridgwater, was re-registered at Bristol on 5 March but also class-expunged from the Lloyds Register in August of that year for non-compliance with the Society's rules following a survey!

Under Bristowe Shippers the *Radstock*, together with the *Roma*, was generally found on the River Ely-Bridgwater service bringing in anything up to 120 tons of coal per voyage mainly to Dunball Wharf where it was off-loaded onto rail for such destinations as the British Cellophane and the Royal Ordnance Factories. This trip could not normally be achieved on one tide and inevitably the ship would sit on the mud off Stert

*Over the years the **Radstock** was a frequent visitor to the Southern Railway's wharf at Fremington on the River Taw where ships of the S&D had often discharged rails. She is seen here on 24 August 1948 in her last days with A.J. Smith before the company went into liquidation and shortly before the ship was laid-up just around the corner at Appledore Quay.* (Craig/Farr collection)

Masters and representative crew members of the Radstock, 1925-1933

MASTERS:	Captain William D. SHARMAN	1925-c1930 (from *Julia (2)* 1925)
	Captain William H. MORSE	c1930-1933 (and in continuation under his ownership until 20 June 1942)
MATE:	?	
ENGINEER:	A. WINTER	
SEAMEN:	William Hill	
	?	
FIREMAN:	Samuel Evans	(ex-S&DJR locomotive fireman)

The crew stayed together until the ship was sold to Captain Morse at the end of 1933 when they dispersed. Sam Evans returned to the railway.

Island to await entry into the river. The ship's master at that time was Captain Holder who usually had his large alsatian dog in the small wheelhouse with him.[45]

Sadly the writing was on the wall for the traditional coal markets and with the advent of more oil-fired electricity generating stations and natural gas coming on stream the trade continued to decline throughout the 1950s and one-by-one the remaining four ships were withdrawn for scrap. *Radstock*, the third of the quartet to go, was declared surplus early in 1958 and on 9 February she made her last voyage to Rees Shipbreaking Industries at Llanelli where she was broken up.[46] Thus ended the final shipping link with the Somerset & Dorset Railway.

*(above) The **Radstock** was well photographed over the years but in this delightful view her latter-day master Captain Holder takes the well-loaded vessel to sea on 14 August 1953 for yet another cross-channel trip when in the ownership of Bristowe Shippers Ltd. Bristowe's retained Smith's funnel colours and the ship looks very smart with her white wheelhouse. The bracing wires have been removed and the navigation lights relocated to the wheelhouse sides. Taking a ship to sea with its hatch covers off and holds open, even on short Bristol Channel journeys such as this, would not be tolerated today. (Keen collection, Bristol Industrial Museum)*

*(right) A fine stern view of the **Radstock** in her later days showing much detail of the quarter-deck as she lays over at Broad Quay, Bristol on 25 August 1955.   (Craig/Farr collection)*

Notes:

GENERAL:

Much of the information contained in this chapter has been taken from or checked against the transcripts of the Bridgwater Ship Registers (SRO DD/FA Volumes 6 to 9) and notes on Somerset Maritime History by Grahame Farr (SRO DD/FA Vol.11/1).

1. PRO Kew. Joint Committee minutes dated 19 October 1875. The ships were not included in the lease of the railway itself.
2. After George Moorsom who had been appointed as secretary to a commission set up in 1849 to make further investigations concerning tonnage measurement. The system advocated in 1852 was incorporated into the 1854 Merchant Shipping Act (Act 17 & 18 Victoria, c.104) which came into force on 1 May 1855. This was also the year in which all ships were given signal codes and Official Numbers (ON) which were allocated at the port of first registry and retained throughout the life of the ship.
3. The Bridgwater Ship Owners and Crew List is derived from details in the Register General of Shipping and Seamen (DD/RSS) and has been indexed by Mr. A. Brown (SRO, Taunton).

Ruby
4. William Patterson's Great Western Yard was situated next to the Albion Yard of Charles Hill & Sons in the floating harbour, Bristol City Docks.
5. From the Mercantile Navy Lists of 1867 and 1868.

Heather Bell
6. The **Heather Bell** has often been confused with a larger steamer of the same name which was built in 1871 for service between Ardrossan and Arran. That vessel was purchased in 1876 by the Port of Portsmouth and Ryde Steam Packet Co. Both vessels are clearly shown together in both the Mercantile Navy List and Lloyds Register under their respective owners.
7. There is conflicting information about the date of sale. In one reference it is stated that Mr. Burt purchased the ship in 1873 but other sources quote 1 May 1871.

Julia (1)
8. It has been suggested that the ship was originally brought to the Bristol Channel by Thomas R. Brown, the well-known Bristol shipowner. There is no evidence to confirm this.
9. Joint Committee minutes dated 29 Oct. 1875 authorised purchase of the vessel from the S&DR, and S&DJR Directors minutes dated 13 Dec. 1875 reports completion of transfer.
10. Information from the Bridgwater Crew Lists (SRO) and the Merchant Navy Lists of 1914 and 1924.
11. Information from Martin Benn, WSS.

Richard and Emily
12. There is a separate report that the Burnham lifeboat was launched on 15 September 1873 to save the **Richard and Emily** and her crew of four. This incident just pre-dates S&DR ownership and seems to confirm that she was already in the Bristol Channel trade.

Leopard
13. PRO RAIL. Joint Committee minutes of 1890 refer.
14. George Dyer probably got the name 'Chatworth' wrong in his memorandum. More likely he was referring to Charles Clatworthy, the resident S&D shipwright.
15. Mercantile Navy Lists of 1900 and 1907 confirm her ownership with confirmation from the transcripts of the Bridgwater Ship Register (SRO DD/FA. Vol.7)

Sherbro
16. Readers are referred to *The Elder Dempster Fleet History 1852-1985* by J. Cowden and J. Duffy for further details of ships with this name of which there were three between 1882 and 1984.

17. Originally shown as **Sherbro'** with the apostrophe.
18. RAIL 626/1-11 series, Minute No.1178 dated 5 March 1884.
19. RAIL 626/1-11 series, Minute No.1186 dated 2 April 1884.
20. *Ibid*. The cost of insurance was £45-11-3.
21. RAIL 626/1-11 series, Minute No.1226 dated 2 July 1884.
22. RAIL 626/1-11 series, Minute Nos.1249 of 8 Oct. 1884 and 1374 of 7 Oct. 1885 refer.
23. RAIL 626/1-11 series, Minute No.1447 dated 6 Oct. 1886.
24. RAIL 626/1-11 series, Minute No.1571 dated 8 Aug. 1888.

Alpha
25. There are some conflicting reports that the ship was not re-registered in Bridgwater until 1905. However both the Bridgwater Ship Register and crew lists prove beyond doubt that this took place on 29 November 1880.
26. RAIL 626/1-11. Minute No.1152 dated 17 July 1924.
27. Ships lying in mud berths are particularly susceptible to the phenomenal suction power of mud. Wise seafarers will pass a wire rope or chain under the hull before the ship grounds on a falling tide to help break the suction as the tide rises. Sudden use of the engines to move the ship along as the tide rises may also help free the hull although masters of steamships were helpless unless steam was raised and the engines were available.
28. RAIL 626/28. Minute No.7633 dated 17 July 1924.
29. RAIL 626/28. Minute No.7708 dated 23 April 1925
30. Lloyds Register of Shipping and S&DRT *Bulletin* No.103.
31. RAIL 626/28. Minute No.7473 dated 29 Jan. 1923.

Julia (2)
32. Related by Captain Luxon's son William to the captain's grandson in 1980 (S&DRT *Bulletin* No.103).
33. RAIL 629/29, Minute No.410 dated 19 Jan. 1934. It would seem that the ship was lying at the New Wharf at Highbridge at which location she was dismantled.
34. Lloyds Register of Shipping and S&DRT *Bulletin* No.103.
35. Lloyds Register of Shipping.
36. Lloyds Register of Shipping. RAIL 626/28, Minute No.7473 dated 29 Jan. 1923 listed Captain Sharman as being 60 years of age, in the service of the S&DJR for just one-and-a-half years and drawing an annual salary of £210.
37. RAIL 626/28, Minute No.7772 dated 21 Jan. 1926 listed Captain Rawlings as being 64 years of age, in the service of the S&DJR for 33 years and drawing an annual salary of £230 in that year.

Radstock
38. RAIL 626/28 Minute No.7748 dated 16 Oct. 1925. In an article written by the S&D's traffic superintendent, George Wheeler, for the *Southern Railway* magazine, June 1929 issue, he states that the ship was launched in August 1925.
39. RAIL 626/28 Minute Nos.7473 dated 29 Jan. 1923 and 7772 dated 21 Jan. 1926.
40. There is no separate minute entry relating to this but it seems that Captain Sharman retired at this time since he was approaching 70 years of age.
41. RAIL 626/29 Joint Conference Minute No.410 dated 19 Jan. 1934 and 626/11 Minute No.4828 dated 6 Feb. 1934; sale of ship reported.
42. W.H. Norman, *Tales of Watchet Harbour*. There are several photographs extant showing aircraft as deck cargo on the ship.
43. W.H. Norman, *op.cit*.
44. Michael Bowyer, *Action Stations, 1. Wartime Military Airfields of East Anglia, 1939-45*.
45. From the memories of Captain Norman Curnoe, Bridgwater harbourmaster from 1953, by courtesy of Alan Hammond.
46. Information supplied by P.R. Gosson. See 'Mighty Miniatures of the Bristol Coal Trade' by R.M. Parsons in *Sea Breezes*, January 1993 for further details of A.J. Smith Ltd.

9 Twilight Years of the Pier

The withdrawal of the **Sherbro** from the Burnham-Cardiff service in mid-1888 marked the end of active interest in Burnham as a seagoing outlet by the S&DJR. Although they now no longer intended to maintain any services, seasonal excursion traffic generated by other operators continued. Aware that these steamers brought some traffic and income to the railway the Joint Committee were, nevertheless, keen to rid themselves of the pier because of ever-increasing maintenance costs.

Nothing noteworthy happened regarding disposal until 1899 when the Joint Committee sought abandonment of the pier. By this time the S&D was only receiving 5/- (25p) a time for each steamer that called. Silting was a constant problem and that, together with the tidal limitations and a structure which by now was in a pretty dilapidated state caused the ship operators to use it only infrequently by 1900. One such vessel which was noted during the early years of the new century was a cattle ship which occasionally called at Burnham from Ireland. An engine would stand at the pier head whilst several cattle wagons were lowered slowly down the incline for loading under the control of wires. There had been trouble in the past with animals on the pier and again there were reports of cattle jumping the barriers on occasions ending up either in the sea or running away along the sands.[1]

Passenger vessels were still calling during the first years of the 20th century, the P. & A. Campbell's paddle

*To confuse the issue, more than one ship could often be found carrying the same name. This is the Bristol-based paddle steamer **Heather Bell** (1871/271grt), not to be confused with the earlier BTH Company steamer of the same name, alongside at Burnham pier in 1901 or 1902. Judging by the number of umbrellas being held by the luckless passengers awaiting embarkation, no doubt many were cursing their luck for choosing such a lousy wet day for an excursion. The ship spent just two seasons on excursion work in this area, ownership having passed to Edwin Hunt of Northants in April 1901. Seen here with her distinctive yellow funnel, black top, black band and with a large blue 'H', the **Heather Bell** was Hunt's only venture into the maritime excursion trade, this lasting less than two years. Early in 1903 she was withdrawn and sold for breaking.*
(Captain James Dew via Robin Atthill collection/SDRT)

steamer **Cambria** (1895/420grt) being one such noted at the pier around 1903, the year in which a serious breech of the structure took place during bad weather on Friday 11 September. This can have done nothing to encourage the Joint Committee to change its mind and although it was repaired they were already locked in battle with the local urban district council to whom the railway wished to dispose this dubious asset. Negotiations did not go well and in 1905 the S&D sought Parliamentary permission to abandon it. This seemed to jog public awareness and a separate company was formed by a group of local residents with a view to carrying out the necessary repairs, then attracting fresh trade. The Burnham Pier Company, as it became then, looked across the water to the Barry Railway Company for help and found a sympathetic management. Under a separate Bill that railway promoted the Burnham (Somerset) Pier Act during the 1907 Parliamentary Session which allowed them to invest £15,000 in the project. According to an article in the September 1907 edition of the *Railway Magazine* the intention of the Barry Railway was to construct a new pier in conjunction with the S&DJR and the report continued:

It is anticipated that when the pier has been erected a steam ferry service will be arranged from Barry connecting with the north and south sides of the Bristol Channel enabling a passenger and perishable goods traffic to be conducted with regularity.

Details of the new structure emerged in another contemporary report and it makes interesting reading:

The New Pier at Burnham is proposed to be erected on the site of the present structure, and to extend seawards in a westerly direction for a distance of about 800 feet from the present Esplanade wall. The approach will be an open space, the new part of the Esplanade being between 60 and 70 feet wide, with an Esplanade wall about 70 feet long. From the entrance to the Pier, for a distance of 125 feet, the Promenade Deck of the Pier will be about 30 feet wide, and slope upwards, so as to give the deck the necessary height above high water level as required by the Board of Trade. Then, for a

The pier ceased to belong to the S&D after 1905 although the occasional ship still called but by 1908, when this view was taken, the traffic had become very infrequent. With the tide well up, P. & A. Campbell's steamer **Waverley** *(1885/258grt) is embarking a sizeable crowd The main line of rails and the short siding to the right are still* in situ *together with many of the mooring piles. Right in the distance, at the end of the 900ft.(277m) slip, the substantial marker post can just be discerned .*
(Captain James Dew via Robin Atthill collection/S&DRT)

distance of 210 feet, it will be 20 feet wide until the Pavilion is reached. Here it will widen out to 80 or 90 feet for a distance of 130 feet. The Pavilion is to be constructed in an ornamental style, and will accommodate about 800 persons, and be equipped as a modern theatre. It will be provided with Balconies and Promenade both inside and out, and with Cloak Rooms and Refreshment Rooms. The Stage and Scenic arrangements will be such as are required by the best concert and theatrical companies. From the Pavilion, the Promenade Deck will continue to the low water line, and there a Pier Head will be constructed, which will berth steamers at practically all states of the tide. Burnham will thus be placed in the premier position of direct communication with the South Wales coast, and will have an advantage possessed by no other resort on the English side of the Bristol Channel – i.e., a steamer can arrive and leave almost at any time of the day or night irrespective of tide. The Pier Head will be fitted with a light tower, which will fulfil a long felt want of mariners

plying to and from Bridgwater and will allay the danger of vessels running on to the present stone and timber structure, which is at present undoubtedly a menace to the navigation of the River Parrett.

There is a certain *déja vu* about all this and one wonders what the older residents of Burnham thought of it all because many of them would have remembered the difficulties and obstacles placed in the way of the Somerset Central Railway when they wanted to create something rather similar. They would also have remembered the difficulties the S&D had in trying to maintain a viable ferry service during the subsequent years and the reasons why it was abandoned. Just why the Barry Railway Company felt they could be more successful where others had failed remains difficult to understand but armed with much enthusiasm they planned to use their new paddle steamer *Barry* (1907/ 497grt) on an all-year-round service between Barry and Burnham.

It is also of interest, perhaps, to note that had this pier been constructed it would have been one of the

The Slip, Burnham.

The local boatmen at Burnham probably made much better use of the pier over the years than did the railway. Here we witness some of the more pleasurable activities at the pier end including those just out for a there-and-back-again stroll! A fair amount of fishing was carried out in this area particularly from Stert (otherwise Steart), the low headland seen opposite, and some of the catch was brought across to be landed at the pier for subsequent sale in the town and surrounding area, an activity which lasted well into the 20th century. (S&DRT)

very last of its type in the country. The notion that every resort must have a grand pier lay very much in the Victorian era and, barring a couple, no new structures of this sort were built after about 1900 so this scheme was very late in the day.

It seems that even the Barry Railway had underestimated the situation but in any case they were hitting other problems with their maritime interests and soon abandoned all hope of running the ferry. Indeed in April 1910 the company disposed of its four paddle steamers, the *Gwalia, Devonia, Westonia* and *Barry*. Thus ended any real chance of providing the little town with a proper pier which so many apparently still wanted.

The Campbell family had been running ships on the Firth of Clyde since the 1850s but it wasn't until 1887, when Captains Peter and Alexander Campbell allowed their *Waverley* (1885/258grt) to come south on a charter, that the famous White Funnel ships were seen in the Bristol Channel. The operation became permanent in the following year and thereafter the fleet of steamers grew as the company embarked upon more and more excursions in competition with a number of other operators, the largest at the time being the Cardiff-based ships of the Edwards and Robertson fleet. The Campbell brothers offered a number of excursions to and from Burnham in the years that

followed, their paddle steamers *Ravenswood* (1891/391grt) and *Lady Margaret* (1895) being just two of the ships advertised to call in 1898 whilst the *Waverley* herself was known to have called at Burnham in 1908, but apart from the Cardiff-Weston seasonal ferry P. & A. Campbell Ltd. (as the company had become in 1893) had little inclination to maintain any other ferry services. Following the collapse of the Barry Railway's shipping venture, however, they also took an interest in the pier but soon came to the conclusion that it was not worth reinstating so by 1910 all excursion traffic had ceased to use it.[2]

There seemed to be little hope that any sensible use could be made of the existing structure and to all intents and purposes the pier was now derelict but with a public obligation for safety the local council had been forced to take responsibility for it. In succeeding years about the only traffic it saw was from the local 'trip round the bay' boatmen. The RNLI, who since 1874 had had a lifeboat station close to the railway station and which had quickly been rail-connected between the boat house and the pier line just east of the Esplanade, had been allowed to use it by the S&D to launch their lifeboat. This concession remained under council ownership until 1930 when Burnham was abandoned as a lifeboat station.[3]

Burnham Lifeboat, 1874-1930 period

As a result of the difficulty in launching the lifeboat across the soft foreshore from the original lifeboat station, a shed under the Esplanade just opposite the Customs House, especially on 15 September 1873 when it was called out to save the ketch *Richard and Emily* and her crew of four, the RNLI decided to build a new lifeboat house alongside the railway between the end of the S&D's long excursion platform at the railway station and the foreshore so that the pier could be used. The building was completed in 1874 and the first lifeboat to use it was the 1869-built, 32ft.(9.85m) *Cheltenham* with a crew of 12. At first it was launched on an ordinary trailer which had been used at the previous house but it was quickly decided to lay in a short railway siding from the building towards the foreshore where it joined the S&D's extension line on to the pier by a point connection. The boat was then mounted on a rail bogie and could be let down the pier in the same way as the railway wagons using the existing wire rope system. Although not stated there must have been occasions during each tide when launching was impossible since the boat was normally floated off its trolley. When the tide was right out the entire end of the pier was well out of the water at its seaward end.

In 1887 the *Cheltenham* was replaced by the larger *John Godfrey Morris*, which was in turn replaced in 1902 by the 'Liverpool' type boat *Philip Beach*. On 11 September 1903 the *Philip Beach* was called out to give assistance to a ship in distress during a tremendous gale. In the course of trying to launch, it was found that the pier had been breached and all efforts had to be abandoned.

Although no longer in S&D ownership from around 1905, the launching facilities remained until the RNLI decided to close the station altogether in 1930. There were several reasons for this but principally because the amount of shipping had been declining in the area for some considerable time and it was also proving difficult to crew the boat. With no further use for the rail connection the siding was taken out shortly afterwards to allow esplanade improvements to continue. The lifeboat house was given to the local Scout troop in 1937.

Two views of the seaward end of Burnham station. (above) The life boat station on the right remained open until 1930 and was still rail-connected when this view of the station was taken.   *(Lens of Sutton)*

(below) This photo was taken from the stop blocks that were put in when the line was cut off from the pier and the Esplanade extended. The former lifeboat station lost its rail connection after it was closed by the RNLI in 1930 and is seen in its converted state for the local Scouts who used it from 1937 until the 1990s. Sitting in front of the building and looking like doors is a grounded coach body.   *(S&DRT)*

Having now found itself in ownership of the pier the local council took the opportunity to make several improvements in the vicinity, and it was at about this time that plans were made to extend the esplanade road across the railway in a southerly direction. With no further use for the pier the sluicing pond was no longer required and this was to be developed into a marine lake. Ironically this redevelopment prompted what was to become the last recorded use of the pier by a ship when the small sand dredger **Manley** (1888/124grt), from Cardiff, discharged two cargoes in 1929 in connection with this work.[4] Thereafter the cut was allowed to silt up completely. The rail siding into the lifeboat house was removed and the former S&D connection to the pier severed just inland from the new esplanade extension road, buffer-stops being fitted.

In succeeding years the pier has seen some preventative maintenance. The rails survived for some time but were progressively removed as repairs were required. In more recent years the timber section at the landward end has been completely renewed and, following the severe storms of December 1981, storm gates were fitted as part of the renewal of the sea defences to prevent any possibility of flooding in the town. The main structure, although now shortened by a couple of hundred feet by Sedgemoor District Council, is still there for everyone to see and walk on. Few people today would probably question why; to most it has always been there, unless, of course you choose to delve into the historical past of Burnham and come across its 'foremost citizen' George Reed who laid the foundation stone all those years ago, when civic

On 28 August 1954, a 12-coach special train was run to celebrate the centenary of the Somerset Central Railway and was hauled by 1896-built Johnson Class 3F 0-6-0 No.43201, formerly S&DJR No.64. Organised by C. & J. Clark and Clark, Son & Morland, it conveyed more than 600 passengers, many of whom were descendants of James Clark the shoe manufacturer of Street and a leading figure in the promotion of the railway. The train ran over the original line from Glastonbury but strangely it was rostered to terminate at Burnham. It is seen here arriving there, even though the short extension from Highbridge had only been in use for 96 years at the time! Still it made a good excuse to spend some time at the seaside for the occupants, many of whom were in period costume.
(S&DRT)

optimism was at its prime. In the end it will go down as one of those typically ambitious railway ventures, similar to so many others throughout the country, which never quite made it for all sorts of pretty obvious reasons. But then the directors of the SCR and its successor, the Somerset & Dorset Railway Company, were always pretty good when it came to optimism!

Notes:

1. S&DRT *Bulletin* No.156.
2. S&DRT File X507. Correspondence G. Luxon/R. Atthill 1966.
3. There was no lifeboat at Burnham until 1994 when an inshore rescue service was instigated by another voluntary group using an inflatable vessel operating from a new boathouse a little to the south of the pier, the latter once again being used to launch it.
4. S&DRT File X507. Correspondence Capt. J. Dew/R. Atthill 1966.

Victorian elegance was a little under-stated when it came to the facilities provided at Burnham, despite the resort's undoubted popularity with day excursionists. This latter-day view, taken inside the train shed, shows the limited passenger accommodation which was available, consisting of a general waiting room, booking hall and office accessed through the nearest door, with the ladies waiting room beyond. Attached to the goods shed are the gentlemen's toilets followed by the very small four-lever signal box which controlled the station loop but not the longer 'excursion' platform loop which was a later addition and necessitated a separate ground frame. The signal box still survives and is now located at Washford on the West Somerset Railway where it has been preserved by the Somerset & Dorset Railway Trust. Judging by the continued use of gas lamps, little has changed since the station was completed about 100 years before, in 1857, and it must have been a particularly cold and draughty place to be when the weather was bad and you were waiting for either a ship to arrive at the adjacent pier or a train from the south. (Lens of Sutton)

The pier still showed some evidence of the rails when seen on 12 January 1967, although renewal of the wooden landward end of the structure with new timbers and repairs elsewhere along its length ensured that all traces would slowly disappear. Just visible on the left is part of the marine lake which replaced the former sluicing pond.
(Chris Handley)

The 900ft. pier in May 1970, viewed from the opposite direction. Again the line of the former rail track is clearly visible with the odd length still in situ. They were originally mounted on longitudinal sleepers set into the cobbles. The long-since silted cut on the right shows the sand to be at the same level as the pier over part of the length, whilst the remains of some of the mooring posts can just be seen. *(Chris Handley)*

With the tide about as far out as it could possibly go there was still a considerable drop at the end of the pier in this May 1970 view. Some attempt has been made to protect the public from walking off the end with the provision of guard rails. *(Chris Handley)*

10 Highbridge Wharf Closure – A Changing Face

When the Dutch coaster *Jola* left Highbridge Wharf in 1948 after discharging her cargo it signalled the end of an era and marked the beginning of the end for many of the small harbours both along the Somerset coastline and in the Bristol Channel as a whole. The New Wharf at Highbridge had opened with the Glastonbury Canal in 1833 and closed officially to shipping in 1949, a working life of just 116 years during which time thousands of tons of coal, iron, steel, timber, stone, flour and other diverse products were to pass through the little harbour. There had always been a coastal trade with the small sailing cargo vessels developing to suit the difficult conditions of the Bristol Channel – the ubiquitous ketch down channel and the Severn Trows which would generally trade from this area up channel to Gloucester and beyond. Highbridge was suited to these vessels and they were to play an important part in the economy of the harbour but it was also to see far larger ships. Firstly the Barques and Barquentines bringing timber in, often from Russia or Scandinavian ports, to be replaced in the course of time with even larger steamships of up to about 1200 gross tons; small by today's standards but large for such a harbour at the head of a winding narrow river.

Trade at Highbridge grew in harness with the railway it was to serve from 1854 but who would have thought in those far off days that this railway would have a life span of only 112 years – just a pinprick in time when put into historical context? The Somerset & Dorset Railway saw its trade peak in the years leading up to the First World War so it is not surprising that traffic through the harbour mirrored it. Imperceptible at first the trade started to ebb away although the war placed a false impression on events as tonnage soared briefly. But in the cold light of the post-war depressive years, trading conditions were bad whilst communication was increasingly improving. The Severn Tunnel had been opened back in the 1880s and this did much to damage the traditional coasting trade along the upper reaches of the Bristol Channel whilst the advent, firstly of the steam coaster, then later of the motor vessel, put paid to the livelihoods of many of the local owner/masters who eked out a living tramping whatever cargoes they could find. They could not compete in their sailing vessels with the higher payloads and shorter delivery times offered. Highbridge Wharf was on the slippery slope.

A panoramic view of the long abandoned harbour at Highbridge taken in October 1969, some 20 years after it was closed to shipping. On the right are the River Brue lower floodgates and sluice (clyce) with Kimber's boatyard in the centre. Considerable silting of the wharf area has taken place although the former deepwater channel is still just visible. Behind the wood and stone quay are the timber storage sheds of Bland's sawmill. H.J. Kimber, or 'Kim' as he was known locally, established his boatbuilding and repair yard in 1927 on an area previously known as Clyce Wharf. Over the years that followed he produced hundreds of small boats including many for the Admiralty during the war years, becoming the last boatbuilding yard in Somerset.
(Chris Handley)

The Second World War did little but offer a reprieve. It is true that the harbour was as busy as ever for the duration but at the same time the marine industry was changing. Ships grew ever bigger whilst road transport entered the picture. It was becoming increasingly obvious that smaller harbours could not handle such large ships, whilst the need to deliver direct to one's doorstep was diminishing; cargo could be off-loaded to rail or road at a convenient port and transported to its final destination. At the end of the war just a handful of traditional sailing craft were still in the coasting trade and the needs of modern industry were beginning to dictate the future. The use of coal, for instance, was quickly giving way to oil and Highbridge was not equipped to take that cargo. It is true that the residual traffic would have continued for another decade or so but there was no longer the tonnage to justify the economics of a badly run-down facility. It made no sense for the newly nationalised railways to invest in its continued upkeep.

Once the decision had been taken to close the harbour, by now badly silted up following little capital investment, British Railways could formally abandon the area. The last known movement out of the harbour was Albert Buncombe's little tug *Rexford* when it was towed away to be scrapped in 1950, leaving just a few yachts and Harold Kimber's boatyard at Clyce Wharf.

Although shipping had ceased, strangely the rail facilities at the Wharf were retained in use and still supported three weekday trains daily in the 1950 timetable. Just four years later, in 1954, Grahame Farr visited the Wharf and wrote:

> having seen the creek when it berthed regular colliers and timber ships and had a steady employment, I was amazed to see how completely the mud had silted the wharves.

In the following year the train service had been cut to just two each day mainly serving Bland's, the timber merchants, since most of the other users had closed their operations. Indeed the sidings at the west end of the Wharf were being used to store crippled or condemned wagons but by the early 1960s even that was no longer required.

Rail traffic was finally discontinued from 2 November 1964 with official closure of the Wharf branch following on 16 May 1965. There was no delay in arranging contracts for the lifting of the rails which followed swiftly from the following July. Ten months later, on Sunday 6 March 1966, the entire Somerset & Dorset Railway system closed and with it came an end of an era.

Highbridge Wharf
Train Arrivals and Departures, from 5 June 1950.

UP

					4.40pm ex Templecombe U.
Evercreech Jcn. N. dep:	11.15am				7.25pm*
Bason Bridge dep:		1.15pm			
Highbridge East arr:					9.20pm
Highbridge Wharf arr:	3.21pm	1.23pm**	2.50pm dep.		9.28pm
Burnham-on-Sea arr:			2.55pm		

* Will not run on Saturdays, also after September 23rd.
** 10 minutes later from Highbridge East to Wharf on Saturdays.

DOWN

Burnham-on-Sea dep:			3.30pm	
Highbridge Wharf dep:	7.17am	12.01pm	3.35pm arr.	5.45pm*
Highbridge East dep:				6.00pm
Bason Bridge arr:	7.25am	12.46pm		6.06pm
Evercreech Jcn.N. arr:	1.05pm			10.45pm to Templecombe U.*

* Will not run on Saturdays, also after September 23rd.

All freight trains Monday to Friday only except where stated.

From the BR Southern Operating Area Working Time Tables of passenger, Milk & Freight Trains, etc. June 5th 1950 until further notice.

Bland's timber yard (originally Sheppard Brothers) was later taken over by Jewson's, but they eventually vacated the site next to the disused wharf and moved their operation to Bridgwater. A few years later the timber sheds were demolished.

Infilling of the harbour took place over a number of years, starting with the easternmost end where the sea lock and upper part were filled during the 1960s. During the late l980s, part of the area at the town end, including the railway trackbed off Newtown Road, succumbed to inevitable redevelopment which included building a new housing estate, whilst part became a compound for Brue Yachts' boatyard (formerly Kimber's). Strangely the top of the bridge and part of the abutments of the old sea lock remained visible together with the top of the New Wharf masonry. By 1985 reclamationof most of the old harbour was complete, leaving just the entrance and a small part of the old wharf visible.

Fifty years on and into the new millennium, it is difficult to imagine just where the harbour was, such has been the extent of change. Even the route of the railway has been totally lost – there is no trace of the level crossing at Church Street, the track bed having long since disappeared under new housing estates and roads, save, that is, for an innocent-looking footpath which will take you to Burnham! Truly, as Sir John Betjeman so poignantly suggested in 1963, Highbridge Wharf's hopes have died and drifted out into the sea.

By October 1969 the only visitors to Highbridge were a few yachts, two of which are seen here, laid up for the winter against the southern bank of the channel. The tremendous silting through years of neglect is plainly evident although traces of the deep water channel surprisingly still survive.

(Chris Handley)

In 1969 the vegetation was such that it was not difficult to stand in the bed of the harbour which had seen so many ships in previous years. The old mooring rings and ladders are clearly visible as are the thriving blackberry bushes on the elevated crane road!

(Chris Handley)

The site of the stacking ground sidings at the west end of the wharf area, again seen in October 1969. Alexander's Eclipse Fuel Company's patent fuel works which manufactured fuel briquettes during the First World War and up to the end of 1924 was still standing at this time. Known as the 'Winkle' locally it was used as a store by the US army during the Second World War but has since been demolished.
(Chris Handley)

Compare this 1969 view, taken from the disused crane road looking east, with earlier views. Only Bland's timber stores still remain in use but even they would eventually be demolished. Much of the area is now covered by housing.
(Chris Handley)

By October 1969 the top end of the harbour had already been filled in but the original entrance into the lock chamber of the Glastonbury Canal, the infamous sea-lock, was still clearly visible, together with the top of the railway-owned bridge which spanned the entrance and at one time carried a short siding across it. A sign close to the bridge forbade locomotives to pass it so one can only assume that the siding had to be shunted by horses. A closer look reveals the bridge number plate, No.283A in the S&DJR series, on the right.   *(Chris Handley)*

Appendix 1
Chronology of Events

DATE	EVENT	REMARKS
1801	Brue Drainage Act	
1803	Brue New Drain at Highbridge completed	
28 May 1827	Glastonbury Navigation & Canal Company Act	
15 August 1833	Glastonbury Canal opened	
17 June 1852	Somerset Central Railway Act	
1 July 1854	Glastonbury Canal closed	
17 August 1854	Somerset Central Railway formally opened	Including Highbridge Wharf extension
30 July 1855	SCR Burnham and Wells Extension Act	
21 July 1856	SCR Extension to Bruton Act	
29 July 1856	Dorset Central Railway Act	
August 1857	SCR Burnham Extension completed	Not opened until 3 May 1858
3 May 1858	SCR Burnham Pier opened	
24 May 1858	Commencement of Burnham-Cardiff ferry service	
3 March 1859	SCR Wells Extension formally opened	
6 August 1860	Burnham Tidal Harbour Act	Burnham Tidal Harbour Company
11 February 1860	First railway-owned ship placed on Burnham ferry	
31 October 1860	Dorset Central Railway formally opened	Wimborne-Blandford
1 September 1862	Somerset & Dorset Railway Company formed	By amalgamation of SCR and DCR
31 August 1863	Channel-to-channel rail link completed by S&DR	
May 1865	S&DR's Poole-Cherbourg ferry service commenced	
29 June 1865	Burnham Tidal Harbour Act, 1865	Extension of time until 1870
June 1866	S&DR lapses into receivership	
February 1867	S&DR's Poole-Cherbourg ferry service suspended	Last service was in 1866
1870	Receivers discharged	
1 August 1870	Burnham Tidal Harbour Act, 1870	Extension of time until 1875
July 1871	S&DR withdraws from direct ownership of railway passenger ships	Burnham-Cardiff ferry maintained by chartered tonnage
21 August 1871	S&DR's Bath Extension Act	
December 1873	S&DR purchases first cargo vessels	
20 July 1874	S&DR's Bath Extension opened	
circa 1875	Burnham Tidal Harbour Co. formally wound up	
1 November 1875	S&DR leased to MR and LSWR jointly	
13 July 1876	S&D Joint Railway. Confirmation of lease	
May 1884	S&DJR purchases passenger vessel for Burnham ferry service	
18 August 1882	Bridgwater Railway Company Act	
July 1888	S&DJR withdraws from Burnham-Cardiff ferry	
21 July 1890	Bridgwater Railway and Wharf open	Operated for LSWR by S&DJR
Circa 1905	S&DJR's Burnham Pier sold to UD Council	
1912	Bridgwater Wharf closed to all shipping	
December 1933	S&DJR withdraws from ownership of cargo vessels	
June 1948	Last commercial cargo landed at Highbridge Wharf	
1949	BR closed Highbridge Wharf to all shipping	
29 October 1951	BR withdraws passenger services Highbridge-Burnham (and Glastonbury-Wells)	Except excursion traffic to Burnham
1 December 1952	BR closes Bridgwater branch	
8 September 1962	Excursion traffic to Burnham discontinued	
20 May 1963	BR withdraws goods traffic to Burnham. Extension closes	
2 November 1964	BR withdraws rail traffic to Highbridge Wharf sidings	
16 May 1965	Highbridge Wharf branch officially closed	
6 March 1966	Somerset & Dorset line officially closed to all traffic	

Appendix 2

Selected List of Ships Noted at Highbridge Wharf

NAME	TYPE	TONS (Gross/Net)	BUILT	REMARKS
ALPHA	Steam Coaster	82g/48n*	1877	b.W.Swan & Son, Maryhill (ON78559). S&D 1879-1925. Twice lengthened 94g/55n 1884, 111g/76n 1905. Reg.Bridgwater. Rail trade. Scrapped 1925.
ADA	Trow	38n	1869	b.Bristol (ON62742). Reg.Gloucester. Dismasted in Bristol Channel 6/1929 and towed into Highbridge by a steam vessel.
ANN	Ketch	54n	1805	b.Dartmouth. Owned by R.Allen, Bridgwater (ON10881).
ANNIE	Ketch	46g/32n	1896	b.J.W.Francis, Milford Haven (ON104117). Reg. Cardigan. Mainly in grain trade. Noted Highbridge in 1937.
ARTHUR	Ketch	62.3g/54.3n	1876	b.H.Fellows & Son, Southtown, Gt.Yarmouth (ON 74713). Owned R.Bound. Reg.Bridgwater. Mainly in brick trade. Stranded 10/7/25. Scrapped Highbridge after 1926.
BERTHA	Steam Cargo	1216g/671n		b.Wood Skinner & Co., Newcastle. Owned in Sweden in 1930s when noted at Highbridge – timber trade.
CODØ	Steam Cargo			Scandinavian but no other details available.
EDWARD BATTERS	Steam Tug	34.1g	1908	b.J.T.Eltringham & Co., South Shields (ON124623). To Bridgwater register 1922. Owner L.W.Nurse for The Bridgwater Steam Towing Co. Ltd. and used on local towage duties. Scrapped Newport 1934.
ELEMORE	Steam Coaster	165g	1915	b.Livingstone & Cooper, Hessle (ON139265). 1937 to A.J.Smith, Bristol. Reg.Bristol. In local coal trade.
ELIZA	Trow	57n	1864	b.Bristol (ON51203). Reg.Gloucester (see Note 1).
FANNY JANE	Ketch	61n	1858	b.J.Gough, Bridgwater (ON10941). Reg.Bridgwater.
FLORA	Trow			Reg.Bristol.
FORSHULT	Steam Cargo	658g/337n	1918	b.Eriksbergs MV Aktieb, Gothenburg (ON6058). Owned by Uddeholms Aktieb (F.Olsson, manager), Uddeholm, Sweden.
GALLEY	Ketch	61n	1825	b. Brinscombe (ON11712).
GERDA	Brig			Baltic trader.
JOHN	Steam Coaster	141g	1849	b.J.T.Price, Neath Abbey (ON26707). Owned by A.J.Smith Ltd., Bristol. Reg.Bristol. In coal trade.
JOLA	Motor Coaster	267g/183n	1935	b.Gebr. Niestern & Co., Delfzijl. Owned by L.Schothorst. Reg. Zuidbroek, Netherlands. Last ship to Highbridge Wharf, 1948.
JULIA (1)	Ketch	69n	1863	b.J.Wright, Milton. S&D 1873-1904. Reg.Bridgwater. Rail trade. Sold 1904.
JULIA (2)	Steam Coaster	197g/78n	1904	b.Mordey, Carney, Southampton (ON111393) for S&D. Reg.Bridgwater. Rail trade. Scrapped 1934.
JUPITER	Barque	610g	1864	b.J.Lange, Vegesack. German owned by SchiffahrtsGes. 'Austra' Reg.Riga, Russia. Timber trade. Noted Highbridge, 1897.
LEOPARD	Steam Coaster	67g/41.8n	1861	b.Hyde & Rowe, Bristol (ON44106). S&D 1874-1896. Reg.Bridgwater. Coal and general cargo. Sold 1896.
LILLY	Barquentine			Reg.Oskarshamn.
LIVONIA	Brigantine	268n	1874	b.by Clow at P.E.Island (ON 24928). Owned by J.Tyrrell. Reg.Newport. Noted Highbridge, c1910.
MARIAN	Ketch	59n	1869	b.J.Gough, Bridgwater (ON56370). Owned T.Rowles Bridgwater. Hulked in R.Brue. Fired and broken up 1939.
MARIE EUGENE	Ketch	51.8g/46.7n		b.Regneville, France, date unknown (ON81531). Noted Highbridge 1897 when in ownership of Clifford Symons, Bridgwater. Scrapped 1927.
MERCATOR	Barquentine	390g/370n	1895	b.M.Holmsen, Haynasch. Owned by M. Weide. Reg.Riga, Russia. Noted Highbridge 1903, Captain P.Walter in command.
MORNING STAR	Schooner	100n	1878	b.Kingston, Elgin (ON70529). Reg.Padstow.
NORAH	Trow	59n	1868	b.J.Gough, Bridgwater (ON56365). Owned B.Pearce, Highbridge.

NAME	TYPE	TONS (Gross/Net)	BUILT	REMARKS
PELLE	Steam Cargo	633g/427n	1890	b.W.Lindbergs AGT, Stockholm. Owned 1930s by Solveborgs Varus & Rederi A/B, Solvesborgs. Danish flagged. Timber trade.
PRIMULA	Steam Cargo	1024g/546n	1918	b.De Haan & Oerlemans, Heusden. Owned 1930s by Skibs A/S Boss (Wahl & Co., Managers), Oslo. Norwegian flagged. Timber trade.
PROVIDENCE	Trow	45n	1892	b.Tewkesbury (ON11694). Reg.Gloucester.
RADSTOCK	Steam Coaster	195g/78n	1925	b.J.Crighton & Co., Saltney, Chester (ON111395) for S&D. Reg.Bridgwater. Rail trade. Sold 1933 and scrapped 1958.
RAILWAY	Ketch	59n	1855	b.J.Higham, Strood (ON25456). S&D 1873-1886. Rail trade. Stranded 1886, total loss.
RAPID	Steam Paddle	53g/16n	1838	b.South Shields (ON10933). Owned by H.Towells, Bridgwater, 1850-1880. Used at Highbridge as a passenger ferry to Cardiff.
REXFORD	Steam Tug	60g/9n	1895	b.Millbay Docks, Plymouth (ON145752). Owned A. Buncombe, Highbridge, c1933-1950. Reg. Poole.
RICHARD AND EMILY	Ketch	82n	1862	b.Chatfield Shipbuilding Yard, Lewes (ON27824). S&D 1873-1886. Rail trade. Sank 1886.
ROYAL FIRTH	Steam Coaster	411g	1921	b.Brown's Shipbuilding & Drydock Co. Ltd., Hull (ON144263). Owned by Border Shipping Co. Ltd., Newcastle (G.T.Gillie & Blair Ltd., Managers). Reg.Glasgow/Newcastle. Rail cargo into Highbridge.
SHERBRO	Steam Passenger	239g/118n	1870	b.J.S.White, W.Cowes (ON73721). S&DJR 1884-1888. Passenger ferry service Burnham-Cardiff summers only. Laid up at Highbridge Wharf during winters.
STAFFA	Steam Coaster	90g/35n	1892	b.J.H.Gilmour, Irvine (ON99838). Originally Glasgow-owned as the NELLIE but renamed in 1925 and passed to O.J.N.Eynon, Angle, Pembs. Reg.Ramsey, Isle of Man. Noted at Highbridge in 1937.
SUNSHINE	Ketch	98.5g/76n	1900	b.Charles Burt, Falmouth (ON111391) for Nurse family. Reg.Bridgwater. Noted Highbridge in 1937 when in ownership of Colthurst Symons & Co. Motorised 1928. Scrapped Genoa 1954.
TWO SISTERS	Ketch	79g/62n	1865	b.Thomas Waters, Bideford (ON47889). Reg.Bideford. Towed in to Highbridge, 1891 by tug having survived terrific storm and loss of rigging. Cargo of oats destined for Poole offloaded.
WILLIAM	Trow	35n	1809	b.Bower Yard, Benthall (ON3912). Reg.Gloucester (see Note 2).
WILLIAM	Trow		1841	b.Coalbrookdale (ON11605). Reg.Bridgwater (see Note 2).
ZILLAH	Steam Coaster	373g	1901	b.Ailsa Shipbuilding Co., Troon (ON111365). Owners Zillah Shipping & Carrying Co. (W.A.Savage, manager) Liverpool. Noted at Highbridge in 1929.

NOTES:

1. There were many vessels registered at Bridgwater and at other local ports with the name ELIZA. The trow ELIZA (ON51203) of Gloucester is a confirmed visitor to Highbridge
2. There were a number of vessels named WILLIAM. Two of them, both trows, were owned at Highbridge at some stage in their long lives and both were ketch rigged. The first was built in 1809 at Bower Yard, Salop (ON3912), Registered in Gloucester and owned eventually by E.Hobbs of Highbridge. The second was built in 1841 at Coalbrookdale (ON11605), registered at Bridgwater and owned first by Benjamin Pearce of Highbridge, then by J.Warren of Bridgwater.

Appendix 3
Selected List of Ships Noted at Burnham Pier

NAME	TYPE	TONS	BUILT	REMARKS
ALPHA	Steam Coaster	82g/48n	1877	b.W.Swan & Son, Maryhill (ON78559). S&D 1879-1925. Twice lengthened 94g/55n 1884, 111g/76n 1905. Reg. Glasgow/Bridgwater. Rail trade. Scrapped 1925.
AVALON	Passenger Paddle Steamer	670g/488n	1865	b.J.& W.Dudgeon, Cubitt Town. Owned by Great Eastern Rly Co. Chartered to BTH Co. 1871. Cardiff ferry service.
BONITA	Steam screw tug	64.7g	1896	b.South Hylton Shipbuilding & Repairing Co., Sunderland (ON108156). Owned by Bridgwater Steam Towing Co. Reg.Bridgwater 1897. Sold 1915. Sunk off Liverpool 3/5/41.
CAMBRIA	Passenger Paddle Steamer	420g/60n	1895	b.H.McIntyre & Co., Alloa (ON102489). Reg.Bristol. Owned by P.& A.Campbell. Excursions.
DIANA	Passenger Paddle Steamer	166g/76n	1851	b.J. Henderson & Sons, Renfrew (ON65308). Reg.Bristol. Chartered to BTH Co. 1871. Cardiff ferry service.
DEFIANCE	Passenger Paddle Steamer	150g/96n	1856	b.Thomas Wingate, Glasgow (ON11542). Owned by BTH Co. (for SCR) 1863-71. Reg.Bridgwater. Sold 1871. Cardiff ferry service.
FLORA	Passenger Paddle Steamer	119g/56n	1851	b.Smith & Rodger, Govan. Owners P.L.Henderson, Liverpool, F.C.Winby, Cardiff, H.Cousins, Cardiff. Chartered to BTH Co. (later S&DR/S&DJR) 1871-78. Scrapped 1879. Cardiff ferry service.
GEORGE REED	Passenger Paddle Steamer	170g/115n	1866	b.J.& W.Dudgeon, Cubitt Town (ON29559). Owned by BTH Co. (G.Reed) for SCR 1866-67. Sold and chartered back until 5/1868. Cardiff ferry service.
HEATHER BELL	Passenger Paddle Steamer	152g/95n	1858	b.J.& G.Thompson, Glasgow (ON22090). Owned by BTH Co. (for SCR) 1864-67. Sold. Cardiff ferry service.
HEATHER BELL	Passenger Paddle Steamer	271g/126n	1871	b.Blackwood & Gordon, Port Glasgow (ON60624). Reg. Portsmouth. Owned by Edwin Hunt. Noted Burnham 1901-2. Excursions. Sold for scrap 1903.
IRON DUKE	Passenger Paddle Steamer	121g/48n	1857	b.T.Wingate & Co., Whiteinch. Owned by Cardiff Steam Nav. Co. First ship to use Burnham pier, 1858.
LADY MARGARET	Passenger Paddle Steamer		1895	b.McMillans, Dumbarton (ON101573). Reg.Cardiff. Owned by P.& A.Campbell 1896-1903. Excursions at Burnham.
MANLEY	Steam Sand Dredger	124g/57n	1888	b.Head & Barnard, Hull (ON94089). Owned by Sessions & Sons. Reg.Cardiff. Last ship known to have used Burnham pier in 1929.
NELSON	Passenger Paddle Steamer	166g/69n	1875	b.Wm.Allsup & Sons, Preston (ON69709). Owned by S.Little, Newport. Chartered to S&DJR 1883. Cardiff ferry service.
PILOT	Steam Paddle Tug	109g/16n	1857	b.Marshall & Co., South Shields. Owned by Cardiff Bute Dock Towing Co. Chart'd to BTH Co. (for SCR) 1863. Cardiff ferry service.
PRINCE OF WALES	Passenger Paddle Steamer	182g/106n	1842	b.N.Tregelles, Neath Abbey. Owned by J.W.Pockett, Swansea. Burnham-Swansea service 1860 and excursions.
RAVENSWOOD	Passenger Paddle Steamer	391g/79n	1891	b.S.McKnight & Co., Ayr (ON98821). Reg.Bristol. Owned by P.& A.Campbell. Excursions to Burnham.
RUBY	Passenger Paddle Steamer	155g/98n	1854	b.J.Henderson & Sons, Renfrew (ON3185). Owned by G.Reed and consortium for SCR. 1859-64. Sold. Cardiff ferry service.
SHERBRO	Passenger Paddle Steamer	239g/118n	1870	b.J.White, West Cowes (ON73721). Owned by MR/LSWR (for S&DJR) 1884-88. Cardiff ferry service and excursions. Sold 1888.
TALIESEN	Passenger Paddle Steamer	158g/85n	1842	b.E.Eyton, Mostyn. Owned by Cardiff Steam Nav. Co. Used on Cardiff ferry 1858-60 on behalf of SCR.
THE LADY MARY	Passenger Paddle Steamer	179g/90n	1868	b.Blackwood & Gordon, Port Glasgow (ON60617). Reg. Glasgow. Operated by J.Boyle. Owned by Bute Trustees, Cardiff. Used on Cardiff ferry service 1882-3 on behalf of SCR.
WATER LILY	Passenger steam-screw ship	52g/32n	1875	b.T.B.Seath & Co., Rutherglen. Owned by S.Little, Newport. Relief ship Cardiff ferry, 1883-7.
WAVERLEY	Passenger Paddle Steamer	258g/52n	1885	b.H.McIntyre & Co., Paisley (ON90053). Reg.Bristol. Owned by P.& A.Campbell. Excursions.
WYE	Passenger Paddle Steamer	108g/54n	1861	b.William Patterson, Bristol (ON29217). Reg.Cardiff. Operated by John Boyle, Cardiff. Used as reserve ship on Cardiff ferry service 1882-3.

Appendix 4
Company Officers with Maritime Responsibilities

As the Somerset & Dorset Railway did not have a marine department the duties associated with the operation of its ships and harbours were shared between the traffic, locomotive and the engineering departments.

Traffic Department

Responsible for the tasking and operation of the ships in conjunction with rail services. Traffic superintendents:

1862-1863	A. Patey
1863-1876	A. Difford
1876-1902	R.A. Dykes
1902-1920	G.H. Eyre
1920-1922	Lt.Col. A.S. Redman
1922-1930	G.H. Wheeler

From 1930 the LMS operated the line directly on behalf of the Joint Committee:

1930-1944	S. Sealy (LMS District Controller, Bath)
1944-1954	S.A. Wilson (Assistant Divisional Superintendent)

From the 1880s until at least 1913 Harry Bastard held the post of Goods Department and Wharf Superintendent at Highbridge and was responsible to the Traffic Superintendent for the day-to-day tasking and operation of the ships and harbour. (Maritime activities ceased in 1948)

Locomotive Department

In addition to its normal duties of building, repairing and maintaining locomotives and rolling stock this department also had responsibility for the maintenance and repair of company ships, arrangement of drydocking and surveys as required. Locomotive Superintendents:

1862-1868	R. Andrews
1868-1874	F.G. Slessor
1874-1883	B.S. Fisher
1883-1889	W.H. French
1889-1911	A.H. Whitaker
1911-1913	M.F. Ryan
1913-1930	R.C. Archbutt

Responsibility passed to the LMS, Derby from 1930 until 1933 when the ships were sold.

Engineering Department

In addition to its major railway responsibilities for the maintenance of track, structures and formation it was also responsible for the maintenance of the harbour at Highbridge, wharves, pier, the sea lock and other associated structures. Also responsible for dredging and maintaining water levels. Civil Engineers:

1852-1862	C.H. Gregory (Engineer-in-Chief 1862-75)
1862-1875	F.G. Slessor (Resident Engineer)
1875-1876	H.S. Chapman
1876-1900	A. Colson
1900-1904	O.A.G. Edwards*
1904-1908	J. Tyler
1908-1916	E.R. Roche
1916	T.E. Maidment (died before taking up appointment)
1917-1930	W.E. Fox (Assistant Engineer to LSW/SR Western District Engineer)

* Appointed Western District Engineer, LSW, at Exeter in 1904 to which subsequent resident engineers reported.

From 1930 the Southern Railway took over full responsibility for civil engineering matters on behalf of the Joint Committee.

Bibliography

Published Books

Atthill, Robin, *The Somerset & Dorset Railway* (David & Charles, 1967)
Atthill, Robin, *The Picture History of the Somerset & Dorset Railway* (David & Charles, 1970)
Bradley, D. & Milton, David, *Somerset and Dorset Locomotive History* (David & Charles, 1973)
Casserley, H.C., *Britain's Joint Lines* (Ian Allan, 1968)
Chapman, Chris, *Secrets of the Levels* (Somerset Books, 1996)
Childs, Bob, *Rochester Sailing Barges of the Victorian Era* (Rochester Sailing Barges Publication, 1993)
Cooke, R.A., *Track Layout Diagrams of the GWR and BR(WR), Section 18* (2nd edition, published by the author, 1980)
Cowden J.E. and Duffy, J.O.C., *Elder Dempster Fleet History, 1852-1985* (Mallett & Bell Publications, 1986)
Cox, Bernard, *Pleasure Steamers* (David & Charles, 1983)
Duckworth & Langmuir, *Railway and Other Steamers* (T. Stephenson & Sons)
Farr, Graham, *Somerset Harbours* (Christopher Johnson, 1954)
Farr, Graham, *West Country Passenger Steamers* (2nd edition, T. Stephenson & Sons, 1967)
Fenton, R.S., *Mersey Rovers* (World Ship Society, 1997)
Fitzhugh, Rod, *Bridgwater and the River Parrett in old Photographs* (Alan Sutton Publishing, 1993)
Fletcher, Ken, *The Somerset Levels & Moors* (Somerset County Council, 1991)
Garner, Russ, *The Somerset & Dorset Joint Railway Locomotive and Rolling Stock Registers, 1886-1930* (The Somerset & Dorset Railway Trust, 2000)
Green, Colin, *Severn Traders* (Black Dwarf Publications, 1999)
Greenhill, Basil, *The Merchant Schooners* (David & Charles, 1962)
Hammond, Alan, *Somerset & Dorset Memories* (Millstream Books, 1993)
Handley, Chris, *Radstock Coal & Steam, Vol.2* (Millstream Books, 1992)
Harrison, J.D., *The Bridgwater Branch* (Oakwood Press, 1981)
Maggs, Colin, *Highbridge in its Heyday* (Oakwood Press, 1973)
Miles, Iain, *Bogs and Inundations* (Somerset Industrial Archaeological Society/Weston Zoyland Engine Trust, 1993)
Murless, Brian, *Somerset Brick and Tile Makers, A Brief History & Gazetteer* (Somerset Industrial Archaeological Society, 1991)
Norman, W.H., *Tales of Watchet Harbour* (published by the author, 1985)
Nurse, James, *The Nurse Family of Bridgwater and Their Ships* (Carmania Press, 1999)
Russell, Ronald, *Lost Canals of England and Wales* (David & Charles, 1971)
Slade, W.J. & Greenhill, Basil, *Westcountry Coasting Ketches* (Conway Maritime Press, 1974)
Storer, Bernard, *The Natural History of the Somerset Levels* (The Dovecote Press, 1985)

Registers and Directories

Lloyds Register of British and Foreign Shipping
Lloyds Register of Shipping
Lloyds Captain's Registers
Lloyds Book of House Flags and Funnels, 1912
Mercantile Navy List and Maritime Directory
Kelly's Directory (various issues)
Shipping Protest Register, 1863-1870
Bridgwater Ship Register (transcript)
Bridgwater Ship Owners and Crew List (transcript)
Whitby's Bridgwater Almanack (various issues)

Periodicals and Newspapers

The Bulletin/Pines Express, Journal of the Somerset & Dorset Railway Trust
Sea Breezes
The Railway Magazine
The Bulletin of the Somerset Industrial Archaeological Society
Somerset Magazine
Bridgwater Mercury